Fodor's

MARTHA'S VINEYARD & NANTUCKET

1st Edition

Where to Stay and Eat
for All Budgets

Must-See Sights
and Local Secrets

Ratings You Can Trust

Excerpted from *Fodor's Cape Cod, Nantucket & Martha's Vineyard*
Fodor's Travel Publications New York, Toronto, London, Sydney, Auckland
www.fodors.com

FODOR'S MARTHA'S VINEYARD & NANTUCKET

Series Editor: Douglas Stallings

Editor: Amy Wang

Editorial Production: Evangelos Vasilakis

Editorial Contributors: Andrew Collins, Sandy MacDonald

Maps & Illustrations: David Lindroth, *cartographer*; William Wu; Bob Blake and Rebecca Baer, *map editors*

Design: Fabrizio LaRocca, *creative director*; Guido Caroti, Siobhan O'Hare, *art directors*; Ann McBride, *designer*; Melanie Marin, *senior picture editor*

Cover Photo: (Nantucket Island): Catherine Karnow

Production/Manufacturing: Matt Struble

SPECIAL SALES

This book is available for special discounts for bulk purchases for sales promotions or premiums. Special editions, including personalized covers, excerpts of existing books, and corporate imprints, can be created in large quantities for special needs. For more information, write to Special Markets/Premium Sales, 1745 Broadway, MD 6-2, New York, New York, NY 10019, or e-mail specialmarkets@randomhouse.com.

AN IMPORTANT TIP & AN INVITATION

Although all prices, opening times, and other details in this book are based on information supplied to us at press time, changes occur all the time in the travel world, and Fodor's cannot accept responsibility for facts that become outdated or for inadvertent errors or omissions. **So always confirm information when it matters,** especially if you're making a detour to visit a specific place. Your experiences—positive and negative—matter to us. If we have missed or misstated something, **please write to us.** We follow up on all suggestions. Contact the Martha's Vineyard & Nantucket editor at editors@fodors.com or c/o Fodor's at 1745 Broadway, New York, NY 10019.

PRINTED IN THE UNITED STATES OF AMERICA

10 9 8 7 6 5 4 3 2 1

Be a Fodor's Correspondent

Your opinion matters. It matters to us. It matters to your fellow Fodor's travelers, too. And we'd like to hear it. In fact, we *need* to hear it. When you share your experiences and opinions, you become an active member of the Fodor's community. Here's how you can help improve Fodor's for all of us.

Tell us when we're right. We rely on local writers to give you an insider's perspective. But our writers and staff editors also depend on you. Your positive feedback is a vote to renew our recommendations for the next edition.

Tell us when we're wrong. We update most of our guides every year. But things change. If any of our descriptions are inaccurate or inadequate, we'll incorporate your changes in the next edition and will correct factual errors at fodors. com *immediately*.

Tell us what to include. You probably have had fantastic travel experiences that aren't yet in Fodor's. Why not share them with a community of like-minded travelers? Share your discoveries and experiences with everyone directly at fodors.com. Your input may lead us to add a new listing or a higher recommendation.

Give us your opinion instantly at our feedback center at www.fodors.com/feedback. You may also e-mail editors@ fodors.com with the subject line "Martha's Vineyard & Nantucket Editor." Or send your nominations, comments, and complaints by mail to Martha's Vineyard & Nantucket Editor, Fodor's, 1745 Broadway, New York, NY 10019.

Happy Traveling!

Tim Jarrell, Publisher

CONTENTS

ABOUT THIS BOOK

Our Ratings

We wouldn't recommend a place that wasn't worth your time, but sometimes a place is so experiential that superlatives don't do it justice: you just have to be there to know. These sights, properties, and experiences get our highest rating, **Fodor's Choice**, indicated by orange stars throughout this book. Black stars highlight sights and properties we deem **Highly Recommended,** places that our writers, editors, and readers praise again and again for consistency and excellence.

Credit Cards

Want to pay with plastic? **AE, DC, MC, V** following restaurant and hotel listings indicate whether American Express, Diner's Club, Master-Card, and Visa are accepted.

Restaurants

Unless we state otherwise, restaurants are open for lunch and dinner daily. We mention dress only when there's a specific requirement and reservations only when they're essential or not accepted—it's always best to book ahead.

Hotels

Unless we tell you otherwise, you can assume that the hotels have private bath, phone, TV, and air-conditioning. We always list facilities but not whether you'll be charged an extra fee to use them, so when pricing accommodations, find out what's included.

Many Listings
★	Fodor's Choice
★	Highly recommended
⊠	Physical address
✛	Directions
⬡	Mailing address
☎	Telephone
🖷	Fax
⊕	On the Web
✉	E-mail
⬛	Admission fee
☉	Open/closed times
Ⓜ	Metro stations
⊟	Credit cards

Hotels & Restaurants
🏨	Hotel
⬐	Number of rooms
♨	Facilities
⫴⦿⫴	Meal plans
✕	Restaurant
⬠	Reservations
↘	Smoking
🍸	BYOB
✕🏨	Hotel with restaurant that warrants a visit

Outdoors
⛳	Golf
⛰	Camping

Other
⊙	Family-friendly
⇨	See also
⊠	Branch address
☞	Take note

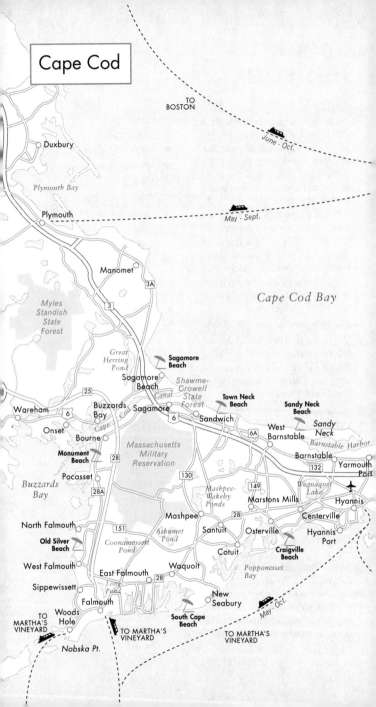

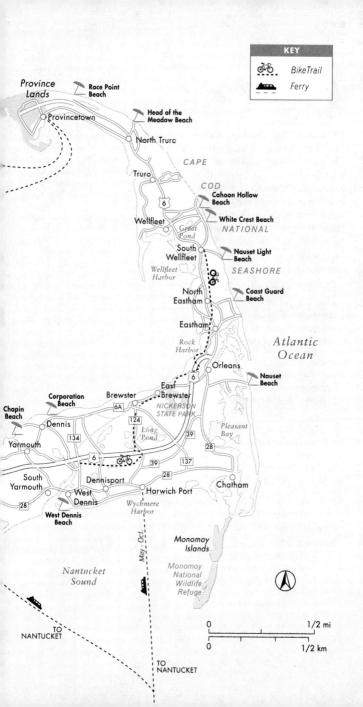

KEY
- BikeTrail
- Ferry

Province Lands

Race Point Beach

Head of the Meadow Beach

Provincetown

North Truro

CAPE

COD

Truro

Cahoon Hollow Beach

White Crest Beach

Wellfleet

Great Pond

NATIONAL

South Wellfleet

Nauset Light Beach

SEASHORE

Wellfleet Harbor

North Eastham

Coast Guard Beach

Eastham

Rock Harbor

Atlantic Ocean

Orleans

Nauset Beach

East Brewster

Corporation Beach

Brewster

6A

NICKERSON STATE PARK

124

Chapin Beach

Dennis

Long Pond

39

Pleasant Bay

134

Yarmouth

6

39

28

137

South Yarmouth

Dennisport

28

West Dennis

Harwich Port

Chatham

28

West Dennis Beach

Wychmere Harbor

May - Oct.

Monomoy Islands

Nantucket Sound

Monomoy National Wildlife Refuge

0   1/2 mi

0   1/2 km

TO NANTUCKET

TO NANTUCKET

WHEN TO GO

Memorial Day through Labor Day (or, in some cases, Columbus Day) is high season on the islands. This is summer with a capital *S,* a time for barbecues, beach bumming, swimming, and water sports. In summer everything is open for business out here, but you can also expect high-season evils: high prices, crowds, and traffic.

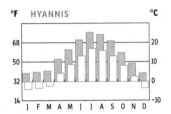

Martha's Vineyard and Nantucket are, however, increasingly year-round destinations. More and more businesses stay open during the winter months.

Climate

The following are average daily maximum and minimum temperatures for Hyannis, which although located on the Cape mainland has a similar climate to the islands. For local weather, coastal marine forecasts, and today's tide times, call the weather line of **WQRC** (☎*508/771–5522*) in Hyannis.

Forecasts **Weather Channel** (⊕*www.weather.com*).

Martha's Vineyard

WORD OF MOUTH

"In Aquinnah, we took numerous photographs of the beautiful cliffs and striking brick lighthouse. The cliffs had colorful strata in the afternoon light. What a gorgeous place!"

—volcam

"I prefer Martha's Vineyard for its more varied terrain and views, beautiful beaches, rolling hills, and indescribable Aquinnah clay cliffs. You can see it all from a tour bus on a day trip."

—Kingajh

By Andrew
Collins

FAR LESS DEVELOPED THAN CAPE COD—thanks to a few local conservation organizations—yet more cosmopolitan than neighboring Nantucket, Martha's Vineyard is an island with a double life. From Memorial Day through Labor Day the quieter, some might say real, Vineyard quickens into a vibrant, star-studded place. Edgartown floods with people who come to wander narrow streets flanked with elegant boutiques, stately whaling captains' homes, and charming inns. The busy main port, Vineyard Haven, welcomes day-trippers fresh off ferries and private yachts to browse in its own array of shops. Oak Bluffs, where pizza and ice-cream emporiums reign supreme, attracts diverse crowds with its boardwalk-town air and nightspots that cater to high-spirited, carefree youth.

Summer regulars have included a host of celebrities over the years, among them William Styron, Art Buchwald, Walter Cronkite, Beverly Sills, Patricia Neal, Spike Lee, and Diane Sawyer. Former president Clinton and his wife, Senator Hillary Clinton, are frequent visitors. Concerts, theater, dance performances, and lecture series draw top talent to the island; a county agricultural fair, weekly farmers' markets, and miles of walking trails provide earthier pleasures.

Most people know the Vineyard's summer persona, but in many ways its other self has even more appeal, for the off-season island is a place of peace and simple beauty. Drivers traversing country lanes through the agricultural center of the island find time to linger over pastoral and ocean vistas, without being pushed along by a throng of other cars, bicycles, and mopeds. In nature reserves, the voices of summer are gone, leaving only the sounds of birdsong and the crackle of leaves underfoot. Private beaches open to the public, and the water sparkles under crisp, blue skies.

Locals are at their convivial best off-season. After the craziness of their short moneymaking months, they reestablish contact with friends and take up pastimes temporarily crowded out by work. The result for visitors—besides the extra dose of friendliness—is that cultural, educational, and recreational events continue year-round.

ABOUT THE RESTAURANTS

From fried fish at roadside stands to boiled lobster and foie gras at fancy French restaurants and a growing array of international influences—Thai, Brazilian, Japanese, Mexican, to name just a few—the Vineyard serves an amazing variety of culinary choices.

The majority of eating establishments, both takeout and sit-down, are concentrated in the three Down-Island towns of Vineyard Haven, Oak Bluffs, and Edgartown. As you travel Up-Island—to West Tisbury, Chilmark, and Aquinnah—choices dwindle, especially when it comes to sit-down dinners. Sadly, Vineyard diners—all-American institutions where you can get an honest, no-frills meal at reasonable prices—are a dying breed. Luckily, you can pick up sandwiches, pastries, and other to-go specialties at a number of places around the island, and with good planning you can eat well on a modest budget and splurge for an elegant dinner.

Most restaurants are open on weekends starting in late spring, and by Memorial Day weekend most are serving daily. Although the season seems to stretch longer each year, most restaurants remain open full time through Columbus Day weekend, then only weekends through Thanksgiving (a small handful of die-hard restaurants remain open year-round). Dress, even for the upscale spots, is casual; a man in a sport jacket is a rare sight. Reservations are highly recommended in summer months.

ABOUT THE HOTELS

The variety of lodging options on Martha's Vineyard ranges from historic whaling captains' mansions filled with antiques to sprawling modern oceanfront hotels to cozy cottages in the woods. When choosing your accommodations, keep in mind that each town has a different personality: Oak Bluffs tends to cater to a younger, active, nightlife-oriented crowd; Edgartown is more subdued and dignified. Chilmark has beautiful beaches and miles of conservation lands, but not much of a downtown shopping area. Vineyard Haven provides a nice balance of downtown bustle and rustic charm. Bear in mind that many of the island's bed-and-breakfasts, set in vintage homes filled with art and antiques, have age restrictions—call ahead if you're traveling with a family. And remember that in July and August, the height of the summer season, minimum stays of as many as four nights may be required. If you're planning to visit for a week or more, consider renting a house. *For more lodging information, including rental properties and B&Bs, (⇨Accommodations in Essentials at the back of this book).*

You should make reservations for summer stays as far in advance as possible; late winter is not too early. Rates in season are very high but can fall by as much as 50% in the

Martha's Vineyard

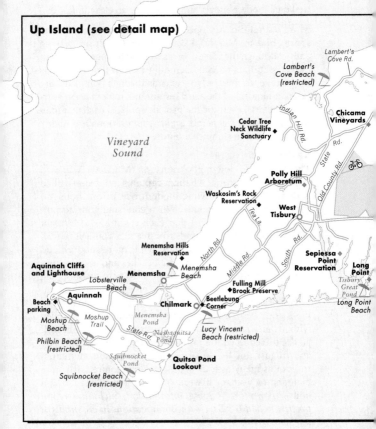

Up Island (see detail map)

Lambert's Cove Rd.

Lambert's Cove Beach (restricted)

Chicama Vineyards

Indian Hill Rd.

State Rd.

Old County Rd.

Cedar Tree Neck Wildlife Sanctuary

Vineyard Sound

Polly Hill Arboretum

Waskosim's Rock Reservation

Tea La.

West Tisbury

North Rd.

Menemsha Hills Reservation

Menemsha Beach

Menemsha

Middle Rd.

South Rd.

Sepiessa Point Reservation

Long Point

Aquinnah Cliffs and Lighthouse

Lobsterville Beach

Fulling Mill Brook Preserve

Beetlebung Corner

Tisbury Great Pond

Long Point Beach

Aquinnah

Chilmark

Beach parking

Moshup Beach

Moshup Trail

Menemsha Pond

State Rd.

Lucy Vincent Beach (restricted)

Philbin Beach (restricted)

Nashaquitsa Pond

Squibnocket Pond

Quitsa Pond Lookout

Squibnocket Beach (restricted)

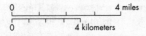

0   4 miles

0   4 kilometers

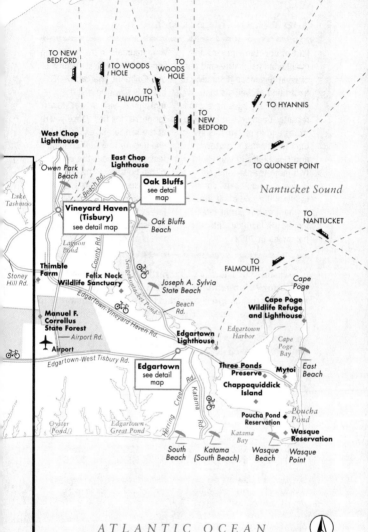

TO NEW BEDFORD

TO WOODS HOLE

TO WOODS HOLE

TO FALMOUTH

TO NEW BEDFORD

TO HYANNIS

TO QUONSET POINT

Nantucket Sound

TO NANTUCKET

West Chop Lighthouse

Owen Park Beach

East Chop Lighthouse

Beach Rd.

Oak Bluffs see detail map

Oak Bluffs Beach

Vineyard Haven (Tisbury) see detail map

Lake Tashmoo

Lagoon Pond

County Rd.

Sengekontacket Pond

TO FALMOUTH

Cape Poge

Thimble Farm

Stoney Hill Rd.

Felix Neck Wildlife Sanctuary

Joseph A. Sylvia State Beach

Beach Rd.

Cape Poge Wildlife Refuge and Lighthouse

Edgartown-Vineyard Haven Rd.

Manuel F. Correllus State Forest

Airport Rd.

Airport

Edgartown-West Tisbury Rd.

Edgartown Harbor

Cape Poge Bay

Edgartown Lighthouse

East Beach

Edgartown see detail map

Herring Creek Rd.

Katama Rd.

Three Ponds Preserve

Mytoi

Chappaquiddick Island

Poucha Pond Reservation

Poucha Pond

Oyster Pond

Edgartown Great Pond

Katama Bay

Wasque Reservation

South Beach

Katama (South Beach)

Wasque Beach

Wasque Point

ATLANTIC OCEAN

KEY	
	Bike Trail
	Ferry

CLOSE UP

The End of the BYOB Era?

Part of how the Vineyard has maintained its charm—and part of what has made it somewhat frustrating as well—is that alcoholic beverages have, until recently, been sold in retail stores and in restaurants in only two towns: Edgartown and Oak Bluffs. In early 2007 two more towns—Vineyard Haven and Aquinnah—voted to allow the sale of alcohol in restaurants but not at retail stores; the law goes into effect beginning in 2008.

At restaurants in the remaining "dry" towns of West Tisbury and Chilmark, you can BYOB, but only if you've had the foresight to visit a "wet" town for provisions first. Once you're at the restaurant, expect to be charged up to $8 for corkage fees (this includes the opening of the bottle and the provision of glasses). There's talk of the remaining towns passing similar laws allowing alcohol sales in restaurants, so call ahead if this is a concern to you.

off-season. The Martha's Vineyard Chamber of Commerce (⇨ *Visitor Information in Martha's Vineyard Essentials at the end of this chapter*) maintains a listing of availability in the peak tourist season, from mid-June to mid-September.

WHAT IT COSTS				
¢	$	$$	$$$	$$$$
RESTAURANTS				
under $10	$10–$16	$17–$22	$23–$30	over $30
HOTELS				
under $90	$90–$140	$140–$200	$200–$260	over $260

Restaurant prices are per person for a main course at dinner. Hotel prices are for a standard double room, excluding 6% sales tax (more in some counties) and 1%–4% tourist tax.

TIMING

Summer is the most popular season on the Vineyard, the time when everyone is here and everything is open and happening. With weather perfect for all kinds of activities, the island hosts special events from the Martha's Vineyard Agricultural Fair to the Edgartown Regatta. Another busy season, fall brings cool weather, harvest celebrations, and fishing derbies. Tivoli Day, an end-of-summer/start-of-fall celebration, includes a street fair. The island does tend to curl up in winter, when many shops and restaurants close. However, for the weeks surrounding the Hanukkah–Christmas–New Year's holidays, the Vineyard puts bells on for all kinds of special events and celebrations, most notably in Edgartown and Vineyard Haven. Spring sees the island awaken from its slumber in a burst of garden and house tours as islanders warm up for the busy season.

NAVIGATING

The island is roughly triangular, with maximum distances of about 20 mi east to west and 10 mi north to south. The west end of the Vineyard, known as Up-Island—from the nautical expression of going "up" in degrees of longitude as you sail west—is more rural and wild than the eastern Down-Island end, comprising Vineyard Haven, Oak Bluffs, and Edgartown. Conservation land claims almost a quarter of the island, with preservationist organizations acquiring more all the time. The Land Bank, funded by a tax on real-estate transactions, is one of the leading groups, set up to preserve as much of the island in its natural state as is possible and practical.

DOWN-ISLAND

Characterizing Martha's Vineyard is a bit like characterizing the taste of milk; it's a complete and unique experience, unlike any other. The three towns that compose Down-Island (the east end of Martha's Vineyard)—Vineyard Haven, Oak Bluffs, and Edgartown—are the most popular and the most populated. Here you can find the ferry docks, the shops, and a concentration of things to do and see, including the centuries-old houses and churches that document the island's history. A stroll through any one of these towns allows you to look into the past while enjoying the pleasures of the present.

VINEYARD HAVEN (TISBURY)

3½ mi west of Oak Bluffs, 8 mi northwest of Edgartown.

Most people call this town Vineyard Haven for the name of the port where the ferry pulls in, but its official name is Tisbury. Not as high-toned as Edgartown or as honky-tonk as Oak Bluffs, Vineyard Haven blends the past and the pres-

CLOSE UP

If You Like

BEACHES

Beaches on the north shore, facing Vineyard Sound, have more gentle waters, and they're also often slightly less chilly, so they are perfect for swimmers and for families. The Vineyard's south shore—from the Aquinnah Cliffs to Katama—is said to be among the longest continuous uninterrupted stretches of white-sand beach from Georgia to Maine. The surf, which crashes in refreshingly chilly waves, is a great place for bodysurfing. A few freshwater beaches at inland ponds provide a change of pace from the salty sea.

Public beaches are split between beaches with free parking—such as the Joseph A. Sylvia State Beach—and several where parking fees are collected—such as Moshup Beach in Aquinnah. Private beaches are reserved for permanent and summer residents, who must obtain parking or resident stickers from the appropriate town hall.

BICYCLING

First the downside: you'll be sharing winding roads with wide trucks and tour buses cruising right by your elbow, inexperienced moped riders, and automobile drivers unfamiliar with the island roads. In addition, most roads are bordered by sand—even those that aren't

near the beach. The bottom line is this: pay attention at all times. And if ever there was a place to commit to wearing a helmet, this would be it.

That being said, you don't have to be an experienced rider to enjoy the paths and roads here. The highest elevation is about 300 feet above sea level, and you can find relatively easy uphill and downhill biking with well-paved bike paths both Down-Island and Up. There are a couple of fun roller-coaster-like dips on the state-forest bike path (watch out for the occasional in-line skater here). Quiet country roads wind up and down gentle hills covered by low-hanging trees that make you feel as though you're riding through a lush green tunnel. The views—across open fields to the Atlantic Ocean, alongside ponds with floating swans, or of sun-flecked meadows where handsome horses graze—will nearly knock you off your bike seat.

Two of the quietest and most scenic roads without paths are North Road, from North Tisbury center all the way to Menemsha; and Middle Road, from its start at Music Street west to Beetlebung Corner, where South Road and Menemsha Cross Road intersect. This ride from Up-Island to the western tip of the island in Aquinnah is challenging—winding and sandy roads with a steep hill or two—but worth the rewards of spectacular views.

FISHING

Huge trawlers unload abundant daily catches at the docks in Vineyard Haven and Menemsha, attesting to the richness of the waters surrounding the island. But some of the most zealous fishing is done by amateurs—the striped bass and bluefish derby in the fall is serious business. One of the most popular spots for sport anglers is Wasque Point on Chappaquiddick. Two others are South Beach and the jetty at the mouth of the Menemsha Basin. Striped bass and bluefish are island stars. Several outfits operate deep-sea fishing trips if surf fishing is not your thing.

HIKING & WALKING

The nature preserves and conservation areas are laced with well-marked, scenic trails through varied terrains and ecological habitats, and the island's miles of uninterrupted beaches are perfect for stretching your legs. At the trailheads of most are small parking areas and bulletin boards with maps and other posted instructions, restrictions, directions, and information. Note that some prohibit dogs; some allow them on a leash.

SHOPPING

With a plethora of unique shops lining picturesque streets, there's nary a chain store in sight (strict zoning laws make this possible). The three main towns—Vineyard Haven, Edgartown, and Oak Bluffs—have the largest concentrations of shops. At the Aquinnah Cliffs, touristy Native American crafts and souvenirs abound during the season, and cottage industries and the odd shop or gallery appear off the main roads in many locations.

A different, more modest shopping experience unfolds at the West Tisbury Farmers' Market, the largest farmers' market in Massachusetts. Elsewhere, some of the antiques stores hidden along back roads brim with the interesting and the unusual.

A specialty of the island is wampum—beads made from black, white, or purple shells and fashioned into jewelry sold at the cliffs and elsewhere. Antique and new scrimshaw jewelry, and jewelry incorporating Vineyard and island-specific designs such as lighthouses or bunches of grapes, are also popular. Many island shops carry the ultra-expensive Nantucket lightship baskets, tightly woven creations of wood and rattan that are now valued collectibles.

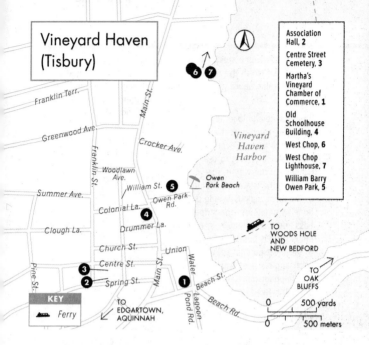

Numbers in the text correspond to numbers in the margin and on the Vineyard Haven map.

ent with a touch of the bohemian. Settled in the mid-1600s when the island's first governor-to-be purchased rights to the land from local Wampanoags, it's the busiest year-round community on Martha's Vineyard. Visitors arriving here step off the ferry right into the bustle of the harbor, a block from the shops and restaurants of Main Street.

Numbers in the text correspond to numbers in the margin and on the Vineyard Haven map.

WHAT TO SEE

2 Association Hall. The stately, neoclassic 1844 building houses the town hall and the Katharine Cornell Memorial Theatre, created in part with funds that Cornell (1898–1974)—one of America's foremost stage actresses in the 1920s, '30s, and '40s and a longtime summer resident—donated in her will. The walls of the theater on the second floor are painted with murals depicting whaling expeditions and a Native American gathering, and the ceiling resembles a blue sky with seagulls overhead. Island artist Stan Murphy painted the murals on the occasion of the town's tercentenary in 1971. The theater occasionally holds performances of plays, concerts, and dances. ✉ *51 Spring St.* ☎ *508/696–4200.*

❸ Centre Street Cemetery. Tall pine trees shade grave markers dating as far back as 1817. Some stones are simple gray slate slabs, and others are carved with such motifs as the death's-head—a skull, common on tombstones of the era. Actress Katharine Cornell, who died in 1974 and whose largesse helped build the theater named for her (housed in the Association Hall), is buried here. ✉ *Centre St. between William and Franklin Sts.*

❶ Martha's Vineyard Chamber of Commerce. If you need to stock up on maps or information on the island, this office is a good place to get your bearings. It's around the corner from the steamship terminal (where you can find a small information booth, open daily 8–8 in season) on Beach Road. ✉ *24 Beach Rd.* ☎ *508/693–0085* ⊕ *www.mvy.com* ☉ *Weekdays 9–5, plus abbreviated weekend hrs in season.*

NEED A BREAK? The delicious breads, pastries, and quick-lunch items at **Black Dog Bakery** (✉ *11 Water St.* ☎ *508/693–4786*) are simply not to be missed—it's a popular stop for good reason.

❹ Old Schoolhouse Building. Built in 1829, this was the first town school and today houses Sail Martha's Vineyard, a program teaching Vineyard children how to sail. Out front, the Liberty Pole was erected by the Daughters of the American Revolution in honor of three patriotic girls who blew up the town's liberty pole in 1776 to prevent it from being taken for use on a British warship. ✉ *110 Main St.*

❻ West Chop. Beautiful and green, the West Chop neighborhood retains its exclusive air and claims some of the island's most distinguished residents. This area, as well as East Chop across the harbor, was largely settled in the late 19th to early 20th century, when the very rich from Boston and Newport built expansive bluff-top "summer cottages." The shingle-style houses, characterized by broad gable ends, dormers, and natural shingle siding that weathers to gray, were meant to eschew pretense, though they were sometimes gussied up with a turret or two. A 2-mi walk, drive, or bike ride along Vineyard Haven's Main Street—which becomes increasingly residential on the way—will take you there.

❼ West Chop Lighthouse. One of two lighthouses that mark the opening to the harbor, the 52-foot white-and-black lighthouse was built of brick in 1838 to replace an 1817 wood building. It's been moved back from the edge of the eroding bluff twice. ✉ *W. Chop Rd. (Main St.)* ⊕*www.marthas-vineyardhistory.com.*

West Chop Woods. This 85-acre conservation area, with marked walking trails through pitch pine and oak, is just south and west of the West Chop lighthouse, with entrances on Main Street and Franklin Street and parking on Franklin.

❺ William Barry Owen Park. For a little relaxation, try the tree-shaded benches in this lovely spot for a picnic. In summer concerts are held at the bandstand. At the end of the lawn is a public beach with a swing set and a close-up view of the boats sailing in and out of the harbor. In the 19th century this harbor was one of the busiest ports in the world, welcoming thousands of vessels each year. Lighthouses still stand at the headlands—West Chop in Vineyard Haven and East Chop in Oak Bluffs—to help bring ships safely into port.

William Street. A stroll down this quiet stretch of white picket fences and Greek Revival houses, many of them built for prosperous sea captains, lets you imagine the town as it was in the 19th century. Now part of a National Historic District, the street was spared when the Great Fire of 1883 claimed much of the old whaling and fishing town.

WHERE TO EAT

$$$–$$$$ ✕ **Le Grenier.** Owner-chef Jean Dupon has been serving classic French food since the late 1970s above the M. V. Bagel Authority at the upper end of Vineyard Haven's downtown. All this time, he's been consistently loyal to the French standards: frogs' legs, sweetbreads, lobster flambéed with calvados, chicken livers Provençale, and tournedos are among the entrées. The decor is hardly stuffy in the French tradition; rather, it's almost backyard casual, with a string of lightbulbs and souvenir wine-bottle corks lining the walls. ✉ *Upper Main St.* ☎ *508/693–4906* ⊕ *www.legrenier restaurant.com* ▭ *AE, MC, V* ⛁ *BYOB* ⊘ *No lunch.*

$$–$$$$ ✕ **Black Dog Tavern.** This island landmark—which is more popular with tourists than locals—lies just steps from the ferry terminal in Vineyard Haven. In July and August, the wait for breakfast (with an expansive omelet assortment) can be as much as an hour from 8 AM on. Why? Partly because the ambience inside—roaring fireplace,

Where to Stay & Eat in Vineyard Haven (Tisbury)

KEY

- ① Hotels
- ❶ Restaurants
- ⛴ Ferry

Restaurants

Artcliff Diner, 7

Beetlebung Coffee House, 3

Black Dog Tavern, 4

Cafe Moxie, 2

Le Grenier, 1

Mediterranean, 8

Net Result, 6

Tropical Restaurant, 5

Hotels

Crocker House Inn, 3

Greenwood House, 2

Hanover House, 5

Mansion House, 4

Martha's Vineyard Family Campground, 6

Thorncroft Inn, 1

dark-wood walls, maritime memorabilia, and a grand view of the water—makes everyone feel so at home. The menu is heavy on local fish, chowders, and chops. Lighter fare is available until 7 PM in the Black Dog Bakery Cafe. ⊠ *Beach St.* ☎ *508/693–9223* ⚓ *Reservations not accepted* ⊟ *AE, D, MC, V* ⓦ *BYOB.*

$–$$$$ ✕ **Cafe Moxie.** Open year-round, this classy restaurant has a handsome wooden bar (though it's a dry town) and local artists' work on the walls. Chef Austin Racine's mussels, steamed in garlic and ginger and served over noodles, are a favorite. For something fancier, try a duck breast wrapped in Swiss chard over a white-bean-and-duck ragout, or herbed gnocchi with garlic, leeks, roasted tomato, and chèvre. Hours tend to vary, so call first. ⊠ *Main St. at Centre St.* ☎ *508/693–1484* ⊟ *D, MC, V* ⓦ *BYOB* ☒ *Closed Mon. No dinner Tues. and Oct.–Apr.*

$–$$$$ ✕ **Mediterranean.** Opened in 2004 by chefs Leslie and Douglas Hewson, this sunny, informal eatery overlooking the harbor has become a favorite with locals for reliable, freshly prepared pan-Mediterranean food—ingredients and recipes reflect Moroccan, Spanish, French, and Italian influences.

Start with the savory artichoke Française sautéed in garlic, herbs, and lemon butter. Excellent main dishes include oven-roasted salt cod with crabmeat, and grilled lamb with a rosemary reduction and a goat cheese–and–tomato tart. Pastry chef Leslie has earned a loyal following with her flaky baklava topped with lemon ice cream. ⊠ *52 Beach Rd.* ☎ *508/693–1617 or 888/693–1617* ⊟ *AE, D, MC, V* 𝅘𝅥*BYOB* ⊗ *No lunch Sun.*

$–$$$ ✕ **Tropical Restaurant.** The house specialty at this roadside restaurant is *rodizio*, a Brazilian style of barbecue where slow-roasted meats—in this case beef, chicken, sausage, pork, and lamb—are carved table-side and served continuously throughout your meal. Along with rice and beans, side dishes include collard greens and yucca. ⊠ *Five Corners* ☎ *508/696–0715* ⊟ *MC, V* 𝅘𝅥*BYOB.*

¢–$$$ ✕ **Net Result.** It may not have quite the ambience of the fish
★ markets in Menemsha, but this simple take-out market and restaurant in a shopping center just outside downtown Vineyard Haven serves some of the best food around, including superb lobster bisque, hefty scallop and oyster platters, steamed lobsters, grilled swordfish sandwiches, and crab salad. There are always additional daily specials that reflect the day's catch, and Net Result also has a sushi counter: the Martha's Vineyard roll is a favorite, packed with tuna, salmon, yellowtail, and avocado and wrapped in seaweed. You can dine at picnic tables outside and view Vineyard Haven's harbor across the busy road. ⊠ *Tisbury Marketplace, 79 Beach Rd.* ☎ *508/693–6071* ⊕ *www.mvseafood.com* ⊟ *MC, V.*

¢–$ ✕ **Artcliff Diner.** This vintage diner has been a year-round breakfast and lunch meeting place for locals since 1943. Owner–chef Gina Stanley, who was on call to make desserts for Blair House when she lived in Washington, D.C., serves anything but ordinary diner fare. She whips up pecan pancakes with real rum raisins for breakfast, and crepes with chèvre, arugula, or almost anything you ask for at lunch. A small porch was added in 2007. ⊠ *39 Beach Rd.* ☎ *508/693–1224* ⊟ *No credit cards* ⊗ *Closed Wed. No dinner.*

¢ ✕ **Beetlebung Coffee House.** This cozy coffeehouse is within easy walking distance of the ferry terminal and downtown shops and restaurants. A hip crowd convenes here for the great sandwiches (try the Taos panini, with flame-roasted New Mexico green chilies, turkey, and cheddar), designer-coffee drinks, and delicious desserts. The breakfast "egg-wich," with Black Forest ham, poached egg, and Vermont cheddar, is a treat. There's an attractive side patio that's perfect on a warm afternoon. ⊠ *32 Beach St.* ☎ *508/696–7122* ⊟ *MC, V.*

WHERE TO STAY

$$$$ ⊡**Crocker House Inn.** This 1924 farmhouse-style inn is
★ tucked into a quiet lane off Main Street, minutes from the ferries and Owen Park Beach. The rooms are decorated casually with understated flair—pastel-painted walls, softly upholstered wing-back chairs, and white-wicker nightstands. Each contains a small, wall-mounted "honor bar," with a disposable camera, sunscreen, and other useful sundries. Three rooms have soothing whirlpool tubs, and two have fireplaces. No. 6, with a small porch and a private entrance, has the best view of the harbor. Breakfast is served at a large farmer's table inside the small common room and kitchen area. Jeff and Jynell Kristal are the young, friendly owners, and Jynell also creates whimsically painted glassware, available for sale. **Pros:** Great owners, short walk from town, easygoing vibe. **Cons:** You pay a premium for this location, decor is more casual than posh, books up quickly in summer. ⊠ *12 Crocker Ave., Box 1658, 02568* ☎ *508/693–1151 or 800/772–0206* ⊕ *www.crocker houseinn.com* ↩ *8 rooms* ⌂ *In-room: Wi-Fi. In-hotel: no elevator, no kids under 12* ⊟ *MC, V* ⊙ *CP.*

$$$$ ⊡**Mansion House.** There has been a hostelry on this Main Street site just above Vineyard Haven Harbor since 1794; today's Mansion House opened in 2003, following a major fire to its predecessor. Apart from the cheerful, summery rooms—some with balconies, gas fireplaces, and soaking tubs—the cupola deck provides a pleasant spot for a respite. It affords sweeping views of the harbor, the town, and the lagoon that stretches between Vineyard Haven and Oak Bluffs. Afternoon cookies and lemonade are served there or you can BYOB. The hotel's Zephrus Restaurant serves reliable American fare and is also a nice spot for cocktails. **Pros:** On-site restaurant and spa, steps from Vineyard Haven shopping and ferry, light-filled rooms. **Cons:** No grounds to speak of, center-of-it-all locale can be a little noisy, not historic. ⊠ *9 Main St., Box 428, 02568* ☎ *509/693–2200 or 800/332–4112* ⊕ *www. mvmansionhouse.com* ↩ *32 rooms, 11 suites* ⌂ *In-room: refrigerator, Wi-Fi. In-hotel: restaurant, room service, pool, gym, spa* ⊟ *AE, D, MC, V* ⊙ *CP.*

$$$$ ⊞ **Thorncroft Inn.** On 2½ wooded acres about 1 mi from the ferry, this inn's main building, a 1918 Craftsman bunga-low, combines fine colonial and richly carved Renaissance Revival antiques with tasteful reproductions to create a somewhat formal environment. Most rooms have work-ing fireplaces and canopy beds; three rooms have two-per-son whirlpool baths, and two have private hot-tub spas. Rooms in the carriage house, set apart from the main house via a breezeway, are more secluded. **Pros:** Short walk from town, antiques galore, carriage-house rooms have lots of privacy. **Cons:** A bit formal and fussy, antiques galore, some rooms are very small given the steep rates. ⊠*460 Main St., Box 1022, 02568* ☎*508/693–3333 or 800/332–1236* ⊞*508/693–5419* ⊕*www.thorncroft.com* ⌂*14 rooms, 1 cottage* ⌂*In-room: refrigerator (some), VCR, Ethernet. In-hotel: restaurant, no kids under 13* ⊟*AE, D, DC, MC, V* ⦿*BP.*

$$–$$$$ ⊞ **Greenwood House.** A low-key bed-and-breakfast on a quiet lane around the corner from Vineyard Haven's pub-lic library, the Greenwood House is one of the better val-ues in town. Affable innkeepers Kathy Stinson and Larry Gomez own this homey, three-story Arts and Crafts–style cottage with classic shingle siding and a shaded yard. The rooms are decorated with a mix of antiques and contem-porary pieces, including brass and four-poster beds, island artwork, and functional but attractive nightstands and bureaus. It's a 10- to 15-minute walk from the ferry and even closer to many shops and restaurants. **Pros:** Easy walk to shops and dining, good value, personal service. **Cons:** Some rooms a bit small, no room phones, beach and water a one-minute walk. ⊠*40 Greenwood Ave., Box 2734, 02568* ☎*508/693–6150 or 866/693–6150* ⊕*www.green-woodhouse.com* ⌂*4 rooms* ⌂*In-room: refrigerator, dial-up. In-hotel: no elevator* ⊟*AE, MC, V* ⦿*BP.*

$$–$$$ ⊞ **Hanover House.** Set on ½ acre of landscaped lawn on a busy road—but within walking distance of the ferry—this three-property, children-friendly inn consists of a classic, home-style B&B, a country inn, and a carriage house. Rooms are decorated with a combination of antiques and reproduction furniture, mostly in the Victorian style, and each has indi-vidual flair: in one, an antique sewing machine serves as the TV stand. The three carriage-house suites have private decks or patios, two have kitchenettes, and one has a gas fireplace. **Pros:** Good value, 10-minute walk to shops and dining, some kitchenettes. **Cons:** Off busy road, no water or beach

views from most units, some stall showers. ⊠*28 Edgartown Rd., Box 2108, 02568* ☎*508/693–1066 or 800/696–8633* ⊕*www.hanoverhouseinn.com* ⤶*12 rooms, 3 suites* ⚮*In-room: kitchen (some), Wi-Fi. In-hotel: no elevator* ⊟*AE, D, MC, V* ⊙*Closed Dec.–Mar.* ◎*BP.*

¢ ⚠**Martha's Vineyard Family Campground.** Wooded sites, a
★ ball field, a camp store, bicycle rentals, and electrical and water hookups are among the facilities at this 20-acre campsite a few miles from Vineyard Haven. A step up from tents are 21 rustic one- or two-room cabins, which come with electricity, refrigerators, gas grills, and combinations of double and bunk beds (but bring your own bedding). The campground also has hookups for trailers. This is the only campsite on the island, so book early; discounts are available for extended stays. No dogs or motorcycles are allowed. **Pros:** Great value, secluded setting, some private cabins. **Cons:** No dogs allowed, 1½-mi walk from town, books up quickly. ⊠*569 Edgartown Rd., Box 1557, 02568* ☎*508/693–3772* ⊟*508/693–5767* ⊕*www.campmvfc.com* ⤶*130 tent sites, 50 RV sites, 21 cabins* ⚮*Refrigerator (some), bicycles, laundry facilities, play area* ⊟*D, MC, V* ⊙*Closed mid-Oct.–mid-May.*

NIGHTLIFE & THE ARTS

The **Vineyard Playhouse** (⊠*24 Church St.* ☎*508/696–6300* ⊕*www.vineyardplayhouse.org*) has a year-round schedule of professional productions. From mid-June through early September, a troupe performs drama, classics, and comedies on the air-conditioned main stage; summer Shakespeare and other productions take place at the natural amphitheater at Tashmoo Overlook on State Road in Vineyard Haven—bring insect repellent and a blanket or lawn chair. Children's programs and a summer camp are also scheduled, and local art exhibitions are held throughout the year. The theater is wheelchair-accessible and provides hearing devices.

SPORTS & THE OUTDOORS

BEACHES

Lake Tashmoo Town Beach (⊠*End of Herring Creek Rd.*) invites swimming in the warm, relatively shallow, brackish lake or in the cooler, gentle Vineyard Sound. There's a lifeguarded area and some parking.

Owen Park Beach (⊠*Off Main St.*), a small, sandy harbor beach, has a children's play area, lifeguards, and a harbor view. The beach straddles a dock that juts into the harbor and is just steps away from the ferry terminal in Vineyard Haven, making it a great spot for some last rays and a dip before you have to kiss the island good-bye.

Tisbury Town Beach (⊠*End of Owen Little Way off Main St.*) is a public beach next to the Vineyard Haven Yacht Club. As at Owen Park Beach, its proximity to the town makes it a perfect out-of-the-way yet near-everything spot for a quick escape from the crowds and a dip.

BICYCLING

Cycle Works (⊠*351 State Rd.* ☎*508/693–6966*) sells all variety of bikes, rents and sells fitness equipment, and has an excellent repair shop.

Martha's Bike Rentals (⊠*4 Lagoon Pond Rd., at Five Corners* ☎*508/693–6593*) rents bicycles, helmets, baby seats, and trailer bikes that attach to the rear of adult bikes to carry kids. It also handles repairs and will deliver and pick up your bike free anywhere on the island.

Martha's Vineyard Strictly Bikes (⊠*24 Union St.* ☎*508/693–0782*) rents a variety of bicycles and baby trailers. It also sells bikes and does repairs.

BOATING

Martha's Vineyard Oceansports (⊠*86 Beach St., Vineyard Haven* ☎*508/693–2838*) rents equipment for a variety of water sports, including wakeboarding, knee boarding, and tubing.

Wind's Up! (⊠*199 Beach Rd.* ☎*508/693–4252 or 508/693–4340* ⊕*www.windsupmv.com*) rents day sailers, catamarans, surfboards, sea kayaks, canoes, and Sunfish, as well as Windsurfers and Boogie boards; the shop also gives lessons.

GOLF

The semiprivate **Mink Meadows Golf Club** (⊠*Golf Club Rd. at Franklin St.* ☎*508/693–0600* ⊕*www.minkmeadowsgc. com*), on West Chop, has 9 holes and ocean views. Reservations can be made 48 hours in advance.

MINIATURE GOLF

At **Island Cove Mini Golf** (⊠*State Rd.* ☎*508/693–2611*) you golf on an 18-hole course with bridges, a cave, sand traps, and a stream that powers a waterfall. The island's only rock-climbing wall is also here.

SHOPPING

All Things Oriental (⊠*123 Beach Rd.* ☎*508/693–8375*) sells new and antique jewelry, porcelains, paintings, furniture, and more, all with an Asian theme.

★ **Belushi Pisano Gallery** (⊠*18 State Rd.* ☎*508/696–8988*), operated by Victor Pisano and Judith Belushi Pisano, is an extension of the Second Chance Foundation, a nonprofit organization that aims to assist artists on Martha's Vineyard during times of financial duress; proceeds from the gallery's sales fund the foundation. It's a handsome space carrying works in all types of media by more than 20 of the island's top artists. There's also a small coffeehouse.

Bowl & Board (⊠*35 Main St.* ☎*508/693–9441*) is summer-home central. It carries everything you need to cozy up in a summer rental.

Bramhall & Dunn (⊠*19 Main St.* ☎*508/693–6437*) carries crafts, linens, hand-knit sweaters, and fine antique country-pine furniture.

Bunch of Grapes Bookstore (⊠*44 Main St.* ☎*508/693–2291*) sells new books and sponsors book signings.

Church Street (⊠*Off Main St.*) is a little enclave of shops including **Fleece Dreams** (☎*508/693–6141*), which sells handmade clothes in sumptuous fabrics; **Good Impressions** (☎*508/693–7682*), which carries rubber stamp supplies and has classes in stamp art and fabric embossing; and **Beadnicks** (☎*508/693–7650*), a bead lover's paradise.

Midnight Farm (⊠*18 Water-Cromwell La.* ☎*508/693–1997*), co-owned by Carly Simon and Tamara Weiss, stocks furniture, clothes, shoes, jewelry, linens, dinnerware, books, soaps, candles, garden supplies, snack foods, and, of course, Carly's books and CDs.

★ Fodor'sChoice **Rainy Day** (⊠*66 Main St.* ☎*508/693–1830*), as the name suggests, carries gifts and amusements that are perfect for one of the island's gloomy rainy days, when you just need a warm, dry diversion. You can find toys, crafts, cards, soaps, and more.

Tisbury Antiques & Interiors (⊠*339 State Rd.* ☎*508/693–8333*) carries a vast selection of 18th- and 19th-century English, French, and Italian antiques, plus fine lighting fixtures, Cornishware, estate jewelry, and vintage books and postcards.

CLOSE UP

Perfect Days

The outings below cover all the towns on the island, but you don't have to. You might want to spend a short time in Vineyard Haven before getting rural Up-Island or heading for a beach. Or you might prefer to go straight to Edgartown to stroll past the antique white houses, pop into a museum or two, and shop. If you just want to have fun, Oak Bluffs, with its harbor scene and nearby beaches, is the place to go. In essence, pick and choose what you like best from what follows. The Vineyard is small enough that you can pick one town as your base and easily explore other areas.

A PERFECT DAY DOWN-ISLAND

Start your day in Vineyard Haven. Historic houses line William Street, and you can find shops and eateries along Main Street. Take a quick jaunt out to **West Chop** for a great view over Vineyard Sound from the lighthouse; then head back through town toward Oak Bluffs via Beach Road. Spend some time wandering the streets of the **Oak Bluffs Campground,** where tightly packed pastel-painted Victorian cottages vie with one another for the fanciest gingerbread trim. Then head into the center of Oak Bluffs for a ride on the Flying Horses, the oldest con-

tinuously operating carousel in the country.

Instead of going to Oak Bluffs from Vineyard Haven, you could head straight to **Edgartown,** where you can spend the afternoon browsing the shops and visiting museums. Take the On-Time ferry to **Chappaquiddick Island** to visit the Mytoi preserve or have a picnic at Three Ponds Preserve. If conservation areas are your thing, the Cape Poge Wildlife Refuge on the island is a must. You'll need a few hours on Chappaquiddick to make the visit worthwhile.

A PERFECT DAY UP-ISLAND

Begin your day with a visit to the **West Tisbury** farms, some of which have pony rides for kids. A stroll amid **Long Point Reservation's** 633 acres of open grassland and heath makes for an engaging morning.

Then drive out to **Aquinnah Cliffs** (formerly Gay Head), one of the most spectacular spots on the island. Go to the lookout at the cliffs for the view, or take the boardwalk to the beach and walk back to see the cliffs and Aquinnah Light from below. Spend some time sunning and swimming at this breathtaking spot. (A note to the modest: the beach attracts nude sunbathers; though it's illegal, officials usually look the other way.)

On your way back from the cliffs, stop in the fishing village of **Menemsha.** You could also stop at the **Winery at Chicama Vineyards** in West Tisbury for a tasting. As the day comes to an end, pick up some seafood and take it to Menemsha Beach for a sunset picnic.

A PERFECT RAINY DAY

After you've assessed that gray skies and steady downpours do not constitute beach weather, start your day curled up with a good book. If you need some good reading material, get up early and visit **Edgartown Books** in Edgartown or **Bunch of Grapes** in Vineyard Haven. **Book Den East,** in a converted barn in Oak Bluffs, is full of rare and fascinating used books. You can also drop by one of the six island libraries.

By late morning, with cabin fever setting in, visit the small handful of island museums. The **Martha's Vineyard Historical Society** houses exhibits in the Captain Pease House, the Gale Huntington Library of History, and the Foster Gallery—all in Edgartown. The **Vincent House Museum,** also in Edgartown, contains displays of early island life. While in Edgartown, have lunch at the cozy **Wharf Pub.**

After lunch, head to the video arcade in Oak Bluffs and, across the street, the **Flying Horses** carousel, both for kids and kids-at-heart. The whole family can unwind at the **Offshore Ale** brewpub, also in Oak Bluffs, where dart enthusiasts can find formidable foes.

By late afternoon and into evening, movies can distract you from the downpour (however, island theaters rarely show matinees earlier than 4 PM). If you're renting a house that has a TV and a VCR or DVD, you're set. There are great video rental shops in the Down-Island towns. If you're Up-Island, try Alley's General Store in West Tisbury and the Harbor Craft Shop in Menemsha. Libraries also have videos for overnight loan, though, depending on the town, you may have to purchase a library card first.

If all else fails, you can always watch the storm through your window and daydream…of sunny days.

The Toy Box (⊠*Tisbury Marketplace, 79 Beach Rd.* ☎*508/693–8182*) is a terrific source of whimsical and imaginative games and toys for kids.

★ Nationally renowned for their distinctive, hand-sculpted metal weather vanes, **Tuck and Holand** (⊠*275 State Rd.* ☎*508/693–3914 or 888/693–3914*) has a studio gallery a 10-minute walk from downtown. Here you can examine Anthony Holand and Travis Tuck's otherworldly creations, including copper Martha's Vineyard wall maps, school-of-bluefish chandeliers, and the signature custom weather vanes.

Wind's Up! (⊠*199 Beach Rd.* ☎*508/693–4340*) sells swimwear, windsurfing and sailing equipment, Boogie boards, and other outdoor gear.

OAK BLUFFS

3½ mi east of Vineyard Haven.

Purchased from the Wampanoags in the 1660s, Oak Bluffs was a farming community that did not come into its own until the 1830s, when Methodists began holding summer revivalist meetings in a stand of oaks known as Wesleyan Grove, named for Methodism's founder, John Wesley. As the camp meetings caught on, attendees built small cottages in place of tents. Then the general population took notice and the area became a popular summer vacation spot. Hotels, a dance hall, a roller-skating rink, and other shops and amusements were built to accommodate the flocks of summer visitors.

Today Circuit Avenue is the center of action in Oak Bluffs, the address of most of the town's shops, bars, and restaurants. Oak Bluffs Harbor, once the setting for a number of grand hotels—the 1879 Wesley Hotel on Lake Avenue is the last of them—is still crammed with gingerbread-trimmed guesthouses and food and souvenir joints. With its whimsical cottages, long beachfront, and funky shops, the small town is more high-spirited than haute, more fun than refined.

Numbers in the text correspond to numbers in the margin and on the Oak Bluffs map.

❾ The **information booth** will help you get your bearings and point the way to the not-to-be-missed spots in Oak Bluffs, with some good tips for gingerbread-trim lovers. ⊠*Lake*

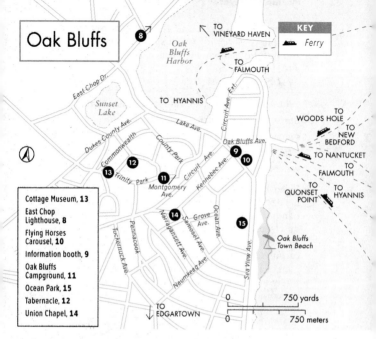

and Oak Bluffs Aves. ☎508/693–4266 ☉*Mid-May–mid-Oct., daily 9–5.*

WHAT TO SEE

⑬ Cottage Museum. For a glimpse at life in Cottage City during its heyday, visit this 1868 Creamsicle-hue cottage near the Tabernacle. The two-story museum exhibits cottage furnishings from the early days, including photographs, hooked rugs, quilts, and old Bibles. The gift shop sells Victorian and nautical items. ✉*1 Trinity Park* ☎508/693–7784 ☎*$1.50 donation requested* ☉*Mid-June–Sept., Mon.–Sat. 10–4.*

East Chop. This is one of two points of land that jut out into the Nantucket–Vineyard sound, creating the sheltered harbor at Vineyard Haven and some fine views. From Oak Bluffs, take East Chop Drive, or you can loop out to the point on your way from Vineyard Haven by taking Highland Drive off Beach Road after crossing the drawbridge.

⑧ East Chop Lighthouse. Spectacular views of Nantucket Sound can be had from this 40-foot structure, which stands high atop a 79-foot bluff. The lighthouse was built out of cast iron in 1876 to replace an 1828 tower (used as part of a semaphore system of visual signaling between the island and Boston) that burned down. ⊠*E. Chop Dr.* ☎*508/627–4441* ☒*$3* ☉*Late June–mid-Sept., Sun. 1 hr before sunset–1 hr after sunset.*

NEED A BREAK? **The Coop de Ville** (⊠*Dockside Marketplace, Oak Bluffs Harbor* ☎*508/693–3420*) **teems with people eager to sample simple fried seafood and raw bar delectables (the oysters are fantastic). Eat out on the patio deck overlooking the water to enjoy the view. It's open May to mid-October.**

🔟 **Flying Horses Carousel.** Handcrafted in 1876 (the horses have real horse hair and glass eyes), this National Historic Landmark—the nation's oldest continuously operating carousel—gives children a taste of entertainment from a TV-free era. On summer evenings or rainy days, however, the carousel can get crowded; you can avoid the crunch by going early in the day. While waiting in line (the wait is rarely longer than 20 minutes or so), you can munch on popcorn or cotton candy or slurp a slushie. The waiting area has a number of arcade games. ⊠*Oak Bluffs Ave.* ☎*508/693–9481* ☒*Rides $1.50, book of 8 tickets $10* ☉*Late May–early Sept., daily 10–10; Easter–late May, weekends 10–5; early Sept.–mid-Oct., weekdays 11–4:30, weekends 10–5.*

⓫ **Oak Bluffs Campground.** Don't miss this 34-acre warren of streets tightly packed with more than 300 Carpenter Gothic Victorian cottages with wedding-cake trim, gaily painted in pastels. As you wander through this fairy-tale setting, imagine it on a balmy summer evening, lighted by the warm glow of hundreds of Japanese paper lanterns hung from every cottage porch. This describes the scene on Illumination Night at the end of the Camp Meeting season—which is attended these days by some fourth- and fifth-generation cottagers. Attendees mark the occasion as they have for more than a century, with lights, song, and open houses for families and friends. Note that because of overwhelming crowds of onlookers in seasons past, the date is not announced until the week before. Ninety-minute tours are conducted Tuesday and Thursday, July and August, at 10 AM. ⊠*Off Circuit Ave.* ☎*508/693–0525* ⊕*www.mvcma. org* ☒*Tour $10.*

⓭ **Ocean Park.** A long stretch of green facing the sea, Ocean Park fronts a crescent of large shingle-style cottages with numerous turrets, breezy porches, and pastel facades. Band concerts take place at the gazebo here on summer nights, and in August the park hosts hordes of island families and visitors for a grand fireworks display over the ocean. ⊠*Sea View Ave.*

⑫ **Tabernacle.** At the center of Trinity Park is this impressive open-air structure of iron and wood, the original site of the Methodist services. On Wednesday at 8 PM in season, visitors are invited to join in on an old-time community sing-along. If you know tunes like "The Erie Canal" or just want to listen in, drop by the Tabernacle and take a seat. Music books are available for a donation. Sunday services are held in summer at 9:30 AM. The 1878 **Trinity Methodist Church** also stands in the park and is open for visits during daylight hours (no tours, however) and, of course, for services on Sunday.

⑭ **Union Chapel.** This octagonal, nonsectarian house of worship was constructed in 1870 for the Cottage City resort folk who lived outside the Campground's 7-foot-high fence. In summer, concerts are held here, as are 10 AM Sunday services. ⊠*Kennebec and Samoset Aves.* ☎*508/693–5350.*

WHERE TO EAT

$$$$ ★ Fodor'sChoice ✕**Sweet Life Café.** Housed in a charming Victorian house, this island favorite's warm tones, low lighting, and handsome antique furniture will make you feel like you've entered someone's home—but the cooking is more sophisticated than home-style. Dishes on the menu are prepared in inventive ways. Duck breast is roasted with a lavender-rosemary-honey glaze, and the gazpacho is a white version with steamed clams, sliced red grapes, and smoked-paprika oil. The desserts are superb; try the warm chocolate fondant with toasted-almond ice cream. There's outdoor dining by candlelight in a shrub-enclosed garden, with heaters for cold nights. The same owners run **Slice of Life** (⊠*50 Circuit Ave.* ☎*508/693–3838*), a more casual, less expensive bakery and café nearby. ⊠*Upper Circuit Ave. at far end of town* ☎*508/696–0200* ⚑*Reservations essential* ⊟*AE, D, MC, V* ⊘*Closed Jan.–Mar.*

$$–$$$$ ✕**Jimmy Seas.** The irresistible fragrance of sautéed garlic wafting out these doors beckons lovers of the "stinking rose." Most dishes come in the pan they're cooked in and are among the biggest portions you'll find on the island. Classic red-sauce Italian dishes include *vongole* (whole littleneck clams) marinara and linguine puttan-

Where to Stay & Eat in Oak Bluffs

Restaurants	Hotels
Jimmy Seas, **5**	Admiral Benbow Inn, **1**
Linda Jean's, **3**	Attleboro House, **2**
Lola's, **7**	Dockside Inn, **5**
Lookout Tavern, **1**	MV Surfside Motel, **6**
Offshore Ale Company, **4**	Oak Bluffs Inn, **3**
Sharky's Cantina, **2**	Oak House, **7**
Smoke 'n Bones, **8**	Pequot Hotel, **4**
Sweet Life Café, **6**	

KEY
1 Hotels
1 Restaurants
Ferry

esca. A brightly colored porch and painted ceilings add to the place's charm, although service can be a little uneven. ⊠*32 Kennebec Ave.* ☎*508/696–8550* ☝*Reservations not accepted* ═*MC, V.*

$$–$$$$ ✕**Lola's.** This festive spot draws a party crowd. On one side, a spirited bar hosts live music; an enclosed patio for dining and a large separate dining room are on another side. Ribs as well as Southern and Louisiana standards such as crawfish étoufée and grilled swordfish with key lime dill sauce fill the long menu; Sunday mornings are reserved for an all-you-can-eat buffet brunch, often with live gospel or jazz. This is more of a scene than a relaxing dining spot. However, the bar is big and welcoming, and the wall mural is full of familiar local faces. Lighter, less expensive fare, such as chicken jambalaya and fried catfish, is available from the pub menu. ⊠*Beach Rd., about 1 mi from Oak Bluffs* ☎*508/693–5007* ⊕*www. lolassouthernseafood.com* ═*DC, MC, V.*

$–$$$$ ✕**Offshore Ale Company.** The island's first and only microbrewery restaurant has become quite popular. There are private wooden booths, and there is dark wood throughout, a dartboard in the corner, and live music throughout the year

(Wednesday-night Irish music jams are a hoot). Take your own peanuts from a barrel by the door and drop the shells on the floor; then order from a menu that includes steaks and burgers, chicken, pasta, gumbo, and fish. However, to truly appreciate the beer, try it with one of the wood-fired brick-oven pizzas. ⊠ *30 Kennebec Ave.* ☎ *508/693–2626* ⊕ *www.offshoreale.com* ⤷ *Reservations not accepted* ⊙ *No lunch Mon. and Tues. Oct.–May* ⊟ *AE, MC, V.*

$-$$$ ×**Smoke 'n Bones.** This is the island's only rib joint, with its own smoker out back and a cord of hickory, apple, oak, and mesquite wood stacked up around the lot. Treats from the smoker include Asian-style dry-rubbed ribs and North Carolina–style pulled pork. The homemade onion rings are addictive. The place has a cookie-cutter, prefab feeling, with all the appropriate touches—neon flames around the kitchen and marble bones for doorknobs. If you're a true rib aficionado, this may not satisfy you, but on the Vineyard it's an offbeat treat. ⊠ *20 Oakland Ave.* ☎ *508/696–7427* ⤷ *Reservations not accepted* ⊙ *Closed Jan.–Mar.* ⊟ *MC, V.*

¢–$$ ×**Lookout Tavern.** There are two things about this easygoing Oak Bluffs seafood joint that make it stand out. First, its rustic dining room affords direct views of the sea and incoming ferryboats—it's truly the perfect "lookout" if you love watching boats ply the island's waters. Second, it serves the usual seafood platters plus first-rate sushi, from the salmon and tuna rolls to more unusual treats, like the Inkwell Roll, with barbecued eel, cucumber, avocado, crab-meat, and seaweed salad. Highlights from the traditional menu include the grilled Cuban sandwich, the snow-crab dinner, fish-and-chips, or the fried scallop plate. ⊠ *8 Seaview Ave. Ext.* ☎ *508/696–9844* ⊟ *AE, D, DC, MC, V.*

¢–$$ ×**Sharky's Cantina.** This small storefront restaurant opened ★ in 2006 to rave reviews. Sharky's serves tasty–somewhat creative–Mexican and Southwestern fare and great drinks, and you may wait awhile to get a table. But once you're in, savor spicy tortilla soup, lobster quesadillas, steak burritos, chicken mole, and gaucho-style skirt steak. There's an extensive margarita list (they're strong here), and for dessert try apple-pie empanadas drizzled with caramel sauce. Limited items from the menu are served until around midnight during the summer season. ⊠ *31 Circuit Ave.* ☎ *508/693–7501* ⊕ *www.sharkyscantina.com* ⤷ *Reservations not accepted* ⊟ *AF, MC, V.*

¢-$ ✕**Linda Jean's.** This is a classic local hangout, a diner that
★ serves food the way a diner should: with hearty helpings and
inexpensive prices. Want breakfast at 6 AM? No problem.
Want breakfast at 11:30 AM? No problem. Tired of the gourmet world and want comfortable booths, friendly waitresses,
and few frills? No problem. The only problem: you may have
to wait—even at 6 AM. ⊠*34 Circuit Ave.* ☎*508/693–4093*
⌂*Reservations not accepted* ⊟*No credit cards.*

WHERE TO STAY

$$$-$$$$ 🏠**Oak Bluffs Inn.** A tan octagonal viewing tower dominates
this rosy-hue Victorian B&B with a veranda on Oak Bluffs'
main street, a short stroll from the beach. Victorian and
country pieces fill the high-ceilinged rooms, all of which
have private baths and gauzy white curtains; one has a four-
poster bed. One very large room in the carriage house can
accommodate three adults or two adults and two kids. **Pros:**
Steps from shops and restaurants, handsome building, well-
chosen antiques. **Cons:** In the thick of the commercial dis-
trict, a tad frilly, location can be a little noisy. ⊠*64 Circuit
Ave., at Pequot Ave., Box 2546, 02557* ☎*508/693–7171 or
800/955–6235* 🖷*508/693–8787* ⊕*www.oakbluffsinn.com*
🛏*9 rooms* ⌂*In-hotel: no elevator* ⊟*AE, MC, V* ⊗*Closed
Nov.–early Apr.* ⚏*CP.*

$$$-$$$$ 🏠**Oak House.** The wraparound veranda of this courtly pas-
★ tel-painted 1872 Victorian looks across a busy street to the
beach and out across Nantucket Sound. Several rooms have
private terraces or balconies; if you're bothered by noise,
ask for a room in back. Ceilings, wall paneling, wainscot-
ing, and furnishings are all in richly painted or polished
oak, and all this well-preserved wood creates an appropri-
ate setting for the choice antique furniture and nautical-
theme accessories. An elegant afternoon tea with cakes and
cookies is served in a glassed-in sunporch. **Pros:** Stunning
decor, romantic and adult-oriented, some rooms have water
views. **Cons:** Some rooms get street noise, old-fashioned
vibe might turn off minimalists, busy location. ⊠*79 Seaview
Ave., Box 299, 02557* ☎*508/693–4187 or 866/693–5805*
⊕*www.vineyardinns.com* 🛏*8 rooms, 2 suites* ⌂*In-hotel:
no kids under 10, no elevator* ⊟*AE, D, MC, V* ⊗*Closed
mid-Oct.–mid-May* ⚏*CP.*

$$-$$$ 🏠**Admiral Benbow Inn.** On a busy road between Vineyard
Haven and Oak Bluffs Harbor—a few blocks from the har-
bor—is this small, endearing B&B. Built for a minister in
1891, the Benbox is decked out with elaborate woodwork,

a comfortable hodgepodge of antique furnishings, and a Victorian parlor with a stunning tile-and-carved-wood fireplace. The rooms are much the same, an eclectic mix of antiques and your grandmother's favorite comfy furniture. You have access to an ice machine and refrigerator in the kitchen. Children of all ages are welcome. **Pros:** Convenient to both Oak Bluffs and Vineyard Haven, beautiful grounds include peaceful gardens and waterscapes, the price is right. **Cons:** Front yard and some rooms view a gas station, on a road with plenty of traffic, no TVs or phones in rooms. ⊠*81 New York Ave., 02557* ☎*508/693–6825* ᗺ*508/693–7820* ⊕*www.admiral-benbow-inn.com* ⌫*7 rooms* ⌂*In-room: no phone, no TV. In-hotel: no elevator, public Internet* ▭*AE, D, MC, V* ⦿*CP.*

$$-$$$ 🖾**Dockside Inn.** This gingerbread Victorian-style inn built in the late 1980s, decked with broad porches, sits right by the dock, steps from the ferry landing and downtown shops, restaurants, and bars. Kids are welcome, and they'll have plenty to do in town and at nearby beaches. Some rooms open onto building-length balconies. **Pros:** Close to everything, very kid-friendly, big porches. Cons. Front of inn right on street, busy location, lots of kids in summer. ⊠*9 Circuit Ave. Ext., Box 1206, 02557* ☎*508/693–2966 or 800/245–5979* ⊕*www.vineyardinns.com* ⌫*17 rooms, 5 suites, 2 apartments* ⌂*In-room: kitchen (some), VCR, Wi-Fi. In-hotel: no elevator* ▭*AE, MC, V* ⊗*Closed late Oct.–mid-May* ⦿*CP.*

$$-$$$ 🖾**Martha's Vineyard Surfside Motel.** These two buildings stand right in the thick of things, steps from restaurants and nightlife, so it tends to get noisy in summer. Rooms are spacious and bright (especially corner units), smartly decorated with carpets, stylish wallpaper, tile floors, and fairly standard but attractive chain-style furnishings that include a table and chairs. Deluxe rooms have water views. Four suites have whirlpool baths, and two are wheelchair-accessible. The staff is helpful and courteous. **Pros:** Affordable by island standards, large rooms, close to dining and shopping. **Cons:** Busy location, more functional than romantic, lots of kids. ⊠*70 Oak Bluffs Ave., Box 2507, 02557* ☎*508/693–2500 or 800/537–3007* ᗺ*508/693–7343* ⊕*www.mvsurfside.com* ⌫*34 rooms, 4 suites* ⌂*In-room: refrigerator, Ethernet. In-hotel: restaurant, no elevator, some pets allowed (fee)* ▭*AE, D, MC, V.*

$$-$$$ ▦**Pequot Hotel.** The bustle of downtown Oak Bluffs is a pleasant five-minute walk past Carpenter Gothic houses from this casual cedar-shingle inn on a tree-lined street. The furniture is quirky but comfortable; the old wing has the most atmosphere. In the main section of the building, the first floor has a wide porch with rocking chairs—perfect for enjoying coffee or tea with the cookies that are set out in the afternoon—and a small breakfast room where you help yourself to bagels, muffins, and cereal in the morning. The hotel is one block from the beaches that line Oak Bluffs–Edgartown Road. **Pros:** Steps from shops and dining, reasonable rates, charmingly offbeat. **Cons:** Dated decor, no room phones, some rooms are small. ✉*19 Pequot Ave., 02557* ☎*508/693–5087 or 800/947–8704* ☎*508/696–9413* ⊕*www.pequothotel.com* ✍*29 rooms, 1 3-bedroom apartment* ⚒*In-room: no phone, Wi-Fi. In-hotel: no elevator* ▤*AE, D, MC, V* ⊘*Closed mid-Oct.–Apr.* ⦿*CP.*

$ ▦**Attleboro House.** This guesthouse, part of the Methodist Association Campground, is across the street from busy Oak Bluffs Harbor. The big 1874 gingerbread Victorian, an inn since its construction, has wraparound verandas on two floors and small, simple rooms with powder-blue walls, lacy white curtains, and a few antiques. Some rooms have sinks. Singles have three-quarter beds, and every room is provided linen exchange (but no chambermaid service) during a stay. The five shared baths are rustic and old but clean. **Pros:** Super affordable, steps from restaurants and shops, sinks in some rooms. **Cons:** Shared bathrooms, zero frills, no Web site. ✉*42 Lake Ave., Box 1564, 02557* ☎*508/693–4346* ✍*11 rooms with shared bath* ⚒*In-room: no TV. In-hotel: no elevator* ▤*AE, D, MC, V* ⊘*Closed Oct.–May* ⦿*CP.*

NIGHTLIFE & THE ARTS

At the **Featherstone Center for the Arts** (✉*Barnes Rd.* ☎*508/693–1850* ⊕*www.featherstonearts.org*), classes are available in photography, watercolor, pottery, printmaking, drawing, stained glass, weaving, and more. In summer, the Musical Mondays program (6:30 to 8 PM) hosts off- and on-island talent. Admission is $5, free for well-behaved kids; performances are on the lawn, so bring a blanket or lawn chair.

Dark and crowded, the **Island House** (✉*11 Circuit Ave.* ☎*508/693–4516*) hosts a mixture of rock, blues, and reggae for younger crowds whose ears crave volume.

The **Lampost** ($\boxtimes$*6 Circuit Ave.* ☎*508/696–9352*) is a good, old-fashioned neighborhood bar with a DJ and dancing. In addition to events such as an '80s night, a Brazilian night, and a Hawaiian night, there are also swing nights. The bar attracts a young crowd.

Lola's ($\boxtimes$*Beach Rd.* ☎*508/693–5007*), a popular restaurant, has a lively bar that hosts local musicians. There's a great pub menu year-round, and you can also get regular restaurant cuisine at the bar.

The island's only family brewpub, **Offshore Ale** ($\boxtimes$*Kennebec Ave.* ☎*508/693–2626*) hosts live Latin, folk, and blues year-round and serves its own beer and ales and a terrific pub menu. Cozy up to the fireplace with a pint on cool nights.

The **Ritz Café** ($\boxtimes$*4 Circuit Ave.* ☎*508/693–9851*) is a popular year-round bar with a pool table that's removed in summer to make way for dancing. There's an eclectic mix of live performances, including rock, blues, and reggae, from Monday through Saturday in summer and on weekends in the off-season.

SPORTS & THE OUTDOORS

BEACHES

Eastville Beach ($\boxtimes$*Over bridge on Beach Rd. leading from Vineyard Haven to Oak Bluffs*) is a small beach where children can swim in the calm waters and dive off the pilings under the drawbridge. From the shore you can watch boats of all sizes passing under the bridge between the lagoon and the harbor.

Joseph A. Sylvia State Beach ($\boxtimes$*Between Oak Bluffs and Edgartown, off Beach Rd.*) is a 6-mi-long sandy beach with a view of Cape Cod across Nantucket Sound. The calm, warm water and food vendors make it popular with families. There's parking along the road, and the beach is accessible by bike path or shuttle bus. Across the street from this barrier beach is Sengekontacket Pond, a popular fishing and shellfishing spot. Even if you don't love beaches, the drive and the expansive vista of the sound and the pond alone will make you at least develop a severe case of infatuation.

Oak Bluffs Town Beach ($\boxtimes$*Between steamship dock and state beach, off Sea View Ave.*) is a crowded, narrow stretch of calm water on Nantucket Sound, with snack stands, lifeguards, roadside parking, and restrooms at the steamship office. One section has been nicknamed Inkwell Beach by the generations of African-Americans who summer on the Vineyard and have been enjoying this stretch for more than a century. A changing area and showers are in this section as well.

BIKING

Ride-On Mopeds and Bikes (✉*Circuit Ave. Exit* ☎*508/693–2076*) rents bicycles and mopeds.

Sun 'n' Fun (✉*28 Lake Ave.* ☎*508/693–5457* ⊕*www.sun nfunrentals.com*) rents bikes, cars, and Jeeps.

BOATING

Martha's Vineyard Oceansports (✉*Dockside Marketplace, Oak Bluffs Harbor* ☎*508/693–8476*) rents a variety of personal watercraft.

FISHING

Dick's Bait & Tackle (✉*New York Ave.* ☎*508/693–7669*) rents gear, sells accessories and bait, and keeps a current copy of the fishing regulations.

The **MV *Skipper*** (✉*Slip 74, Oak Bluffs Harbor Bulkhead* ☎*508/693–1238* ⊕*www.mvskipper.com*) runs morning and afternoon guided fishing tours around the island's waters, with tackle, bait, and bags to bring home your catch included. Fluke, scup, black sea bass, and tautog are among the common catches on these popular tours.

GOLF

Farm Neck Golf Club (✉*County Rd.* ☎*508/693–3057*), a semiprivate club on marsh-rimmed Sengekontacket Pond, has a driving range and 18 holes in a championship layout. Reservations are required 48 hours in advance.

KAYAKING

Carolyn "Chick" Dowd runs great kayaking tours and offers expert instruction through her company, **Island Spirit Sea-Kayak Adventures** (☎*508/693–9727* ⊕*www.islandsspirit. com*). Tours range from day trips around Cape Pogue to evening sunset and full-moon paddles.

SHOPPING

Book Den East (✉*71 New York Ave.* ☎*508/693–3946*) stocks 20,000 out-of-print, antiquarian, and paperback books.

B*tru (⊠40 *Circuit Ave.* ☎508/693–5222) sells wonderfully stylish, offbeat, funky clothing and accessories.

If you're looking for out-of-the-ordinary, **Craftworks** (⊠42 *Circuit Ave.* ☎508/693–7463) carries outrageous painted furniture, ceramic figures, folk art, and home accessories—all handmade by American artists.

Laughing Bear (⊠33 *Circuit Ave.* ☎508/693–9342) carries women's clothing made of Balinese or Indian batiks plus jewelry and accessories from around the world.

The favored destination of sweet tooths, **Murdick's Fudge** (⊠5 *Circuit Ave.* ☎888/553–8343) also does a brisk mail-order business and has locations in Vineyard Haven and Edgartown as well. The company has been turning out delicious fudge in many flavors (including the strangely tasty Cape Cod cranberry variety), plus tasty brittle, since 1887.

The **Secret Garden** (⊠41 *Circuit Ave.* ☎508/693–4759), set in a yellow gingerbread cottage, has a complete line of Shelia collectibles—miniature wooden versions of Camp Ground houses and other island landmarks.

ART GALLERIES

Cousen Rose Gallery (⊠71 *Circuit Ave.* ☎508/693–6656) displays works by many island artists, including Myrna Morris, John Breckenridge, Marietta Cleasby, Deborah Colter, Lynn Hoefs, Ray Prosser, and Renee Balter. In summer be sure to inquire about children's art classes.

Dragonfly Gallery (⊠*Dukes County and Vineyard Aves.* ☎508/693–8877) changes shows weekly and holds artist receptions—featuring jazz pianist John Alaimo—every other Saturday in summer from 4 to 7 PM. Check the local papers for a schedule of artists.

EDGARTOWN

6 mi southeast of Oak Bluffs.

Edgartown has long been the Vineyard's toniest spot. Ever since Thomas Mayhew Jr. landed here in 1642 as the Vineyard's first governor, the town has served as the county seat. Plenty of settlers inhabited the area, making it the island's first colonial settlement, but the town was not officially named until 1652. First called Great Harbour, it was renamed for political reasons some 30 years later, after the three-year-old son of the Duke of York.

Once a well-to-do whaling port, Edgartown has managed to preserve the elegance of that wealthy era. Lining the streets are 18th- and 19th-century sea captains' houses, many painted white with black shutters, set among well-manicured gardens and lawns. Plenty of shops as well as other sights and activities here occupy the crowds who walk the streets. A stroll is definitely the best way to absorb it all.

Numbers in the text correspond to numbers in the margin and on the Edgartown map.

㉒ A good place to stop for directions or suggestions is the **Edgartown Visitors Center,** which has information, restrooms, and snacks in season. ⊠*Church St.* ☎*No phone.*

WHAT TO SEE

☾ **Capt. Francis Pease House.** This 1850s Greek Revival houses a permanent exhibit of Native American, prehistoric, pre-Columbian, and later artifacts, including arrowheads and pottery, plus changing exhibits from the collection. The Children's Gallery presents changing exhibits created by children, and the museum shop sells books, maps, jewelry, and island crafts. ⊠*School St.* ☎*508/627–4441.*

Carriage Shed. A number of vessels and vehicles live here, among them a whaleboat, a snazzy 1855 fire engine with stars inlaid in wood, and an 1830 hearse, considerably less ornate than the fire engine. The shed also houses some peculiar gravestones that mark the eternal resting places of an eccentric poet's strangely beloved chickens. In the yard outside are a replica of a 19th-century brick tryworks, used to process whale oil from blubber aboard ship, and the 1,008-prism Fresnel lens installed in the Aquinnah Lighthouse (⇨*see Aquinnah*) in 1854 and removed when the light was automated in 1952. Each evening the lens lamp is lighted briefly after sundown. The toolshed contains harvesting tools used both on land and at sea in the early 19th century. ⊠*School St.* ☎*508/627–4441.*

⓴ **Dr. Daniel Fisher House.** A truly elegant sight is this graceful mansion with a wraparound roof walk and a small front portico with fluted Corinthian columns. It was built in 1840 for one of the island's richest men, who was a doctor, the first president of the Martha's Vineyard National Bank, and the owner of a whale-oil refinery, a spermaceti (whale-oil) candle factory, and a gristmill, among other pursuits. The good doctor came to a portion of his fortune through

CLOSE UP

A Brief History of the Vineyard

1

Martha's Vineyard was first settled by Europeans in 1642 and developed into a community of farmers and fishermen. In the early 1800s, the basis of the island's economy shifted to whaling. Never as influential as Nantucket or New Bedford, Martha's Vineyard nonetheless held its own. Especially during the industry's golden age, between 1830 and 1845, captains built impressive homes with their profits. These, along with many graceful houses from earlier centuries, still line the streets of Vineyard Haven and Edgartown, both former whaling hubs. The industry went into decline after the Civil War, but by then revenue from tourism had picked up, and those dollars just keep flooding in.

The story of the Vineyard's development as a resort begins in 1835, when the first Methodist Camp Meeting—a two-week gathering of far-flung parishes for group worship and fellowship—was held in the Oak Bluffs area, then isolated and undeveloped. From the original meeting's 9 tents, the number grew to 250 by 1857. Little by little, returning campers built permanent platforms arranged around the central preachers' tent. Then the odd cottage popped up in place of a tent. By 1880, Wesleyan Grove, named for Methodism's founder, John Wesley, was a community of about 500 tiny cottages, most built in Gothic Revival styles. Lacy filigree insets of jigsaw-cut detail work—known as gingerbread—began to appear on cottage facades, and the ornamented look came to be known as Carpenter Gothic.

Meanwhile, burgeoning numbers of cottagers coming to the island each summer helped convince speculators of its desirability as a resort destination, and in 1867 developers laid out a separate secular community alongside the Camp Ground. Steamers from New Bedford, Boston, New York, and elsewhere brought in fashionable folk for bathing and taking in the sea air, for picking berries, or for playing croquet. Grand hotels sprang up around Oak Bluffs Harbor. A railroad followed, connecting the town with the beach at Katama. The Victorian seaside resort was called Cottage City before its name changed to Oak Bluffs.

More than 300 of the Camp Ground cottages remain. And just as Edgartown and Vineyard Haven reflect their origins as whaling ports, so Oak Bluffs—with its porch-wrapped beach houses and a village green where families still gather to hear the town band play in the gazebo—evokes the days of Victorian summer ease, of flowing white dresses and parasols held languidly against the sun.

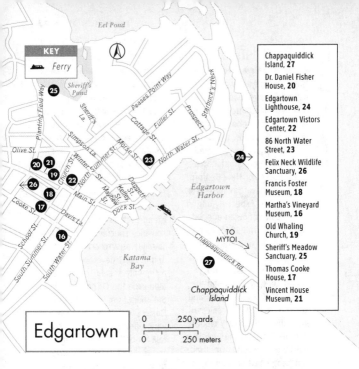

KEY

🚢 Ferry

Chappaquiddick
Island, **27**

Dr. Daniel Fisher
House, **20**

Edgartown
Lighthouse, **24**

Edgartown Vistors
Center, **22**

86 North Water
Street, **23**

Felix Neck Wildlife
Sanctuary, **26**

Francis Foster
Museum, **18**

Martha's Vineyard
Museum, **16**

Old Whaling
Church, **19**

Sheriff's Meadow
Sanctuary, **25**

Thomas Cooke
House, **17**

Vincent House
Museum, **21**

Edgartown

0   250 yards

0   250 meters

marriage—as a wedding gift, his generous but presumably eccentric father-in-law presented him with the bride's weight in silver. The house is now used for functions and office space, and you can gain access only on Liz Villard's Vineyard History Tours. ⊠*99 Main St.*

㉔ Edgartown Lighthouse. For a great view (but seaweedy bathing), stop by the Edgartown Lighthouse, surrounded by a public beach. The white cast-iron tower was floated by barge from Ipswich, Massachusetts, in 1938. ⊠*Off N. Water St..*

㉓ 86 North Water Street. The architecturally pristine, much-photographed upper part of North Water Street is lined with many fine captains' houses. You can seemingly always discover an interesting detail on this stretch that you never noticed before—like a widow's walk with a mannequin poised, spyglass in hand, watching for her seafaring husband to return. The 1832 house where this piece of whimsy can be seen stands at No. 86, which the Society for the Preservation of New England Antiquities maintains as a rental property.

1

NEED A BREAK? If you need a pick-me-up, pop into **Espresso Love** (⊠*3 S. Water St.* ☎*508/627-9211*) for a cappuccino and a homemade raspberry scone or blueberry muffin. If you prefer something cold, the staff also makes fruit smoothies. Light lunch fare is served: bagel sandwiches, soups, and delicious pastries and cookies—all homemade, of course. It's by the Edgartown bus station.

㉖ Felix Neck Wildlife Sanctuary. The Massachusetts Audu-
Ⓒ bon Society preserves this 350-acre sanctuary, 3 mi outside Edgartown toward Oak Bluffs and Vineyard Haven. There are 2 mi of hiking trails traversing marshland, fields, woods, seashore, a butterfly garden, and waterfowl and reptile ponds. Naturalist-led events include sunset hikes, stargazing, snake or bird walks, and canoeing. ⊠*Off Edgartown–Vineyard Haven Rd.* ☎*508/627-4850* ☞*$4* ☉*Center June–Aug., Mon.–Sat. 8–4, Sun. 10–3; Sept.–May, Tues.–Sat. 8–4, Sun. noon–4. Trails daily sunrise–7 PM.*

⑱ Francis Foster Museum. A small collection of whaling implements, scrimshaw, and navigational instruments can be found here, in addition to many old photographs, among them images of 110 19th-century Edgartown whaling masters. The **Dale Huntington Reference Library and Foster Maritime Gallery** is also in the building, with genealogical records, rare island books, and ships' logs from the whaling days, as well as some publications for sale. ⊠*School St.* ☎*508/627-4441.*

⑯ Martha's Vineyard Museum. Stop at this complex of build-
★ ings and lawn exhibits to orient yourself historically before making your way around town. The opening hours and admission listed below apply to all the buildings and exhibits—including the Thomas Cooke House, the Francis Foster Museum, the Capt. Francis Pease House, and the Carriage Shed—and the Huntington Reference Library of Vineyard History, which contains archives of oral history, letters, and law documents. The museum sells an excellent Edgartown walking-tour booklet full of anecdotes and the history of the people who have lived in the town's houses over the past three centuries; you can purchase the booklet at the entrance gatehouse in summer or at the library in winter. ⊠*Cooke and School Sts.* ☎*508/627–4441* ⊕*www.marthasvineyardhistory.org* ☞*$7* ☉*Mid-Mar.–mid-June and early Oct.–late Dec., Wed.–Fri. 1–4,*

Sat. 10–4; mid-June–early Oct., Tues.–Sat. 10–5; early Jan.–mid-Mar., Sat. 10–4.

⑲ Old Whaling Church. In addition to a six-column portico and unusual triple-sash windows, this massive building—opened in 1843 as a Methodist church, now a performing-arts center—has a 92-foot clock tower that can be seen for miles. The simple, graceful interior is brightened by light from 27-foot-tall windows and still contains the original box pews and lectern. Aside from attending performances, you can get inside only if you join one of the historical walking tours run by Vineyard History Tours. ⊠*89 Main St.* ☎*508/627–8619 for tour.*

㉕ Sheriff's Meadow Sanctuary. A pleasant walking trail circles an old ice pond at the center of 17 acres of marsh, woodland, and meadow. One of the area's many wildlife preserves, Sheriff's Meadow contains a variety of habitats. ⊠*Planting Field Way* ☎*508/693–5207* ⊕*www.sheriffsmeadow.org.*

⑰ Thomas Cooke House. This is the one Vineyard Museum property open only from mid-June to mid-October. The house itself is part of the display, evoking the past with its low doorways, wide-board floors, original raised-panel woodwork with fluted pilasters, and hearths in the summer and winter kitchens. Docents answer questions about the 12 rooms, whose exhibits reveal the island's history with furniture, tools, costumes, portraits, toys, crafts, and various household objects. One room is set up as a 19th-century parlor, illustrating the opulence of the golden age of whaling with such period pieces as a pianoforte. Upstairs are ship models, whaling paraphernalia, old customs documents, and a room tracing the evolution of the Camp Meeting through photographs and objects. ⊠*School St.* ☎*508/627–4441.*

㉑ Vincent House Museum. A tour of this weathered-shingle farmhouse—built in 1672, it's the island's oldest dwelling—takes you along a time line that starts with the sparse furnishings of the 1600s and ends in a Federal-style parlor of the 1800s. ⊠*Main St.* ☎*508/627–4440* ⊕*www.mv preservation.org/tours.html* ⊡*Museum $5* ⊗*May–mid-Oct., Mon.–Sat. 10:30–3.*

1

WHERE TO EAT

$$$$ ✕**Atria.** One of the island's more urbane venues, Atria feels
★ like a big-city bistro and cocktail lounge, with a swank
dining room, glam crowd, and artful food presentations.
Chef Christian Thornton uses eclectic, globally influenced
ingredients to come up with such entrées as cracklin' pork
shank with collard greens and sour cream–mustard sauce;
and grilled lamb T-bones with Tuscan-style white beans,
roasted tomatoes, grilled artichokes, and a red-wine reduction. Top starters include steak tartare with crisp shallots,
capers, truffle oil, and aged balsamic vinegar; and braised-
veal-cheek ravioli with stuffed squash blossoms, shaved
Parmesan, and truffle oil. The chocolate-molten cake with
cappuccino ice cream is a great finish. There's jazz certain
evenings. ✉*137 Main St.* ☎*508/627–5850* ⊕*www.atri-
amv.com* ☰*AE, MC, V.*

$$$–$$$$ ✕**Alchemy Bistro and Bar.** According to the menu, the dic-
tionary meaning of *alchemy* is "a magic power having as its
asserted aim the discovery of a panacea and the preparation
of the elixir of longevity"—lofty goals for a French-style
bistro. This high-class version has elegant gray wainscot-
ing, classic paper-covered white tablecloths, old wooden
floors, and an opening cut into the ceiling to reveal the
second-floor tables. The only things missing are the patina
of age, experience, cigarette smoke—and French working
folk's prices—but you can expect quality and imagination.
One example is the fried cornmeal-dusted soft-shell crab
with lemon risotto, sweet peas, and artichokes. The alco-
hol list, long and complete, includes cognacs, grappas, and
beers. ✉*71 Main St.* ☎*508/627–9999* ☰*AE, MC, V.*

★ **Fodor's**Choice ✕**Detente.** A dark, intimate wine bar and res-
$$$–$$$$ taurant with hardwood floors and rich banquette seating,
Detente serves more than a dozen wines by the glass as
well as numerous half bottles. Even if you're not much of
an oenophile, it's worth a trip just for the innovative food,
much of it from local farms and seafood purveyors. Try
the complex starter of ahi tuna tartare with toasted pine
nuts, vanilla-pear puree, ginger, and arugula salad, fol-
lowed by such choice entrées as roasted venison loin with
thyme spaetzle, sautéed Swiss chard, blue cheese, roasted
figs, and a port reduction; or lemon-honey–basted halibut
with potato au gratin, truffled leek puree, roasted arti-
chokes, and oven-dried tomatoes. ✉*Nevin Sq. off Water
St.* ☎*508/627–8810* ⊕*www.detentewinebar.com* ☰*AE,
MC, V* ⊗*Closed Tues. and Jan.–mid-Apr. No lunch.*

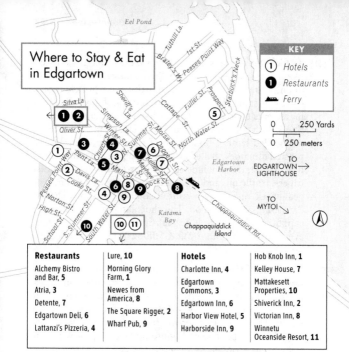

Where to Stay & Eat in Edgartown

KEY
① Hotels
❶ Restaurants
⛴ Ferry

Restaurants		Hotels	
Alchemy Bistro and Bar, **5**	Lure, **10**	Charlotte Inn, **4**	Hob Knob Inn, **1**
Atria, **3**	Morning Glory Farm, **1**	Edgartown Commons, **3**	Kelley House, **7**
Detente, **7**	Newes from America, **8**	Edgartown Inn, **6**	Mattakesett Properties, **10**
Edgartown Deli, **6**	The Square Rigger, **2**	Harbor View Hotel, **5**	Shiverick Inn, **2**
Lattanzi's Pizzeria, **4**	Wharf Pub, **9**	Harborside Inn, **9**	Victorian Inn, **8**
			Winnetu Oceanside Resort, **11**

★ **Fodor's**Choice ✕**Lure.** The airy restaurant at Winnetu Oceans-
$$$–$$$$ ide Resort draws plenty of discerning diners, including
plenty of nonhotel guests, to sample some of the most
exquisite and creatively prepared seafood on the island. It's
the only dining room with a south-facing water view, and
it's a stunning one at that. The staff here is young, eager
to please, and friendly, and chef Mark Goldberg, previ-
ously of Boston's famed Mistral restaurant, knows his way
around a kitchen. You won't find a better lobster dish on
the island than Lure's tender butter-poached version topped
with roasted corn and fava beans and served alongside but-
tery corn bread. Locally caught fluke with littleneck clams,
leeks, smoked bacon, and a rich chowder broth is another
star. Finish off with the molten Valrhona chocolate cake
with vanilla ice cream and raspberry coulis. ✉*Katama Rd.*
☎*508/627–3663* ═*AE, D, MC, V* ☻*No lunch.*

$$–$$$$ ✕**The Square Rigger.** Locals are loyal to this old-school comfort food spot because it tends to stay open seven days a
week until January. Grilled lamb chops, pork chops, and
swordfish are on the menu along with other hearty fare—
the lobster-stuffed lobster is justly famous for its size and

1

richness, and a hefty portion of prime rib with a popover is served Thursday through Sunday. It's just right for a night out with the family. ⊠*The Triangle, 225 State Rd.* ☎*508/627–9968* ▭*AE, MC, V.*

$–$$$ ✕**Lattanzi's Pizzeria.** Albert and Cathy Lattanzi's big brick oven gets fired up by 2:30 PM, and the pizza that slides out come evening is delicious—baby clams with plum tomatoes, oregano, spinach, roasted garlic, and Asiago cheese is just one example. The more formal adjacent restaurant serves traditional, deftly prepared Italian specialties, such as Tuscan-style steak with black peppercorns, lemon, and olive oil. ⊠*Old Post Office Sq.* ☎*508/627–9084 for pizzeria, 508/627–8854 for restaurant* ⊕*www.lattanzis.com* ▭*D, DC, MC, V* ◷*No lunch at restaurant. Restaurant closed Sun. and Mon. Oct.–June.*

$–$$$ ✕**Wharf Pub.** The name may sound generic, and the menu tends toward the predictable—shrimp scampi, prime rib, burgers, and steaks—but this lively bar and grill in the heart of Edgartown earns kudos for its well-prepared food, inviting dining room and pair of bars, and easygoing vibe. Standouts include the grilled flank steak with fries and a horseradish cream sauce, and the Cobb salad with ham and chicken. You can tune in to a game on the TV or mingle with locals. It's nothing fancy, but this year-round mainstay is consistently reliable and a great bet for singles, groups of friends, and—especially during the day—families. ⊠*Lower Main St.* ☎*508/627–9966* ▭*AE, D, MC, V.*

$–$$ ✕**Newes from America.** Sometimes a nearly subterranean, darkened scene feels right on a hot summer afternoon, in which case the Newes is the perfect spot for an informal lunch or dinner. Inside there's plenty of wood and greenery and many things "olde." The food is mostly Americana (burgers and fries), though some slightly more international dishes like Roquefort Stilettos (French bread, Roquefort cheese, and bacon) and chicken burritos have made their way onto the menu. There's a massively inclusive list of microbrewed beers, and the staff is well equipped to make recommendations. The Newes is open from 11 AM until midnight every day of the year except Christmas. ⊠*23 Kelly St.* ☎*508/627–4397* ⬧*Reservations not accepted* ▭*AE, D, MC, V.*

¢–$ ✕**Morning Glory Farm.** Fresh farm greens in the salads and
★ vegetables in the soups; homemade pies, cookies, and cakes; and a picnic table and grass to enjoy them on make

this an ideal place for a simple country lunch. ✉ *W. Tisbury Rd.* ☎*508/627–9003* ☐*No credit cards.*

¢ ✕**Edgartown Deli.** A no-frills place with a down-home, happy feeling, this deli has walls and a glass counter plastered with specials written on multicolored paper. Brightly lighted booths fill one side of the room, and customers line up at the counter for orders to go. Breakfast specials, served from 8 until 10:45, include egg, cheese, and *linguiça* (garlicky Portuguese sausage) on a roll. Lunch sandwiches include corned beef and Swiss, roast beef, turkey, pastrami, or steak and cheese. ✉*52 Main St.* ☎*508/627–4789* ⚇*Reservations not accepted* ☐*No credit cards* ⊗*Closed Nov.–Apr. No dinner.*

WHERE TO STAY

$$$$ ★ Fodor'sChoice ▥**Charlotte Inn.** From the moment you walk up to the dark-wood Scottish barrister's check-in desk at this regal 1864 inn, you'll be surrounded by the trappings and customs of a bygone era. Guests' names are handwritten into the register by the dignified and attentive staff. Beautiful antique furnishings, objets d'art, and paintings fill the property—the book you pick up in your room might be an 18th-century edition of Voltaire, and your bed could be a hand-carved four-poster. All rooms have hair dryers and robes; rooms in the carriage house have fireplaces and French doors that open into the brick courtyard as well as private patios. The elegant atmosphere that pervades the property extends to the inn's swank restaurant, the Catch. **Pros:** Over-the-top lavish, quiet yet convenient location, beautifully landscaped. **Cons:** Expensive, can feel overly formal, intimidating if you don't adore museum-quality antiques. ✉*27 S. Summer St., 02539* ☎*508/627–4751 or 800/735–2478* ☐*508/627–4652* ⊕*www.relaischateaux.com* ↪*21 rooms, 2 suites* ♿*In-room: Ethernet. In-hotel: restaurant, no elevator, no kids under 14* ☐*AE, MC, V* ⁙*CP.*

$$$$ ▥**Harbor View Hotel.** The centerpiece of this historic hotel ★ that underwent a massive overhaul in 2007 is a gray-shingle, 1891 Victorian building with wraparound veranda and a gazebo. Accommodations are also in a complex of nearby buildings in a residential neighborhood. The contemporary town houses have cathedral ceilings, decks, kitchens, and large living areas with sofa beds. Rooms in other buildings are laid out like upscale motor-lodge units but have the same fine decor and plush in-room amenities, from CD

1

clock radios to L'Occitane bath products. A beach, good for walking, stretches ¾ mi from the hotel's dock, and the sheltered bay is a great place for kids to swim. Packages and theme weekends are available. The hotel is also home to the Coach House restaurant, a worthy spot for a full meal that also has an excellent, lighter bar menu. Plans for 2008 include a full-service spa. **Pros:** Great harbor views, not far from restaurants, recently renovated. **Cons:** A few blocks from commercial district, less intimate than a B&B, steep rates. ⊠*131 N. Water St., Box 7, 02539* ☎*508/627–7000 or 800/225–6005* ☎*508/742–1042* ⊕*www.harborview.com* ☞*102 rooms, 22 suites* ⌂*In-room: kitchen (some), refrigerator, Wi-Fi. In-hotel: 2 restaurants, room service, tennis courts, pool, gym, spa, concierge, laundry service* ▤*AE, DC, MC, V.*

$$$$ ☱**Hob Knob Inn.** This 19th-century Gothic Revival inn blends the amenities and service of a luxury hotel with the ambience and charm of a small B&B. It's a short walk to the harbor, on the main road into town—but far enough out to avoid crowds. Rooms are gracious and quite large by island standards; the upper floors have dormer windows. Art and antiques help capture the island's rural, seaside charm, and many rooms overlook the spectacular gardens. The inn also runs fishing trips and charters on its 27-foot Boston Whaler. Full breakfast and lavish afternoon tea are included. **Pros:** Spacious rooms, afternoon tea included, easy walk to harbor yet slightly removed from crowds. **Cons:** Steep rates, service can sometimes feel a bit impersonal, near but not overlooking harbor. ⊠*128 Main St., 02539* ☎*508/627–9510 or 800/696–2723* ☎*508/627–4560* ⊕*www.hobknob.com* ☞*17 rooms, 1 suite* ⌂*In-room: Wi-Fi. In-hotel: gym, bicycles, no elevator, no kids under 10* ▤*AE, MC, V* ⋈*BP.*

$$$$ ☱**Kelley House.** In the center of town, this sister property of the Harbor View combines services and amenities with a country-inn feel. The 1742 white clapboard main house and the adjacent Garden House are surrounded by pink roses. Large suites in the Chappaquiddick House and the two spacious town houses in the Wheel House have porches (most with harbor views) and living rooms. The Newes from America, a dark and cozy spot with original hand-hewn timbers and ballast-brick walls, serves typical pub victuals and microbrewed beers on tap. **Pros:** Lots of historic charm, pretty gardens, some harbor views. **Cons:** On street with lots of pedestrian traffic, pricey, frequent wedding locale. ⊠*23*

*Kelley St., Box 37, 02539 ☎508/627–7900 or 800/225–6005
🖷508/627–8142 ⊕www.kelley-house.com ⌨52 rooms, 8
suites, 2 town-house units ♿In-room: kitchen (some), Ethernet. In-hotel: restaurant, bar, tennis courts, pool, laundry
service ⊟AE, DC, MC, V ⊘Closed mid-Oct.–Apr. ⦿CP.*

$$$$ ⊞**Mattakesett Properties.** This attractive resort complex,
which is part of the nearby Winnetu Oceanside Resort,
sits close to South Beach. Mattakesett differs from the
Winnetu in that all of its units are owner-furnished town
houses and condominiums with three to four bedrooms;
guests at either property can use the amenities at both. All
homes have fireplaces and decks. The children's programs
are extensive, and the pool and barbecue grills make this
a favorite for families. Bookings at Mattakesett are taken
on a per-week basis only. A vintage fire truck and livery are
used to shuttle you around the area. **Pros:** Access to Winnetu facilities, fairly good value for large families, great for
kids. **Cons:** Some units more nicely decorated than others, a
longish walk from town, lots of kids in summer. ✉*Katama
Rd., RFD 270, 02539 ☎508/627–4747 or 978/443–1733
⊕www.winnetu.com/mattakesett.htm ⌨92 units ♿In-
room: kitchen, Ethernet (some), Wi-Fi (some). In-hotel:
tennis courts, pool, gym, children's programs (ages 3–12),
laundry facilities, no elevator ⊟AE, MC, V ⊘Mattakesett
closed Nov.–Apr.*

$$$$ ⊞**Shiverick Inn.** This inn is set in a striking 1840 former
★ doctor's home with mansard roof and cupola. Rooms are
airy and bright, with high ceilings, lots of windows, eclectic
American and English antiques, and Oriental rugs. Beds
are mostly queen-size with canopies or carved four-posters.
Nine rooms have fireplaces or woodstoves. A full breakfast
and tea are served. There's a second-floor library with high-
speed Internet and a stereo, as well as a terrace and a first-
floor flagstone garden patio. It's about a five-minute walk
to downtown. **Pros:** Quiet yet convenient location, ultra-
cushy beds and linens, lovely gardens. **Cons:** No phones in
rooms, not ideal for young kids, no water views. ✉*5 Pease's
Point Way, at Pent La., Box 640, 02539 ☎508/627–3797
or 800/723–4292 🖷508/627–8441 ⊕www.shiverickinn.
com ⌨11 rooms ♿In-room: no phone. In-hotel: no elevator, public Internet ⊟AE, D, MC, V ⦿BP.*

$$$$ ★ Fodor'sChoice ☆**Winnetu Oceanside Resort.** A departure from most properties on the island, the contemporary Winnetu—styled after the grand multistory resorts of the gilded age—both encourages families and provides a contemporary seaside-resort experience for couples. This all-suites property has units that can sleep up to 11 guests. All have kitchens and decks or patios with views. Room decor is stylish and modern but casual enough so that kids feel right at home. The resort arranges bicycling and kayaking trips, lighthouse tours, and other island activities. The General Store carries snacks, and the superb Lure restaurant, the only one on the island with a south-facing water view, prepares tasty box lunches for the beach. (It's open to the public and specializes in gourmet fish fare.) The staff will stock your kitchen in advance of your arrival on request and can arrange a wide range of island tours and activities, from bike trips to yoga classes. Clambakes are held on the grounds on Wednesday evening. In summer all stays must be a minimum of three nights. **Pros:** Outstanding staff, tons of activities, fantastic restaurant. **Cons:** Pricey, a longish walk from town, lots of kids in summer. ⊠*Katama Rd., RFD 270, 02539* ☎*508/627–4747 or 978/443–1733* ⊕*www.winnetu.com* ⇨*22 suites* ⌂*In-room: kitchen, VCR, Ethernet (some), Wi-Fi (some). In-hotel: restaurant, tennis courts, pools, gym, concierge, children's programs (ages 3–12), laundry facilities* ⊟*MC, V* ⊗*Closed Dec.–mid-Apr.*

$$$–$$$$ ☆**Victorian Inn.** White with the classic black shutters of the
★ town's historic homes and fronted by ornate columns, this appropriately named inn sits a block from the downtown harbor; it was built as the home of 19th-century whaling captain Lafayette Rowley. Today the inn's three floors are done in dark woods and bold floral wallpapers, with rugs over wood floors. Several rooms hold handmade reproduction four-poster beds. Breakfast, served in season in the brick-patio garden, includes creative muffins and breads. **Pros:** Top-notch staff, super romantic, close to restaurants. **Cons:** You'd better love high-style Victoriana, not geared to families, lots of pedestrian traffic. ⊠*24 S. Water St., 02539* ☎*508/627–4784* ⊕*www.thevic.com* ⇨*14 rooms* ⌂*In-room: Wi-Fi. In-hotel: no elevator, no kids under 8* ⊟*MC, V* ⦿*BP.*

$$–$$$$ ☆**Harborside Inn.** Edgartown's only true waterfront accommodation, with boat docks at the end of its nicely landscaped lawn, this large inn provides a central town location, harbor-view decks, and plenty of amenities. Seven

two- and three-story buildings sprawl around formal rose beds, brick walkways, a brick patio, and a heated pool. Rooms have colonial-style but modern furnishings, brass beds and lamps, and textured wallpapers. Some units have terraces facing Edgartown Harbor. **Pros:** Steps from restaurants and shops, immaculate rooms, lovely gardens. **Cons:** In center of Edgartown action and crowds, it's run as condo-time-share, lots of kids in summer. ⊠*3 S. Water St., Box 67, 02539* ☎*508/627–4321 or 800/627–4009* ☐*508/627–7566* ⊕*www.theharborsideinn.com* ⇨*87 rooms, 3 suites* ⌂*In-room: refrigerator, Ethernet. In-hotel: pool* ⊟*AE, MC, V* ⊗*Closed mid-Nov.–mid-Apr.*

$–$$$$ ▥**Edgartown Inn.** The inside of the former home of whaling captain Thomas Worth still evokes its late-18th-century origins. In fact, its cozy parlor and antiques-filled rooms look as if the captain still lives here. The inn was also the spot where Nathaniel Hawthorne wrote much of his "Twice Told Tales" during a stay. Many an Edgartonian joins inn guests in the paneled dining room or back garden for breakfast in summertime. **Pros:** Great value, main inn building is rich in history, close to Edgartown shopping and dining. **Cons:** No Internet access, doesn't accept credit cards, least-expensive rooms have shared baths. ⊠*56 N. Water St., 02539* ☎*508/627–4794* ☐*508/627–9420* ⊕*www.edgartowninn.com* ⇨*20 rooms, 4 with shared bath* ⊟*No credit cards.*

$$–$$$ ▥**Edgartown Commons.** This condominium complex of seven buildings, which includes an old house and motel rooms set around a busy pool, is just a couple of blocks from town. Studios and one- or two-bedroom condos all have full kitchens, and some are very spacious. Each has been decorated by its individual owner, so the decor varies—some have an older look, others are new and bright. Definitely family-oriented, the place is abuzz with kids; rooms away from the pool are quieter. **Pros:** Nice big pool, full kitchens in units, great for families. **Cons:** Decor varies according to each unit's owner, lacks historical character, lots of kids. ⊠*20 Pease's Point Way, Box 1293, 02539* ☎*508/627–4671 or 800/439–4671* ☐*508/627–4271* ⊕*www.edgartowncommons.com* ⇨*35 units* ⌂*In-room: no phone, kitchen (some), some Wi-Fi. In-hotel: pool, laundry facilities, no elevator, public Wi-Fi* ⊟*AE, MC, V* ⊗*Closed mid-Oct.–Apr.*

NIGHTLIFE

The **Atria Bar** (⊠*137 Main St.* ☎*508/627–5850*) is off the beaten path, but it's a quiet, comfortable place to escape the summer crowds. Enjoy one of the clever drinks, including the Aunt Katherine Manhattan (Maker's Mark and sweet vermouth, served neat), and the Espresso Martini (Stoli vanilla vodka, Kahlúa, Tia Maria, and a shot of fresh espresso).

Outerland (⊠*Martha's Vineyard Airport, Edgartown–West Tisbury Rd.* ☎*508/693–1137*) books music acts such as Medeski, Martin and Wood, Ben Lee, Kate Taylor, and the Derek Trucks Band.

The Wharf (⊠*Lower Main St.* ☎*508/627–9966*) is a great spot for tasty food and a terrific place for cocktails, people-watching, and listening to live rock and pop music.

SPORTS & THE OUTDOORS

BEACHES

Bend-in-the-Road Beach (⊠*Beach Rd.*), Edgartown's town beach, is a protected area marked by floats adjacent to Joseph A. Sylvia State Beach. Backed by low, grassy dunes and wild roses, the beach has calm, shallow waters; some parking; and lifeguards. It's on the shuttle-bus and bike routes.

Lighthouse Beach is accessible from North Water Street or by continuing toward downtown Edgartown from Little Beach. The beach wraps around the Edgartown Lighthouse, a classic backdrop for wedding pictures. Though you will have no privacy, as many strollers pass along here, it commands a great view of all of Edgartown Harbor.

Little Beach (⊠*End of Fuller St.*) is a little-known beach that looks like a crooked pinkie that points into Eel Pond, a great place for bird-watching (be careful of the fenced-off piping plover breeding grounds in the dunes). From here you can look across and see the lighthouse at Cape Poge, at the northern tip of Chappaquiddick. This is a good beach for quiet sunbathing and shallow water wading. There's limited parking along Fuller Street. From Pease's Point Way, turn right onto Morse Street, then left onto Fuller.

South Beach (⊠*Katama Rd.*), also called Katama Beach, is the island's largest and most popular. A 3-mi ribbon of sand on the Atlantic, it sustains strong surf and occasional dangerous riptides, so check with the lifeguards before swimming. Also check the weather conditions, as fog can quickly turn a glorious blue-sky morning here into what seems like an afternoon in London. There's limited parking.

BICYCLING

Several bike paths lace through the Edgartown area, including a path to Oak Bluffs that has a spectacular view of Sengekontacket Pond on one side and Nantucket Sound on the other.

Edgartown Bicycles (⊠*Upper Main St.* ☎*508/627–9008* ⊕*www.edgartownbicycle.com*) provides a full array of rentals and repairs.

R.W. Cutler Bike (⊠*1 Main St.* ☎*508/627–4052* ⊕*www.marthasvineyardbikerentals.com*) rents and repairs all types of bicycles.

Wheel Happy (⊠*8 S. Water St.* ☎*508/627–5928*) rents bicycles and will deliver them to you.

FISHING

Coop's Bait and Tackle (⊠*147 W. Tisbury Rd.* ☎*508/627–3909* ⊕*www.coopsbaitandtackle.com*) sells accessories and bait, rents fishing gear, books fishing charters, and keeps a current listing of fishing regulations.

The annual **Martha's Vineyard Striped Bass & Bluefish Derby** (☎*508/693–0728* ⊕*www.mvderby.com*), from mid-September to mid-October, presents daily, weekly, and derby prizes for striped bass, bluefish, bonito, and false albacore catches, from boat or shore. The derby is a real Vineyard tradition, cause for loyal devotion among locals who drop everything to cast their lines at all hours of day and night in search of that prizewinning whopper. Avid fisherfolk come from all over the rest of the country, too, to cast their fates to the fishing gods.

SHOPPING

Claudia (⊠*35 Winter St.* ☎*508/627–8306*) brings you back to another era with its clever windows, antique display cases, and fabulous French fragrances. You'll find designer, vintage-looking, and fine gold and silver jewelry in a variety of price ranges.

David Le Breton, the owner of **Edgartown Books** (⊠*44 Main St.* ☎*508/627–8463*), is a true bibliophile. He carries a large selection of current and island-related titles and will be happy to make a summer reading recommendation.

The **Edgartown Scrimshaw Gallery** (✉*43 Main St.* ☎*508/627–9439*) showcases a large collection of scrimshaw, including some antique pieces.

Pick up fine tea accoutrements, chocolates, and gourmet items at **English Butler** (✉*22 Winter St.* ☎*508/627–1013*), a dainty boutique that hosts cheeky tea parties (gossip is encouraged) on Wednesday nights.

In the Pink (✉*33 Main St.* ☎*508/627–1209*) harks back to the 1960s when Edgartown had one of the signature stores for Lilly Pulitzer's perky pink and powder blue summer wear, which was de rigueur at the Edgartown Yacht Club. Lilly Pulitzer bathing suits, shorts, slacks, skirts, blouses, and handbags are all on sale here. There's also a branch in Vineyard Haven.

The **Old Sculpin Gallery** (✉*58 Dock St.* ☎*508/627–4881*) is the Martha's Vineyard Art Association's headquarters.

CHAPPAQUIDDICK ISLAND

❷ *1 mi southeast of Edgartown.*

A sparsely populated area with many nature preserves, Chappaquiddick Island makes for a pleasant day trip or bike ride on a sunny day. The "island" is actually connected to the Vineyard by a long sand spit that begins in South Beach in Katama. It's a spectacular 2¾-mi walk, or you can take the ferry ($10 for car and driver and $3 for each additional passenger), which departs about every five minutes from 7 AM to midnight daily, June to mid-October, and less frequently from 7 AM to 11:15 PM, mid-October to May.

WHAT TO SEE

Cape Poge Wildlife Refuge. On the easternmost shore of Chappaquiddick Island is this conglomeration of habitats, more than 6 square mi of wilderness where you can swim, walk, fish, or just sit and enjoy the surroundings. Its dunes, woods, cedar thickets, moors, salt marshes, ponds, tidal flats, and barrier beach serve as an important migration stopover and nesting area for numerous sea- and shorebirds. The best way to get to the refuge is as part of a naturalist-led **jeep drive** (☎*508/627–3599*).

Dike Bridge. This bridge at the end of Dike Road is infamous as the scene of the 1969 accident in which a young woman died in a car driven by Ted Kennedy. The rickety bridge has been replaced, after having been dismantled in 1991, but for ecological reasons, vehicle access over it is limited. There's a ranger station on the bridge that is manned June to September.

★ Fodor'sChoice **Mytoi.** The Trustees of Reservations' 14-acre preserve is a serene, beautifully tended, Japanese-inspired garden with a creek-fed pool spanned by a bridge and rimmed with Japanese maples, azaleas, bamboo, and irises. A boardwalk runs through part of the grounds, where you're apt to see box turtles and hear the sounds of songbirds. There are few more enchanting spots on the island. The garden was created in 1958 by a private citizen. Restroom facilities are available. ⊠*Dike Rd., ⅕ mi from intersection with Chappaquiddick Rd.* ☎*508/627–7689* ⊠*Free* ☉*Daily sunrise–sunset.*

Poucha Pond Reservation. Near the southeast corner of theisland, these 99 acres encompass a variety of environments. Trails wander among shady pitch pine and oak forests and around a marshy pond on onetime farmland. One trail end has a great view of the pond, Dike Bridge, and the East Beach dunes in the distance. Bring binoculars for the birds—terns, various herons, gulls, plovers—and repellent for the mosquitoes. ⊠*4 mi from Chappaquiddick ferry landing* ☎*508/627–7141* ⊠*Free* ☉*Daily sunrise–sunset.*

Three Ponds Preserve. It's no wonder this 226-acre preserve is a popular, scenic picnicking spot. Mown grasses surround a serpentine pond with an island in its center and a woodland backdrop behind—a truly lovely setting. Across the road are fields, woods, and another pond.

★ **Wasque Reservation.** Pronounced *wayce*-kwee, this 200-acre reservation is mostly a vast beach. Closing off the south end of Katama Bay, this is where Chappaquiddick connects to the mainland Vineyard. You can fish, sunbathe, take the trail by Swan Pond, walk to the island's southeasternmost tip at Wasque Point, or dip into the surf—use caution, as the currents are strong. Wasque Beach is accessed by a flat boardwalk with benches overlooking the west end of Swan Pond. It's a pretty walk skirting the pond, with ocean views on one side and poles for osprey nests on the other. Atop a bluff is a pine-shaded picnic grove with a spectacular, practically 180-degree panorama. ⊠*At east end of Wasque Rd., 5 mi from Chappaquiddick ferry landing* ☎*508/627–7260* ⊠*Cars $3, plus $3 per adult late May–mid-Sept.; free rest of yr* ☉*Property 24 hrs. Gatehouse late May–mid-Oct., daily 9–5.*

SPORTS & THE OUTDOORS

BEACHES

East Beach, one of the area's best beaches, is accessible by car from Dike Road. There's a $3 fee to enter the beach. **Wasque Beach,** at the Wasque Reservation, is an uncrowded ½-mi sandy beach with a parking lot and restrooms. The surf and currents are sometimes strong.

UP-ISLAND

Much of what makes the Vineyard special is found in its rural reaches, in the agricultural heart of the island and the largely undeveloped lands south and west of the Vineyard Haven–to–Edgartown line known as Up-Island. Country roads meander through woods and tranquil farmland, and dirt side roads lead past crystalline ponds, abandoned cranberry bogs, and conservation lands. In Chilmark, West Tisbury, and Aquinnah, nature lovers, writers, artists, and others have established close, ongoing summer communities. In winter the isolation and bitter winds generally send even year-round Vineyarders from their Up-Island homes to places in the cozier Down-Island towns.

Numbers in the text correspond to numbers in the margin and on the Up-Island map.

WEST TISBURY

❷❽ *8 mi west of Edgartown, 6½ mi south of Vineyard Haven.*

Founded in the 1670s by settlers from Edgartown, among them the son of Myles Standish and the son-in-law of the *Mayflower* Aldens, West Tisbury was known for its first 200 Westernized years simply as Tisbury. Most important among the settlement's advantages over Down-Island outposts was a strong-flowing stream that ran into a pond, creating a perfect mill site—a rarity on the Vineyard. Farming, especially sheep farming, became Tisbury's mainstay.

West Tisbury retains its rural appeal and maintains its agricultural tradition at several active horse and produce farms. The town center looks very much the small New England village, complete with a white, steepled church. Half the 5,146-acre Manuel F. Correllus State Forest lies within the town limits.

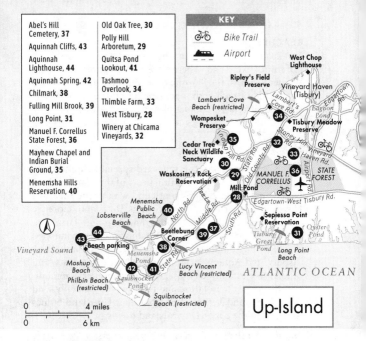

KEY

🚲 Bike Trail

✈ Airport

West Chop Lighthouse

Ripley's Field Preserve

Vineyard Haven (Tisbury)

Lambert's Cove Beach (restricted)

Wompesket Preserve

Tisbury Meadow Preserve

34

Cedar Tree Neck Wildlife Sanctuary

35

32

33

Waskosim's Rock Reservation

30

29

MANUEL F. CORRELLUS

36

STATE FOREST

Mill Pond

28

Edgartown–West Tisbury Rd.

Menemsha Public Beach

40

Lobsterville Beach

Sepiessa Point Reservation

44

Beetlebung Corner

39 **37**

31

43 Beach parking

38

Vineyard Sound

Menemsha Pond

Lucy Vincent Beach (restricted)

Tisbury Great Pond

Long Point Beach

Oyster Pond

Moshup Beach

42 **41**

ATLANTIC OCEAN

Philbin Beach (restricted)

Squibnocket Pond

Squibnocket Beach (restricted)

0 _____ 4 miles

0 _____ 6 km

Up-Island

WHAT TO SEE

Cedar Tree Neck Wildlife Sanctuary. Among the 312 hilly acres of unspoiled West Tisbury woods managed by the Sheriff's Meadow Foundation are a sphagnum bog and a pond. The sanctuary has interesting flora, including bayberry and swamp azalea bushes, tupelo, sassafras, and pygmy beech trees. Wooded trails lead to a stony but secluded North Shore beach (swimming, picnicking, and fishing prohibited), and from the summit of a headland are views of Aquinnah and the Elizabeth Islands. To get here, follow Indian Hill Road off State Road for 2 mi, and then turn right 1 mi on Obed Daggett Road, an occasionally steep, rocky dirt road to the parking lot. ⊠*Indian Hill Rd.* ☎*508/693–5207* ⊕*www.sheriffsmeadow.org* 🎟*Free* ⊙*Daily 8:30–5:30.*

32 **Chicama Vineyards.** The fruit of the Mathiesen family's labors is this rather unique island undertaking. From 3 acres of trees and rocks, George—a broadcaster from San Francisco—his wife, Cathy, and their six children have built a fine vineyard. They started in 1971 with 18,000 vinifera vines, and today the winery produces nearly 100,000 bottles a year from Chardonnay, Cabernet, and other European grapes. Chenin blanc, Merlot, and a cranberry dessert wine are among their 10 or more tasty varieties. A shop selling their wine, along with herbed vinegars, mustards, jellies, and other foods prepared on the premises, is open year-round. ✉*Stoney Hill Rd.* ☎*508/693–0309* ⊕*www. chicamavineyards.com* ✆*Free tours and tastings* ☉*Late May–mid-Oct., Mon.–Sat. 11–5, Sun. 1–5, tours at 2 and 4; call for off-season hrs and tastings.*

Field Gallery. An unusual sight awaits here, where the late Tom Maley's ponderous white sculptures, such as a colonial horse and rider or a whimsical piper, are displayed on a wide lawn. Inside there are changing summer exhibitions of island artists' work, which is for sale. ✉*1050 State Rd.* ☎*508/693–5595.*

③① **Long Point.** With 632 acres of open grassland and heath, this Trustees of Reservations preserve provides a lovely walk with the promise of a refreshing swim at its end. The area is bounded on the east by freshwater Homer's Pond, on the west by saltwater Tisbury Great Pond, and on the south by fantastic, mile-long South Beach on the Atlantic Ocean. Long Cove Pond, a sandy freshwater swimming pond, is an ideal spot for bird-watchers. ✉*Mid-June–mid-Sept., turn left onto unmarked dirt road (Waldron's Bottom Rd., look for mailboxes) ³/₁₀ mi west of airport on Edgartown–West Tisbury Rd.; at end, follow signs to Long Point parking lot. Mid-Sept.–mid-June, follow unpaved Deep Bottom Rd. (1 mi west of airport) 2 mi to lot* ☎*508/693–7392* ✆*Mid-June–mid-Sept., $10 per vehicle plus $3 per adult; free rest of yr* ☉*Daily 9–6.*

③⑥ **Manuel F. Correllus State Forest.** At the center of the island
★ is this 5,000-acre pine and scrub-oak forest crisscrossed with hiking trails and circled by a paved but rough bike trail (mopeds are prohibited). You can also find a 2-mi nature trail, a 2-mi par fitness course, and horse trails. The West Tisbury side of the state forest joins with an equally large Edgartown parcel to virtually surround the airport. ✉*Headquarters on Barnes Rd. by airport* ☎*508/693–2540* ✆*Free* ☉*Daily sunrise–sunset.*

Martha's Vineyard Glassworks. Watch glass being blown—a fascinating process—by glassmakers who have pieces displayed in Boston's Museum of Fine Arts. Their work is also for sale. ✉*529 State Rd., North Tisbury* ☎*508/693–6026.*

35 Mayhew Chapel and Indian Burial Ground. Deep in the woods off a dirt road, the chapel and burial ground are suffused with history. The tiny chapel, built in 1829 to replace an earlier one, and a memorial plaque are dedicated to the pastor Thomas Mayhew Jr., leader of the original colonists who landed at Edgartown in 1642. Mayhew was noted for his fair dealings with the local Wampanoags. Within a few years, he had converted a number of them to Christianity. Called Praying Indians, they established a community here called Christiantown.

An overgrown wildflower garden grows near the chapel. Beyond the boulder with the plaque are rough-hewn stones marking Native American grave mounds—the dead are not named, for fear of calling down evil spirits. Behind the chapel is the beginning of the Christiantown Woods loop trail, which leads to a lookout tower. You can find a map at the head of the trail. ⊠*Off Indian Hill Rd., off State Rd.*

Mill Pond. This is a lovely spot graced with swans—at the right time of year you might see a cygnet with the swan couple. The small building nearest the pond has been a grammar school, an icehouse, and a police station. The mill stands across the road. Originally a gristmill, it opened in 1847 to manufacture island wool for pea coats, which whalers wore. The Martha's Vineyard Garden Club uses the building now. The pond is just around the corner from the town center on the way toward Edgartown. ⊠*Edgartown–West Tisbury Rd.*

Music Street. Named for the numerous parlor pianos bought with the whaling money of successful sea captains, Music Street is lined with the oldest houses in West Tisbury.

NEED A BREAK? Step back in time with a visit to **Alley's General Store** (⊠*State Rd.* ☎*508/693-0088*), the heart of town since 1858. Alley's sells a truly general variety of goods: everything from hammers to housewares and dill pickles to sweet muffins as well as great things you find only in a country store. There's even a post office inside. Behind the parking lot, Garcia's at Back Alley's serves tasty sandwiches and pastries to go year-round.

New Ag Hall. Built in 1996, about a mile from the Old Agricultural Hall, this is the setting for various shows, lectures, dances, and potluck dinners. A yearly county fair—including a woodsman contest, dog show, games, baked goods and jams for sale, and, of course, livestock- and produce-judging—is held here in late August. ✉ *35 Pan-handle Rd.* ☎ *508/693–9549.*

Old Agricultural Hall. Though the 1859 building near town hall no longer functions as the town center, the **West Tisbury Farmers' Market**—Massachusetts' largest—is held here Wednesday and Saturday in summer. The colorful stands overflow with fresh produce, most of it organic—a refreshing return to life before fluorescent-lit, impersonal supermarkets. ✉ *South Rd.* ☎ *508/693–9549.*

30 Old Oak Tree. This massive, much-loved member of the *quercus* family is thought to be about 150 years old, and it's a perennial subject for nature photographers. Its limbs twist into the sky and along the ground where it stands, near the intersection of State and North roads.

Place on the Wayside. This memorial to Thomas Mayhew Jr. stands along Edgartown–West Tisbury Road, just east of the airport entrance on the south side of the road. A plaque identifies the spot where Mayhew had his "last worship and interview with them the Wampanoags before embarking for England" in 1657, never to return: the ship was lost at sea. Wampanoags passing this spot would leave a stone in Mayhew's memory, and the stones were later cemented together to form the memorial.

29 Polly Hill Arboretum. Horticulturist and part-time Vineyard
★ resident Polly Hill, now in her nineties, has over the years tended some 2,000 species of plants and developed nearly 100 species herself on her old sheep farm in West Tisbury. A rich and expansive collection of flora and serene walking trails are the attractions of her eponymous arboretum. On site are azaleas, tree peonies, dogwoods, hollies, lilacs, magnolias, and more. Hill raised them from seeds without the use of a greenhouse, and her patience is the inspiration of the arboretum. Now run as a nonprofit center, the arboretum also runs guided tours, a lecture series, and a visitor center and gift shop. ✉ *809 State Rd.* ☎ *508/693–9426* ⊕ *www.pollyhillarboretum.org* ✐ *$5* ⊙ *Grounds daily sunrise–sunset. Visitor center late May–mid-Oct., daily 9:30–4; guided tours by appointment.*

Ripley's Field Preserve. For an idea of what the island must have looked like 200 years ago, come to Ripley's Field. This preserve established in the 1950s spreads over undulating, glacier-formed meadows and woodland. A windmill and wildflowers are pleasant attractions. The preserve connects

via old cart paths to Tisbury Meadow and Wompesket preserves in North Tisbury. A parking area and bike rack are
on the left. ⊠*John Hoft Rd., off north end of Lambert's
Cove Rd., 2/3 mi from State Rd.*

Sepiessa Point Reservation. Bird-watchers in particular will
be in paradise here. The reservation covers 164 acres on
splendid Tisbury Great Pond, with expansive views, walking trails around coves and saltwater marshes, horse trails,
swimming, and a boat launch. On the pond beach, watch
out for razor-sharp oyster shells. Beaches across the pond
along the ocean are privately owned. ⊠*New La., which
becomes Tiah's Cove Rd., off W. Tisbury Rd.* ☎*508/627–
7141* ⊘*Free* ☉*Daily sunrise–sunset.*

❹ **Tashmoo Overlook.** Just outside the center of Vineyard
Haven, on the way to West Tisbury, this overlook surveys a
public meadow leading down to Lake Tashmoo and Vineyard Sound beyond. Across the lane from the meadow is
the amphitheater where the Vineyard Playhouse holds summer productions. ⊠*State Rd. and Spring St.*

❸ **Thimble Farm.** In season you can pick your own strawberries, raspberries, and flowers here—or also buy preboxed
fruit if you're not feeling quite so agrarian. The farm also
sells cut flowers, melons, pumpkins, hydroponic tomatoes,
and other produce. ⊠*Stoney Hill Rd.* ☎*508/693–6396*
☉*June–early Oct., Tues.–Sun. 10–5.*

Tisbury Meadow Preserve. One of the rare meadows open
for hiking on the island, this 83-acre preserve isn't being
farmed but is mowed to keep it from reverting to woodland. An old farmstead sits on the property, and the back
acres are wooded except for an 18th-century cart path.
You can walk Tisbury Meadow in less than an hour or
combine it with two other areas, the Wompesket and Ripley's Fields preserves across State Road, for a longer hike.
⊠*Trailhead on east side of State Rd., ½ mi south of Tashmoo Overlook.*

Wompesket Preserve. Bordering part of Merry Farm,
Wompesket includes an interesting wet meadow and ponds
that are good for birding. The walk to the 18-acre area
overlooks the farm and the Atlantic in the distance. To get
here, follow marked dirt roads from Ripley's Field or Tisbury Meadow Preserve. ⊠*Red Coat Hill Rd.*

1

WHERE TO STAY & EAT

★ Fodor'sChoice ✕⊡ **Lambert's Cove Inn and Restaurant.** A nar-
$$$–$$$$ row road winds through pine woods and beside creeper-
covered stone walls to this posh, handsomely designed inn
surrounded by gardens and old stone walls. In 2005 genial
innkeepers Scott Jones and I. Kell Hicklin bought what had
been a slightly fading 1790 farmhouse inn and gave it a
clean, crisp makeover. The richly appointed rooms each
have decorative schemes and antiques based on grand East
Coast resort towns, from Key West to Bar Harbor. Those
in the outbuildings are airy and a bit more contemporary,
some with decks and porches. Guests receive free passes
to beautiful and private Lambert's Cove beach. Fireplaces
and hardwood floors lend warmth to the stellar contempo-
rary restaurant ($$–$$$; reservations essential), where you
might dine on crab cakes with caper aioli and shaved-fennel
salad, or a main course of braised veal cheeks with sweet
corn–English pea risotto and a Madeira wine reduction.
Pros: Smart and contemporary decor, fantastic restaurant,
serene and verdant grounds. **Cons:** Need a car to explore
island from here, not for budget travelers, total seclusion
is a drawback if you love being in center of action. ⊠*Off
Lambert's Cove Rd.* ⊕*R.R. 1, Box 422, Vineyard Haven
02568* ☎*508/693–2298* ⊟*508/693–7890* ⊕*www.lamberts
coveinn.com* ⇨*17 rooms* ⚄*In-room: DVD, Ethernet. In-
hotel: restaurant, tennis court, pool, no elevator* ⊟*AE,
MC, V* |⊙|*BP.*

¢ ⊺**Martha's Vineyard International Hostel.** The only budget,
roof-over-your-head alternative in season, this hostel is one
of the country's best. The large, common kitchen is outfit-
ted with multiple refrigerators and stoves (barbecue grills
are available, too), the common room has a fireplace and
plenty of books, and you can catch wind of local events on
the bulletin board. Morning chores are required in summer.
The hostel runs summer programs on island history, as well
as nature tours. It's near a bike path, and 2 mi from the air-
port and about 3 mi from the nearest beach. Buses stop out
front. **Pros:** It's cheap, it's just off a bike path, it's a fun place
to meet young and active backpackers. **Cons:** Hostel vibe
not for everyone, you need to rely on bus or bike to get to
restaurants and towns, prepare to enjoy doing those morn-
ing chores during high season. ⊠*Edgartown–West Tisbury
Rd., Box 158, 02575* ☎*508/693–2665* ⊕*www.usahostels.
org* ⇨*78 dorm-style beds* ⚄*In-hotel: laundry facilities, no
elevator* ⊟*MC, V* ⊗*Closed mid-Oct.–mid-Apr.*

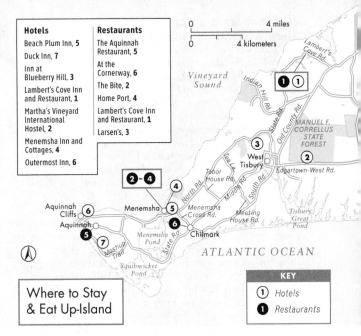

Hotels

Beach Plum Inn, **5**

Duck Inn, **7**

Inn at
Blueberry Hill, **3**

Lambert's Cove Inn
and Restaurant, **1**

Martha's Vineyard
International
Hostel, **2**

Menemsha Inn and
Cottages, **4**

Outermost Inn, **6**

Restaurants

The Aquinnah
Restaurant, **5**

At the
Cornerway, **6**

The Bite, **2**

Home Port, **4**

Lambert's Cove Inn
and Restaurant, **1**

Larsen's, **3**

KEY

① *Hotels*

❶ *Restaurants*

Where to Stay
& Eat Up-Island

SPORTS & THE OUTDOORS

BEACHES

To reach **Cedar Tree Neck Wildlife Sanctuary,** take Indian Hill
Road to Obed Daggett Road, a dirt road that leads to the
trailhead of this Sheriff's Meadow Foundation conservation area. From the ample parking area, the trailhead leads
through an enchanted forest down a hill, across a tiny footbridge, and over dunes to a long beach with giant boulders.
This is not a swimming beach, but it invites long, contem-
plative walks.

Lambert's Cove Beach (✉*Lambert's Cove Rd.*), one of the
island's prettiest, has fine sand and clear water. The Vineyard Sound–side beach has calm waters good for children
and views of the Elizabeth Islands. In season it's restricted
to residents and those staying in West Tisbury.

Long Point, a Trustees of Reservations preserve, has a beautiful beach on the Atlantic, as well as freshwater and saltwater ponds for swimming, including the brackish Tisbury
Great Pond. Restrooms are available.

Sepiessa Point Reservation (⊠*Off Tiah's Cove Rd.*) is a 164-acre area of the Land Bank Commission. A long walk along Tiah's Cove leads to a beach, at the southerly point, alongside Tisbury Great Pond. Across the pond you can see the ocean. The very narrow beach is delightful, though not for laying out a towel and sunbathing. Those with canoes or kayaks can put in at the trailhead and paddle across the pond to a barrier beach for picnicking and swimming. There's parking for only a few cars at the trailhead.

Uncle Seth's Pond is a warm freshwater pond on Lambert's Cove Road, with a small beach right off the road. Seth's is popular with families—toddlers enjoy frolicking in the shallow waters along the shore—as well as with the lap swimmers crisscrossing the pond. Parking is very limited.

HORSEBACK RIDING

Arrowhead Farm (⊠*Indian Hill Rd.* ☎*508/693–8831*) has riding lessons for adults and children year-round, as well as children's summer horsemanship programs. The farm has an indoor ring and leases horses and has trail rides.

Crow Hollow Farm (⊠*Tiah's Cove Rd.* ☎*508/696–4554* ⊕*www.crowhollowfarm.com*) has trail rides for experienced riders only, plus lessons and clinics.

Manuel F. Correllus State Forest (⊠*Access off Barnes Rd., Old County Rd., and Edgartown–West Tisbury Rd.*) is laced with horse trails open to the public, but it has no stables.

Pond View Farm (⊠*Off New Lane* ☎*508/693–2949* ⊕*www. pondviewfarm.com*) holds a summer camp for children 6 and up and gives riding lessons.

SHOPPING

Forget-Me-Not Antiques (⊠*State Rd.* ☎*508/693–1788*) sells European pine furniture, including Hungarian country hutches and cupboards and tables.

The **Granary Gallery at the Red Barn** (⊠*Old County Rd.* ☎*508/693–0455* ⊕*www.granarygallery.com*) displays early-American furniture and exhibits artworks by island and international artists.

CHILMARK

38 *5½ mi southwest of West Tisbury.*

A rural, unspoiled village with scenic ocean-view roads, rustic woodlands, and no crowds, Chilmark draws chic summer visitors and, hard on their heels, stratospheric real-estate prices. Lucy Vincent Beach (residents only in summer) here is perhaps the island's most beautiful. Laced with ribbons of rough roads and winding stone fences that once separated fields and pastures, Chilmark reminds visitors what the Vineyard was like in an earlier time, before developers took over.

WHAT TO SEE

37 **Abel's Hill Cemetery.** Longtime summer resident and writer Lillian Hellman, one of many who continued the Vineyard's tradition of liberal politics, is buried here, as is John Belushi, in an unmarked grave. A boulder, engraved with the comedian's name, sits near the entrance. A few steps away is a headstone sporting a skull and crossbones, with the notation "Here Lies the Body of John Belushi. I May Be Gone but Rock and Roll Lives On"; common knowledge is that it's a decoy placed to deter overzealous fans from finding the actual burial site. Visitors often leave, as tokens of remembrance, empty champagne bottles, cigarette butts, flowers, and notes. ⊠*South Rd.*

Beetlebung Corner. The black gum trees that grow here used to be used to make wooden mallets and plugs for casks (called "beetles" and "bungs"). Today, this crossroads marks Chilmark's town center. Here are the town's public buildings, including the firehouse and the post office, as well as the **Chilmark Community Center** (☎*508/645–9484*), where events such as town meetings, auctions, children's activities, and chamber music concerts take place. In summer, a general store, a clothing boutique, a restaurant and breakfast café, a gallery, and a bank turn the little crossroads into a minimetropolis. ⊠*Middle, State, South, and Menemsha Cross Rds.*

NEED A BREAK? The **Chilmark Store** (⊠ *7 State Rd.* ☎*508/645–3655*) serves up pizza, burgers, salads, and deli sandwiches—it's a solid take-out lunch spot. If you've bicycled into town, the wooden rockers on the porch may be just the place to take a break—or find a picnic spot of your own nearby to enjoy a fish burger or a slice of the pizza of the day. It's open from May to mid-October.

❸❾ Fulling Mill Brook. This 50-acre conservation area is jointly owned by the Land Bank and the town. Its easy walking trail slopes gently down toward the lowlands along the brook, where there are boulders to sit and sun on, and a bike rack at the property's edge at South Road.

Waskosim's Rock Reservation. Bought by the Land Bank in 1990 from a developer who had planned to build 40 houses on it, this reservation comprises diverse habitats—rolling green hills, wetlands, oak and black-gum woods, and 1,500 feet of frontage on Mill Brook—as well as the ruins of an 18th-century homestead. Waskosim's Rock itself was deposited by the retreating glacier 10,000 years ago and is said to resemble the head of a breaching whale. It's one of the highest points on the Vineyard, situated on a ridge above the valley, from which there's a panoramic view of more than 1,000 acres of protected land. At the trailhead off North Road, a map outlines a 3-mi hike throughout the 166 acres. ⊠*Parking areas on North Rd.* ☎*508/627–7141* 🖃*Free* ☉*Daily sunrise–sunset.*

WHERE TO STAY & EAT

$$$–$$$$ ✕**At the Cornerway.** Jamaican chef Deon Thomas brings cuisine rich in his home island's flavors to this American-style bistro. Adventurous diners can try braised goat shoulder with prunes and pearl onions; those with less exotic tastes can choose from offerings like oven-crisped orange duck with a chambord drizzle, and roasted grouper curry with lime-mango chutney. Whichever pleases your palate, make sure to finish with either the coconut bread pudding or chocolate rum cake. If you want to be able to hear your dinner companions, ask for a corner seat away from the atrium. The acoustics are terrible in this barnlike structure that once hosted square dances. ⊠*Beetlebung Corner* ☎*508/645–9300* ⊕*www.atthecornerway.com* 🖃*AE, MC, V* 🍽*BYOB.*

$$$–$$$$ ✕🔲**Inn at Blueberry Hill.** Exclusive and secluded, this cedar-shingle retreat on 56 acres of former farmland puts you in the heart of the rural Vineyard. The restaurant, Theo's ($$–$$$$), is relaxed and elegant, with fresh, health-conscious food that is thoughtfully prepared. You might dine on maple-spiced duck breast with sweet-potato gnocchi, or seared sea scallops with a basil-grapefruit-tarragon beurre blanc. A Continental breakfast is included in the

room rate, and a box lunch is available for a picnic on the beach (the inn runs a guest shuttle to Lucy Vincent and Squibnocket beaches). Rooms are sparsely but tastefully decorated with simple island-made furniture; most have glass doors that open onto terraces or private decks. There's a large parlor-library with a fireplace. **Pros:** Lots of privacy, many rooms have terraces with views, terrific restaurant. **Cons:** Not a great choice for children, a long drive from town centers, Wi-Fi in common room but not individual guest rooms. ⊠*74 North Rd., 02535* ☎*508/645–3322 or 800/356–3322* ✆*508/645–3799* ⊕*www.blueberryinn. com* ⇨*25 rooms* ♿*In-hotel: restaurant, tennis court, pool, gym, airport shuttle, public Wi-Fi, no kids under 12, no elevator* ⊟*AE, MC, V* ⊘*Closed Nov.–Apr.* ⦿*CP.*

SPORTS & THE OUTDOORS

BEACHES

Chilmark Pond Preserve (⊠*Off South Rd.*), on the south side of the road about 3 mi from West Tisbury Center, is an 8-acre Land Bank property at the foot of Abel's Hill (look for the white post with the Land Bank signage). From a landing at the bottom of the driveway, you reach the north side of magnificent Chilmark Lower Pond. You can either plant yourself right there or, if you bring your own canoe, kayak, small rowboat, or inflatable raft, you can paddle a short distance across the pond to 200 feet of Land Bank–owned Atlantic Ocean beach. If you're not a Chilmark resident or Chilmark summer renter with a beach pass, this is the only public Atlantic Ocean beach access in town. There's parking for about 10 cars.

★ Fodor'sChoice **Lucy Vincent Beach** (⊠*Off South Rd.*), on the south shore, is one of the island's most beautiful. The wide strand of fine sand is backed by high clay bluffs facing the Atlantic surf. Keep walking to the left (east, or Down-Island) to reach the unofficial nude beach. Walking to the right, toward the private Windy Gates beach, is restricted to those who own beachfront property here. All others are prohibited. There's great bodysurfing for all ages in these waters. In season, Lucy Vincent is restricted to town residents and visitors with passes. Off-season a stroll here is the perfect getaway. Parking is available.

A narrow beach that is part smooth rocks and pebbles, part fine sand, **Squibnocket Beach** (⊠*Off South Rd.*), on the south shore, provides an appealing boulder-strewn coastline and gentle waves. Surfers know this area for its good waves. Tide-pool lovers can study marine life close up. During the high season, this beach is restricted to residents and visitors with passes.

FISHING

Flashy Lady Charters (⊠*Menemsha Harbor* ☎*508/645–2462* ⊕*www.flashyladycharters.com*) leads inshore charters twice a day, for trolling bass and blues. It's the only charter boat with the guarantee "no fish—no charge."

Menemsha Blues Charters (⊠*Basin Rd., Menemsha Harbor* ☎*508/645–3778* ⊕*www.menemshabluescharters.com*) runs bass, bluefish, and bonita charters out of Menemsha.

Sortie Charters (⊠*Charter Dock, Basin Rd., Menemsha Harbor* ☎*508/645–3015* ⊕*www.sortiecharters.com*) leads inshore trolling excursions and jigging for bass and blues twice daily. You can also take a scenic trip for lunch and a leisurely stroll around fabled Cuttyhunk Island.

SHOPPING

★ **Chilmark Chocolates** (⊠*State Rd.* ☎*508/645–3013*) sells superior chocolates and what might just be the world's finest butter crunch, which you can sometimes watch being made in the back room.

★ **Martha's Vineyard Glassworks** (⊠*683 State Rd.* ☎*508/693–6026*) makes a great stop not just to browse the colorful, stunningly crafted contemporary glass pieces but also to watch the artists at work in the glass-blowing studio.

MENEMSHA

★ *1½ mi northwest of Chilmark.*

A fishing village unspoiled by the "progress" of the past few decades, Menemsha is a jumble of weathered fishing shacks, fishing and pleasure boats, drying nets and lobster pots, and parents and kids pole-fishing from the jetty. Though the picturesque scene is not lost on myriad photographers and artists, this is very much a working village. The catch of the day, taken off boats returning to port, is sold at markets along Dutcher's Dock. Romantics bring picnic suppers to the public Menemsha Beach to catch perfect sunsets over the water. If you feel you've seen this town before, you probably have: it was used for location shots in the film *Jaws*.

WHAT TO SEE

40 Menemsha Hills Reservation. A 210-acre Trustees of Reservations property, including a mile of rocky shoreline and high sand bluffs along Vineyard Sound, Menemsha Hills is very different from most other island conservation areas. Its hilly walking trails through scrub oak and heathland have interpretive signs at viewing points, and the 309-foot Prospect Hill, the island's highest, affords excellent views of the Elizabeth Islands and beyond. Call ahead about naturalist-led tours. ⊠*Off North Rd., 1 mi east of Menemsha Cross Rd.* ☎*508/693–7662* ⊟*Free* ☉*Daily sunrise–sunset.*

WHERE TO STAY & EAT

$$$$ ✕**Home Port.** A classic seafood-in-the-rough experience since the 1930s, this breezy seasonal island institution serves absolutely the freshest lobster around (including a hefty 3-lb. lobster that'll set you back $60), plus steamers, scallops, smoked bluefish pâté, and local fish. The fishing nets and other nautical paraphernalia hanging on the knotty-pine walls bring you back to a bygone era. Sailors from all around southern New England savor the chance to pull into Menemsha for a meal at this stalwart, where commoners often rub shoulders with celebs. You can also get your meal to go and enjoy it on the lawn or by the dock overlooking the harbor. ⊠*At end of North Rd.* ☎*508/645–2679* ⊕*www.homeportmv.com* ⟁*Reservations essential* ⊟*MC, V* ⎆*BYOB* ☉*Closed mid-Oct.–mid-Apr. No lunch.*

★ FodorśChoice ✕**Larsen's.** Basically a retail fish store, Larsen's
¢–$$ has a raw take-out counter and will also boil lobsters for you. Dig into a plate of fresh littlenecks or cherrystones. Oysters are not a bad alternative. There's also seafood chowder and a variety of smoked fish and dips. Bring your own bottle of wine or beer, buy your dinner here, and then set up on the rocks, the docks, or the beach: there's no finer alfresco rustic dining on the island. Larsen's closes at 6 PM weekdays, 7 PM weekends. ⊠*Dutcher's Dock* ☎*508/645–2680* ⊟*MC, V* ⎆*BYOB* ☉*Closed mid-Oct.–mid-May.*

¢–$ ✕**The Bite.** Fried everything—clams, fish-and-chips, you name it—is on the menu at this simple, roadside shack, where two outdoor picnic tables are the only seating options. Small, medium, and large are the three choices: all of them are perfect if you're craving that classic seaside fried lunch. But don't come on a rainy day, unless you want to get wet—the lines here can be long. To beat the crowds, try arriving between traditional mealtimes. The best advice, however,

CLOSE UP

Martha's Vineyard Trivia

1

The year-round population of the island is about 15,000. On any given day in summer, the population increases fivefold, to an estimated 75,000.

Some four decades after the island was charted in 1602, Bay Colony businessman Thomas Mayhew struck a deal with the Crown and purchased Martha's Vineyard, as well as Nantucket and the Elizabeth Islands, for £40.

Jeanne and Hugh Taylor, the latter the brother of recording star James Taylor, operate the Outermost Inn, by the light-house in Aquinnah.

Total shoreline: 126 mi. Total land area: 100 square mi.

Martha's Vineyard was formed more than 20,000 years ago as great sheets of ice, as thick as 2 mi, descended from the frigid northern climes into what is now New England, pushing great chunks of earth and rock before them. When the glaciers melted and receded, the island, as well as Nantucket and Cape Cod, remained in their wake.

When residents say they are going "Up-Island," they mean they're heading to the western areas of Aquinnah, Chilmark, Menemsha, and West Tisbury. The designation is based on nautical terminology, where heading west means going "up" in longitude. "Down-Is-land" refers to Vineyard Haven, Oak Bluffs, and Edgartown.

During the height of the 19th-century whaling era, it was considered good luck to have an Aquinnah Wampanoag on board. The Wampanoags were renowned as sailors and har-pooners. Town residents voted to change the name of Gay Head to Aquinnah in 1997, and the official change was signed into law on May 7, 1998.

The North American continent's last heath hen, an eastern prai-rie chicken, died in a forest fire on Martha's Vineyard in 1932. A monument to it stands in the State Forest just off the West Tisbury–Edgartown Road.

West Tisbury resident, farmer, and sailor Joshua Slocum be-came the first man to sail solo around the world. He set out in 1895 in his 36-foot sloop and returned three years later. Ten years later he was lost at sea.

Despite the fact that Great Harbour was renamed Edgar-town after the young son of the Duke of York, the unfor-tunate three-year-old died one month before the name became official.

is be patient and don't arrive too hungry. The Bite is open 11 AM–3 PM in spring and fall and until 8:45 PM in summer. ⊠ *29 Basin Rd.* ☎ *509/645–9239* ⊕ *www.thebitemenemsha. com* ⊟ *No credit cards* ⊗ *Closed Oct.–late May.*

$$$–$$$$ ✕⬜**Beach Plum Inn.** This mansard-roof inn, bought by the
★ nearby Menemsha Inn in 2005, is surrounded by 7 acres
of lavish formal gardens and lush woodland; it sits on a
bluff over Menemsha Harbor. The floral-theme rooms—
five in the main house and six in cottages—have gorgeous
furnishings, and some have whirlpool tubs; in the Daffo-
dil room, bathed in shades of yellow and blue, you can
find a hand-painted queen bed and a romantic balcony.
A vaulted, beamed ceiling rises over the bedroom of the
secluded Morning Glory Cottage. As romantic settings go,
it's hard to beat the restaurant ($$$$) here, with its knock-
out harbor views, especially at sunset. For dinner, consider
such memorable fare as pan-seared scallops with orange-
mango-fennel salad, and the mixed grill of lamb chop with
rhubarb compote, filet mignon, orange-infused duck, and
chicken-apple sausage with truffle risotto. **Pros:** Gardens
will blow you away, short walk to Menemsha, superb res-
taurant. **Cons:** A bit of a drive from any major towns, pub-
lic Wi-Fi but none in rooms, pricey. ⊠*North Rd., 02552*
☎*508/645–9454 or 877/645–7398* ⊕*www.beachpluminn.
com* ➫*11 rooms* ♿*In-room: refrigerator, dial-up. In-hotel:
tennis court, gym, concierge, public Wi-Fi, no elevator*
⊟*AE, D, MC, V* ⊗*Closed Nov.–Apr.* ⍑*BP.*

$$$–$$$$ ⬚**Menemsha Inn and Cottages.** For 40 years the late *Life*
photographer Alfred Eisenstaedt returned to his cot-
tage on the hill here for the panoramic view of Vineyard
Sound and Cuttyhunk beyond the trees below. These cot-
tages, which are owned by the neighboring Beach Plum
Inn, all have screened porches, fireplaces, and kitchens,
tumble down a hillside behind the main house, and vary
in privacy and views. You can also stay in the 1989 inn
building or the pleasant Carriage House. All rooms have
private decks, most with sunset views. Suites include sitting
areas, desks, and big tiled baths. A continental breakfast
is served in a solarium-style breakfast room with a deck
facing the ocean. Passes and shuttle transportation to both
Squibnocket and Lucy Vincent beaches are provided. **Pros:**
Wonderfully secluded locale on 14 acres, short walk to
Menemsha, sunset views from private decks. **Cons:** Not for
the budget-minded, need a car to explore island from here,
public Wi-Fi but none in rooms. ⊠*North Rd., Box 38,
02552* ☎*508/645–2521* ⊕*www.menemshainn.com* ➫*15
rooms, 11 cottages, 1 2-bedroom house* ♿*In-room: kitchen
(some), refrigerator (some), VCR, dial-up. In-hotel: tennis*

court, gym, public Wi-Fi, no elevator =MC, V ⊘*Closed Dec.–mid-Apr.* ⦿CP.

SPORTS & THE OUTDOORS

BEACHES

Great Rock Bight Preserve (⊠*On North Rd., about 1 mi from Menemsha Hills Reservation*) is a Land Bank–managed tract of 28 acres. Parking is at the end of a ½-mi dirt road; it's a ½-mi walk to the beach, a secluded sandy cove of about 1,300 feet. It's well worth the trek.

Menemsha Beach (⊠*Adjacent to Dutcher's Dock*) is a pebbly public beach with gentle surf on Vineyard Sound and, with views to the northwest, a great place to catch the sunset. This is an active harbor for both commercial and sport fishermen; you'll be able to catch an eyeful of the handsome yachts and smaller boats. There are always anglers working the tides on the jetty, too. On-site are restrooms and lifeguards. Snack stands and restaurants are a short walk from the parking lot, which can get crowded in summer (there's room for about 60 cars).

AQUINNAH

6½ mi west of Menemsha, 10 mi southwest of West Tisbury, 17 mi southwest of Vineyard Haven.

Aquinnah, formerly called Gay Head, is an official Native American township. In 1987, after more than a decade of struggle in the courts, the Wampanoag tribe won guardianship of 420 acres of land, which are held in trust by the federal government in perpetuity and constitute the Aquinnah Native American Reservation. In 1997 the town voted to change the town's name from Gay Head back to its original Native American name, Aquinnah (pronounced a-*kwih*-nah), Wampanoag for "Land Under the Hill." Although the name has changed, it will take some time for the state and Martha's Vineyard authorities to convert road signs, maps, and other documents to the new name—so you can expect minor confusion. Some private businesses that use the name Gay Head might elect to retain it, so keep in mind that Gay Head and Aquinnah refer to the same place.

The "center" of Aquinnah consists of a combination fire and police station, the town hall, a Tribal Council office, and a public library, formerly the little red schoolhouse.

Because the town's year-round population hovers around 650, Aquinnah children attend schools in other towns.

WHAT TO SEE

43 ★ Fodor'sChoice **Aquinnah Cliffs.** A National Historic Landmark and part of the Wampanoag reservation land, these spectacular cliffs are the island's major tourist attraction, as evidenced by the tour bus–filled parking lot. Native American crafts and food shops line the short approach to the overlook, from which you can see the Elizabeth Islands to the northeast across Vineyard Sound and Noman's Land Island, part wildlife preserve, part military-bombing practice site, 3 mi off the Vineyard's southern coast.

If you've reached a state of quiet, vacationland bliss, keep in mind that this *is* a heavily touristed spot, and it might turn out to be a shock to your peace of mind. When you come, consider going to Aquinnah Lighthouse first, then down and around to the beach and cliffs.

There's no immediate access to the beach from the light— nothing like an easy staircase down the cliffs to the sand below. To reach the cliffs, park in the Moshup Beach (⇨ *Sports & the Outdoors*) lot by the lighthouse loop, walk 5-plus minutes south on the boardwalk, then continue another 20 or more minutes on the sand to get back around to the lighthouse. The cliffs themselves are pretty marvelous, and you should plan ahead if you want to see them. It takes a while to get to Aquinnah from elsewhere on the island, and in summer the parking lot and beach fill up, so start early to get a jump on the throngs. Although the lot costs $15 a day, you'll get $10 of your deposit back if you stay only an hour and $5 if you stay two, which is plenty of time to see the cliffs, have a meal, or do a little shopping. ⌂ *State Rd.*

44 **Aquinnah Lighthouse.** The brick lighthouse, stationed precariously atop the rapidly eroding cliffs, is open to the public on summer weekends at sunset, weather permitting. Across from the lighthouse parking area, you'll see the historic Vanderhoop Homestead (⊕ *www.vanderhoop homestead.org*), a handsome 1880s house that's currently being restored. Plans are to turn the house into community cultural center and museum on Aquinnah's rich history. ⌂ *Lighthouse Rd.* ☎ *508/645-2211* ⌂ *$2.*

42 **Aquinnah spring.** The spring's water, channeled through a roadside iron pipe, is cold enough to slake a cyclist's thirst on the hottest day. Feel free to fill a canteen. Locals come from all over the island to fill jugs. The spring is on the left, clearly visible from the road, 1/10 mi past the Aquinnah town line sign. ⊠*State Rd.*

Cranberry Lands. This area of cranberry bogs gone wild is a popular nesting site for birds. No humans can nest here, but you can drive by and look. A scenic route worth the trip is West Basin Road, which takes you along the Vineyard Sound shore of Menemsha Light and through the bogs. At the end of the road, with marshland on the right and low dunes, grasses, and the long blue arc of the bight on the left, you get a terrific view of the quiet fishing village of Menemsha, across the water. **Lobsterville Road Beach** here is public, but public parking is limited to three spots, so get here early if you want one of them.

❹ Quitsa Pond Lookout. Quitsa Pond Lookout has a good view of the adjoining Menemsha and Nashaquitsa ponds, the woods, and the ocean beyond. ⊠*State Rd.*

WHERE TO STAY & EAT

$$–$$$$ ✕**The Aquinnah Restaurant.** At the far end of the row of fast-food take-out spots and souvenir shops at the Gay Head Cliffs is this restaurant owned and operated by members of the Vanderhoop and Madison families, native Wampanoags. The family took back the lease in 2000 after a four-year hiatus, and the restaurant has regained its reputation as a homey place to eat. For breakfast try the Tomahawk Special, two homemade fish cakes covered with salsa on top of poached eggs with melted cheddar cheese. The lunch menu includes sandwiches, burgers, and healthy-sounding salads. Dinner entrées include sautéed shrimp, scallops, and lobster with rotini in a Chardonnay sauce, and striped bass in a mussel-and-saffron sauce. The home-baked pies (banana cream, pecan, or fruit) come wrapped in a moist and flaky crust. ⊠*State Rd.* ☎*508/645–3867* ▤*MC, V* ⊘*Closed mid-Oct.–mid-Apr.*

$$$$ ✕▦**Outermost Inn.** This rambling, sun-filled inn by the ★ Aquinnah Cliffs stands alone on acres of moorland, a 10-minute walk from the beach. The house is wrapped in windows revealing views of sea and sky in three directions, and there are great views of the Aquinnah Lighthouse from the wide porch and patio. The inn is clean and contemporary, with white walls and polished light-wood floors. Each room has a phone, and one has a whirlpool tub. The restaurant, open to the public, serves dinner nightly in

summer and is all prix fixe at $72 (reservations are essential, and it's BYOB). **Pros:** Spectacular setting high atop Gay Head Cliffs, daily trips available on the inn's catamaran, wonderful food. **Cons:** Location is far from bigger towns on island, steep rates, not suitable for young kids. ⊠*Lighthouse Rd., R.R. 1, Box 171, 02535* ☎*508/645–3511* 🖷*508/645–3514* ⊕*www.outermostinn.com* ⇩*7 rooms* ⌂*In-room: no a/c, dial-up. In-hotel: restaurant, no elevator, no kids under 12* ⊟*AE, D, MC, V* ⊙*Closed mid-Oct.–mid-May* ⦿*BP.*

$–$$ 🛏 **Duck Inn.** The Duck Inn, originally an 18th-century home
★ built by Native American seafarer George Belain, sits on a bucolic 5-acre bluff overlooking the ocean, with the Aquinnah Lighthouse standing sentinel to the north. The eclectic, fun interior blends peach stucco walls, Native American rugs and wall hangings, and ducks. Three upstairs rooms come with balconies; a suite in the stone-wall lower level (cool in summer, warm in winter) has views of the rolling fields; and a small attached cabin (closed in winter) with separate bath is the least expensive room. The first floor's common room, with a working 1928 Glenwood stove, piano, and fireplace, is the heart of the inn. Massage and facial therapies are available, and the healthful breakfast fare includes waffles with strawberries and omelets or chocolate crepes. This inn is informal—kids and pets are welcome—and one night is free with a week's stay. **Pros:** A good value on this part of the island, totally secluded, ocean views. **Cons:** A longish drive from any large town, an informal operation with no Web site, peaceful setting isn't ideal if you like lots of bustle. ⊠*10 Duck Pond Way, off State Rd., Box 160, 02535* ☎*508/645–9018* 🖷*508/645–2790* ⇩*4 rooms, 1 suite* ⌂*In-hotel: some pets allowed* ⊟*MC, V* ⦿*BP.*

SPORTS & THE OUTDOORS

BEACHES

Lobsterville Beach encompasses 2 mi of beautiful sand and dune beach directly off Lobsterville Road on the Vineyard Sound. It's a seagull nesting area and a favorite fishing spot. Though the water tends to be cold, and the pebbles along the shore make getting in and out difficult, the beach is protected and suitable for children. The view looking east—of Menemsha Harbor, the rest of the Vineyard, and the Elizabeth Islands across the sound—makes you feel like you're surrounded by the Greek islands. Given the limited parking (for about eight cars), this is an ideal stop-off for cyclists exploring this area of the island.

Moshup Beach (⊠*At intersection of State Rd. and Moshup Trail*) is, according to the Land Bank, "probably the most glamorous" of its holdings, because the beach provides access to the awesome Aquinnah Cliffs. The best views of the cliffs and up to the lighthouse are from a 25-plus-minute walk via boardwalk and beach. On clear days Noman's Land looms like a giant mirage. There's a drop-off area close to the beach, but you still must park in the lot and walk to the sand. The island shuttle bus stops here, too, and there are bike racks on the beach. Come early in the day to ensure both a quieter experience and an available parking spot. Keep in mind that climbing the cliffs is against the law—they're eroding much too quickly on their own. It's also illegal to take any of the clay with you. There's a parking fee of $15 from Memorial Day to Labor Day.

Philbin Beach, off Moshup Trail, is restricted to town residents or renters with a lease. It's a nice, wide beach with a wild Atlantic Ocean challenging you to master it. Beach passes can be obtained from the **Aquinnah town hall** (⊠*65 State Rd.* ☎*508/645–2300*).

FISHING

Conomo Charters (⊠*10 Old South Rd.* ☎*508/645–9278*), under Captain Brian Vanderhoop, leads striped-bass and bluefish trips.

Menemsha Creek Charters (☎*508/645–3511*), run by Captain Hugh Taylor, leads two trips a day aboard the catamaran *Arabella* for swimming and picnicking for up to 40 people at a time. Day trips to Cuttyhunk depart at 10:30 AM and return at 3:30 PM; daily sunset cruises are also available.

Tomahawk Charters (☎*508/645–3201*), with Captain Buddy Vanderhoop at the helm, specializes in striped-bass fishing trips as well as bluefish, tuna, bonita, and sharks. Captain Lisa Vanderhoop also leads fishing charters especially for kids.

MARTHA'S VINEYARD ESSENTIALS

To research prices, get advice from other travelers, and book travel arrangements, visit www.fodors.com.

TRANSPORTATION

BY AIR
⇨ *Air Travel in Essentials in the back of this book.*

BY BIKE
Martha's Vineyard offers superb terrain for biking—you can pick up a map that shows the island's many dedicated bike paths from the chamber of commerce. Several shops throughout the island rent bicycles, many of them close to the ferry terminals. Martha's Vineyard Strictly Bikes rents bike racks for your car.

Bike Rentals **DeBettencourt's** (✉*Circuit Ave. Exit, Oak Bluffs* ☎*508/693–0011*). **Edgartown Bicycles** (✉*Upper Main St., Edgartown* ☎*508/627–9008*). **Martha's Vineyard Strictly Bikes** (✉*24 Union St., Vineyard Haven* ☎*508/693–0782*).

BY BOAT & FERRY
⇨ *Boat & Ferry Travel in Essentials in the back of this book.*

BY BUS
The big buses of the Martha's Vineyard Transit Authority (VTA) provide regular service to all six towns on the island, with frequent stops in peak season and very limited service in winter. The fare is $1 per town, including the town of departure. One-day ($6), three-day ($15), one-week ($25), and one-month ($40) passes are available on the buses or at the Edgartown Visitors Center. The VTA also has two free in-town shuttle-bus routes, one in Edgartown and one in Vineyard Haven.

Bus Information **Martha's Vineyard Transit Authority** (*VTA* ☎*508/693–9940* ⊕*www.vineyardtransit.com*).

BY CAR
Traffic can be a challenge on Martha's Vineyard, especially in season, but driving can be worth the hassle if you really want to see the whole island and travel freely among towns. Bringing a car over on the ferry in summer, however, requires reservations far in advance, costs almost double what it does in the off-season, and necessitates standing in long lines—it's sometimes easier and more economical to rent a car once you're on the island, and then only for the

days when you plan to explore. Where you stay and what you plan on seeing can greatly influence your transportation plans; discuss the different options for getting around Martha's Vineyard with your innkeeper or hotel staff as soon as you've booked a room.

Note that permits, fees, and certain equipment are needed for driving on Katama Beach and Wasque Reservation. Contact the chamber of commerce or park rangers for details.

You can book rentals on Martha's Vineyard through the Woods Hole ferry terminal free phone. The agencies listed below have rental desks at the airport. Cost is $80–$170 per day for a sedan; renting a four-wheel-drive vehicle costs around $150 per day (seasonal prices fluctuate widely).

Martha's Vineyard Agencies **AAA Island** (☎508/627–6800 or 800/627–6333 ⊕www.mvautorental.com). **Adventure Rentals** (✉Beach Rd., Vineyard Haven ☎508/693–1959 ⊕www.adventure-rentalsmv.com).

BY TAXI

Taxis meet all scheduled ferries and flights, and there are taxi stands by the Flying Horses Carousel in Oak Bluffs, at the foot of Main Street in Edgartown, and by the steamship office in Vineyard Haven. Fares range from $6 within a town to $35–$42 one-way from Vineyard Haven to Aquinnah.

Rates double between 1 AM and 7 AM. Note that limousine companies often provide service both on- and off-island.

Martha's Vineyard Taxi Companies **AdamCab** (☎508/627–4462 or 800/281–4462 ⊕www.adamcab.com). **All Island Taxi** (☎508/693–2929 or 800/693–8294). **Atlantic Cab** (☎508/693–7110 or 877/477–8294). **Mario's** (☎508/693–8399).

CONTACTS & RESOURCES

TOURS

Liz Villard's Vineyard History Tours leads walking tours of Edgartown's "history, architecture, ghosts, and gossip," including a stop at the Vincent House. Tours are run from April through December; call for times. Liz and her guides also lead similar tours of Oak Bluffs and Vineyard Haven. Walks last a little more than an hour.

Contacts **Vineyard History Tours** (☎508/627–8619).

VISITOR INFORMATION

The Martha's Vineyard Chamber of Commerce is two blocks from the Vineyard Haven ferry. The chamber information booth by the Vineyard Haven steamship terminal is open late May to the last weekend in June, Friday–Sunday 8–8; July–early September, daily 8–8; and early September–mid-October, Friday–Sunday 8:30–5:30. The chamber itself is open weekdays 9–5. There are also town information kiosks on Circuit Avenue in Oak Bluffs and on Church Street in Edgartown.

Tourist Information **Martha's Vineyard Chamber of Commerce** (⊠ *Beach Rd.* ✆ *Box 1698, Vineyard Haven 02568* ☎ *508/693–4486 or 800/505–4815* ⊕ *www.mvy.com*).

Nantucket

WORD OF MOUTH

"I keep going back to Nantucket for the natural beauty of its beaches, the sense of being far away from the mainland, and the smell of Rosa rugosa everywhere outside of town."

—MarieF

"It's not for everyone. The prices are out of control: gas, houses, rents, meals, goods and services, ferry tickets for your auto, etc., etc. But for many of us, it's the BEST."

—rhkkmk

By Andrew
Collins
& Sandy
MacDonald

FOR THE FIRST TIME since its golden age as a world-renowned whaling capital in the early 1800s, the tiny island of Nantucket is decidedly on a roll. Modest shingled cottages that might have gone begging for a buyer a few decades ago now fetch an easy million. The 800-plus pre-1840 structures that compose the core of town—a National Landmark Historic District—only rarely change hands, and then at exalted prices. As for the trophy houses—mega-mansions built in the hinterlands for rich arrivistes—they're consistently off the charts, setting new records only to break them.

And yet its ascending chic has little to do with what attracts most people to Nantucket in the first place, or keeps them coming back. The allure has more to do with how, at the height of summer, a cooling fog will drift in across the multihue moors or the way rambling wild roses, the gaudy pink Rosa rugosa, perfume a hidden path to the beach.

Essentially Nantucket is *all* beach—a boomerang-shape sand spit consisting of detritus left by a glacier that receded millennia ago. Off Cape Cod, some 26 mi out to sea, the island measures 3½ by 14 mi at its widest points, while encompassing—such are the miracles of inlet and bay—about 80 mi of sandy shoreline, all of it open, as a matter of local pride, to absolutely everyone.

The small commercial area of Nantucket Town is the center of island activity, just as it has been since the early 1700s. It's only a few square blocks of mostly historical buildings, lovingly restored inns, and boutiques and galleries leading up from the pretty harbor and waterfront, where the ferries dock. Beyond it, quiet residential roads fan out to points around the island; Siasconset (known locally as 'Sconset) lies 8 mi to the east, Surfside 3 mi to the south, and Madaket 6 mi west of town. Thus far, the outlying areas appear relatively rural; however, increasing "infill" threatens the idyll.

Still, on a day when sun scintillates on sand and the thrumming waves hint at an eternal rhythm, it's hard to imagine that anything could ever go too terribly wrong here. As summer succeeds summer, children will continue to construct their fanciful if foredoomed sand castles and marvel over the odd treasures the tides drag in. Adults will gladly play along, if allowed, remembering their own seemingly endless days of summer and imagining more of the same for their children's children and so on and on. Perfection can be surprisingly simple, after all, and even if Nantuck-

et's current cachet should fade, the island's timeless pleasures will endure.

ABOUT THE RESTAURANTS

For such a tiny island, Nantucket is rife with great restaurants—"world class" would be no exaggeration. Of course,
with New York–level sophistication come New York–level
prices. And whereas the titans of industry who flock here
for a bit of high-rent R&R might not blink at the prospect
of a $40 or even $50 entrée, the rest of us must sometimes
suppress a nervous gulp. Is it worth it? Again and again, in
venues that vie for the title of most recherché, the answer
is yes.

New American fever hit Nantucket about two decades ago
and shows no signs of abating. Often, the chefs brought
in to dazzle at established front-runners decide to stay on
and open places of their own. Thus, the restaurant scene is
constantly expanding and improving.

Even though the island itself isn't agriculturally equipped
to furnish much more than a bit of produce and some
homegrown herbs and greens (lovely as they can be), New
England's top greengrocers are on tap to provide regional
delicacies. The seafood, naturally, is nonpareil, especially
local scallops in season. So don't let the prices deter you.
The general excellence of Nantucket's restaurants seems to
have a trickle-down effect: even many of the more modest
eateries pack unexpected panache.

In any month other than July or August, call ahead to
check hours of operation, which tend to shrink. Dining
off-season used to be a dicey proposition, but in the past
few years, enough talented resident chef-owners have set
up shop so that the options even in the dead of winter can
be mighty inviting. For restaurants, we list months closed;
otherwise, it's safe to assume that places are open year-
round. And, by the way, smoking is prohibited in all Nantucket restaurants.

Reservations can be hard to come by in high season, as well
as popular weekends such as December's Christmas Stroll
and the Daffodil Festival in April, so plan and make dinner reservations well ahead. The better restaurants can get
booked up weeks in advance. (We mention only when reservations are absolutely essential.) Or consider alternative
time slots: the odds will be in your favor if you're willing
to eat unfashionably early or decadently late.

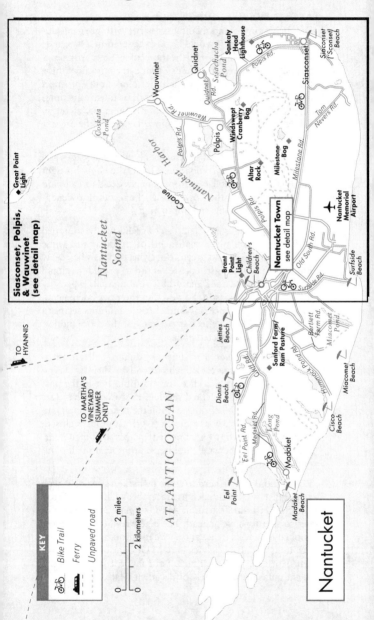

Siasconset, Polpis, & Wauwinet (see detail map)

Great Point Light

Coskata Pond

Nantucket Sound

Nantucket Harbor

Coatue

Wauwinet

Quidnet

Wauwinet Rd.

Quidnet Rd.

Sesachacha Pond

Polpis Rd.

Polpis

Windswept Cranberry Bog

Sankaty Head Lighthouse

Siasconset

Siasconset ('Sconset) Beach

Tom Nevers Rd.

Milestone Bog

Altar Rock

Milestone Rd.

Polpis Rd.

Brant Point Light

Children's Beach

Nantucket Town see detail map

Nantucket Memorial Airport

Old South Rd.

Surfside Rd.

Surfside Beach

TO HYANNIS

TO MARTHA'S VINEYARD (SUMMER ONLY)

ATLANTIC OCEAN

Eel Point

Dionis Beach

Jetties Beach

Eel Point Rd.

Madaket Rd.

Madaket

Madaket Beach

Long Pond

Cliff Rd.

Sanford Farm/ Ram Pasture

Hummock Pond Rd.

Bartlett Farm Rd.

Miacomet Pond

Cisco Beach

Miacomet Beach

KEY
Bike Trail
Ferry
Unpaved road

0   2 miles
0   2 kilometers

Nantucket

A Paradise in Crisis?

Whereas elsewhere along the New England coast private interests have carved prime beachfront into exclusive enclaves, Nantucketers are resolved that the beaches should remain accessible to the general public. A half dozen or so town-supervised beaches have amenities such as snack bars and lifeguard stations. The rest are the purview of solitary strollers—or, unfortunately, ever-growing convoys of dune-destroying SUVs. Nantucket's laissez-faire approach to beach management poses a delicate and perhaps ultimately untenable balancing act. So far islanders seem shockingly sanguine about the escalating presence of cars on their pristine beaches, even as they carp about congestion in town.

This is but one of the issues that percolate to the surface every April, during a weeklong town meeting that draws a good portion of the island's 12,000 year-round residents (the summer population expands to five times that figure). Far more immediate are concerns about overbuilding. The level of concern is such that, in 2000, Nantucket made the National Trust for Historic Preservation's list of Most Endangered Historic Places, a dubious honor at best. At present the island is too prosperous for its own good—a paradise in crisis. But residents are actively addressing these and other concerns and are building consensus for a Comprehensive Plan that will include affordable housing and sustainable businesses.

ABOUT THE HOTELS

From small bed-and-breakfasts to the island's few surviving grand hotels, Nantucket knows the value of hospitality. A unique "product" plus good service—as busy as this little island gets—are the deciding factors that keep visitors coming back year after year.

The majority of lodgings are in town, convenient to the shops and restaurants; the downside is that you may be subjected to street noise on summer evenings. Those seeking quiet might prefer the inns on the periphery of town, a 5- to 10-minute walk from Main Street. The most remote inns, in Sconset and Wauwinet, also tend to be among the most expensive. Families with children will probably want to consider the larger, less formal hotels, since many of the small, historic B&Bs are furnished with antiques—not an ideal match for rambunctious little ones. Or for smokers, for that matter: an ever-increasing number of inns are smoke-free.

Nantucket is notoriously expensive, so don't expect to find many bargains in terms of lodging, especially in summer. The best rates can be found in the off-season; however, the spring and fall shoulder seasons are also growing in popularity, and such special-event weekends as the Daffodil Festival in late April and Christmas Stroll in early December command peak-season rates. Most inns charge upward of $150 a night in summer, and many go higher—way higher in the case of the Wauwinet and White Elephant, whose cottages can fetch in a night what others charge per week.

Although many islanders remain nonplussed by such lofty prices, both venues tend to be booked solid and actually offer good value for the type of clientele they attract. The only truly "budget" facility you'll find is the youth hostel, which is also the only option for roughing it, since camping is prohibited anywhere on-island. In any case, this is not a place to pinch pennies: Nantucket is all about charm and comfort, at an admittedly steep price. If you plan to stay, come prepared to splurge.

If you're stranded for some reason or want to make your day trip a last-minute overnight, check with Nantucket Visitor Services at 25 Federal Street (☎508/228–0925, ⊕*www.nantucket.net/town/departments/visitor.html*): they track cancellations daily and might be able to refer you to an inn with newly available rooms.

For more lodging information on rental properties and B&Bs, see Accommodations in Essentials at the back of this book.

WHAT IT COSTS				
¢	$	$$	$$$	$$$$
RESTAURANTS				
under $10	$10–$16	$17–$22	$23–$30	over $30
HOTELS				
under $90	$90–$140	$140–$200	$200–$260	over $260

Restaurant prices are per person for a main course at dinner. Hotel prices are for a standard double room, excluding 6% sales tax (more in some counties) and 1%–4% tourist tax.

NAVIGATING

More than a few visitors debark from the ferries only to find themselves mildly disoriented. Although it's true that the journey from Hyannis to Nantucket is pretty much southward, by the time the boat rounds Brandt Point to enter the Nantucket Town harbor, it's facing due west. Nantucket Town's Main Street, at the core of the historic district, has an east–west orientation, stemming from Straight Wharf out to Madaket Road, which proceeds 6 mi west to Madaket Beach. Milestone Road, accessed from a rotary at the end of Orange Street off Main Street, is a straight, 8-mi shot to the easternmost town of Sconset (formally, Siasconset).

To find your way to the south-shore beaches or among the hillocks of Polpis—Altar Rock is the island's highest point, at a mere 100 feet—you'll want to use a map. The bike shops along the piers and the Nantucket Visitor Services and Information Bureau, at 25 Federal Street in the center of town, provide a useful assortment of maps for free.

NANTUCKET TOWN

30 mi southeast of Hyannis, 107 mi southeast of Boston.

At the height of its prosperity in the early 19th century, the little town of Nantucket was the foremost whaling port in the world. Shipowners and sea captains built elegant mansions, which today remain remarkably unchanged, thanks to a very strict building code initiated in the 1950s. The entire town of Nantucket is now an official National Historic District encompassing more than 800 pre-1840 structures within 1 square mi.

Given its compact nature, Nantucket definitely merits consideration as a day trip—a prospect made easier by the introduction of fast ferries (the crossing now takes an hour) from Hyannis. Day-trippers usually take in the architecture and historical sites and browse the pricey boutiques. After dining at one of the many delightful restaurants, you can hop a ferry back—or, if you're not in a hurry, stay the night at one of the town's luxurious historic inns.

Nantucket Town has one of the country's finest historical districts, with beautiful 18th- and 19th-century architecture and a museum of whaling history.

If You Like

ARCHITECTURE

In addition to Nantucket's cranberry bogs and roadside daffodils, there are dozens of lovely and interesting man-made sights to see, from a working windmill to a trio of lighthouses; from the Quaker Friends Meeting House to centuries-old Greek Revival town houses. In fact, in 1972, the entire island was declared a historic district—800 buildings predate the Civil War—and it's one of the country's finest. Look for the 2½-story typical Nantucket house, immediately identifiable by its gabled roof, roof walks, and wind-proofing white cedar shingles, which in no time weather to their familiar mottled lead gray.

CULTURAL ACTIVITIES & EVENTS

Intellectual curiosity is as alive today on Nantucket as it was in the mid-18th century, when citizens flocked to the Atheneum's Great Hall to hear such speakers as Melville, Emerson, and Thoreau. Today the roster runs to Paul Theroux, Anna Quindlen, and other nationally known names. Nantucket supports a semi-professional, homegrown theater company, which can be counted on for gripping performances. While plans percolate for a permanent performing arts center, plays often go up in a handful of church halls, which may also host concerts. On Friday evenings in summer, a scattering of art galleries hold their openings, and you can wander from one to the next, feasting on the art and complimentary canapés. As for cinema, Nantucket has two distinctive venues covering Hollywood's latest blockbusters as well as independents—and a popular, annual film festival in late June. Christmas Stroll, held the first weekend of December, is the centerpiece of the festive holiday season that is fast becoming as busy as summer. Many businesses and restaurants stay open right up until New Year's.

SHOPPING

Ever since sea captains initiated the China Trade in the early 1800s, Nantucket has enjoyed pride of place as a market for luxury goods from around the world. Today the town supports an active—one might even say hyperactive—retail scene. Chain stores have for the most part been kept at bay—in 2006, citizens voted to bar new franchises from the island. The 19th-century storefronts are packed with recherché boutiques proffering *très cher* goods, from fashion to furnishings and everything in between.

★ **Fodors**Choice The **Nantucket Historical Association (NHA)**
(☎*508/228–1894 NHA* ⊕*www.nha.org*) maintains an
assortment of venerable properties in town, many of them
described below, including the gloriously expanded Whaling Museum. An $18 pass gets you into all of the associ-
ation's site's.

*Numbers in the text correspond to numbers in the margin
and on the Nantucket Town map.*

WHAT TO SEE

❶ African Meeting House. Nantucket's only public building constructed and occupied by African-Americans in
the 19th century is one of nine sights associated with the
island's African-American heritage. (All are on the self-
guided Black Heritage Trail tour, a free pamphlet available
at Nantucket Visitor Services and NHA sites.) As far back
as the early 1700s, there was a small African-American
population on Nantucket; the earliest blacks were slaves
of the island's first settlers. When the island abolished
slavery in 1773, Nantucket became a destination for free
blacks and escaping slaves. The African Meeting House
was built in the 1820s as a schoolhouse, and it functioned
as such until 1846, when the island's schools were inte-
grated. The building was later used as a church and social
center. A complete restoration has returned the site to its
authentic 1880s appearance. Rooms for lectures, concerts,
and readings help to preserve the contributions and experiences of African-Americans on Nantucket. ⊠*29 York
St.* ☎*508/228–9833* ⊕*www.afroammuseum.org* ⊠*Free*
⊙*July and Aug., Tues.–Sat. 11–3, Sun. 1–3.*

㉜ Brant Point Light. The 26-foot-tall, white-painted beauty has
views of the harbor and town. The point was the site of
the second-oldest lighthouse in the country (1746), though
the present, much-photographed light was built in 1902.
In fact, the existing lighthouse is the 10th to occupy this
historic spot; its reassuring beacon is visible from 10 mi
offshore. ⊠*End of Easton St., across footbridge.*

㉑ Coffin houses. The two attractive brick homes, the Henry
Coffin House and the Charles G. Coffin House, face each
other and were built for brothers. The Coffins were wealthy
shipping agents and whale-oil merchants who used the same
mason for these 1830s houses and the later Three Bricks.

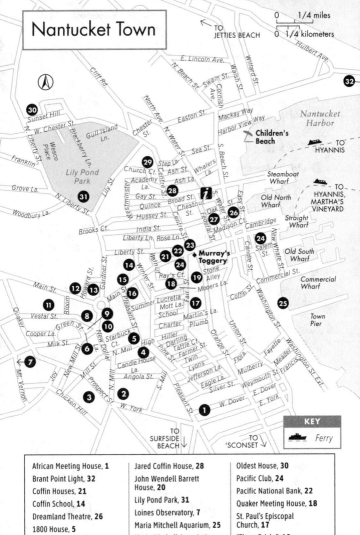

Nantucket Town

0   1/4 miles
0   1/4 kilometers

← TO JETTIES BEACH

Nantucket Harbor

E. Lincoln Ave.
N. Beach St.
Swain St.
Willard St.
Hulbert Ave.
Cliff Rd.
Cornish Ave.
Walsh St.
North Ave.
N. Water St.
Chester St.
Easton St.
Mackay Way
Harbor View Way
Children's Beach
Sea St.
S. Beach St.
Whalers La.
→ TO HYANNIS
Steamboat Wharf
Sunset Hill
W. Chester St.
Gull Island Ln.
Blackberry Ln.
Wesco Place
N. Liberty St.
Franklin
Lily Pond Park
Step La.
Ash St.
Ash La.
Old North Wharf
→ TO HYANNIS, MARTHA'S VINEYARD
Church Ct.
Centre St.
Grove La.
Academy La.
Gay St.
Quince
Broad St.
Chestnut St.
Easy St.
Straight Wharf
N. Liberty St.
Lily St.
Woodbury La.
Westminster
Hussey St.
India St.
Oak St.
S. Water St.
Madison Ct.
Cambridge
Brooks Ct.
Liberty Ln.
Rose Ln.
Centre St.
New White St.
Old South Wharf
Liberty St.
Salem St.
Murray's Toggery
Stone Alley
Candle St.
Main St.
Howard St.
Gardner St.
Walnut
Winter St.
Ray's Ct.
Moors La.
Washington St.
Commercial St.
Commercial Wharf
Bloom
Pleasant St.
Summer
Lucretia Mott La.
Fair St.
Martin's La.
Coffin St.
Vestal St.
Green St.
School
Charter
Plumb
Union St.
Town Pier
Quaker La.
Cooper La.
Milk St.
Starbuck Ct.
N. Mill
High
Hiller
Darling
Tattle Ct.
Farmer St.
Flora
Mulberry
Fayette
Meader St.
Washington St. Ext.
Mt. Vernon
New Mill St.
Candle House La.
Pine
Twin
Lyons
Orange St.
Weymouth La.
E. Dover
Joy
Chicken Hill
Mill St.
Prospect St.
N. Mill St.
Angola St.
Jefferson La.
Eagle La.
Silver St.
E. York
W. York
S. Mill
S. Pleasant St.
W. Dover
E. York
↓ TO SURFSIDE BEACH
↓ TO 'SCONSET
→ (32)

KEY
⛴ Ferry

The houses are privately owned and not open to the public. ⊠75 and 78 Main St.

⓮ Coffin School. The impressive Greek Revival building was built in 1854 to house a school founded three decades earlier by Admiral Sir Isaac Coffin to train the youth of Nantucket (at the time, half the inhabitants were Coffin descendants) in the ways of the sea. It's now home to the Egan Institute of Maritime Studies, whose mission is to "advance the study and appreciation of the history, literature, art, and maritime traditions of Nantucket" through changing art exhibits, publications, and nautical instruction. At the evening lecture series in summer, you can hear the fascinating tales of such ships as the *Essex*, which inspired Herman Melville's writing as well as founding director's Nathaniel Philbrick's 2000 best seller, *In the Heart of the Sea*. ⊠4 Winter St. ☎508/228–2505 ⊕www. eganinstitute.org ⊴Free ⊙Late May–mid-Oct., daily 1–5.

㉖ Dreamland Theatre. This handsome wooden theater, which was purchased in fall 2007 by a nonprofit preservation foundation after two years of disuse, was built as a Quaker meetinghouse in 1829 and then became a straw factory and, later, an entertainment hall. It was moved to Brant Point as part of the grand Nantucket Hotel in the late 19th century and was floated across the harbor by barge in about 1905 to its present location—a good illustration of early Nantucketers' penchant for the multiple uses of dwellings, as well as the relocation of houses. Trees (and therefore lumber) were so scarce that Herman Melville wrote in *Moby-Dick* that "pieces of wood in Nantucket are carried about like bits of the true cross in Rome." The current owners plan to keep it going as a summer cinema and also consider ways to use it as a performance space. ⊠17 S. Water St. ☎508/228–5356.

❺ 1800 House. Once the residence of the high sheriff, not a rich whaling family, the typical Nantucket home remains an example of how the other half lived at the time of its construction. The house has a six-flue chimney and is currently used by the NHA as a learning and education center—a variety of arts and crafts classes are offered. ⊠4 Mill St. ☎508/228–1894 ⊕www.nha.org/1800house.

⓭ Fire Hose Cart House. Built in 1886 as one of several neighborhood fire stations—Nantucketers had learned their lesson after the 1846 conflagration—the minimuseum displays a small collection of fire-fighting equipment used in the 18th century, including dousing buckets and a hand-pumped fire cart. ⊠8 Gardner St. ☎508/228–1894 ⊕www.nha.org ☜NHA History ticket only $6 ☉Late May–early Sept., daily 10–5.

㉙ First Congregational Church. Nantucket's largest and most
★ elegant church is also known as the Old North Church. Its tower—whose steeple is capped with a weather vane depicting a whale catch—rises 120 feet, providing the best island view. On a clear day the reward for climbing the 92 steps (with many landings as rest stops) is a panorama encompassing Great Point, Sankaty Head Lighthouse, Muskeget and Tuckernuck islands, moors, ponds, beaches, and the winding streets and rooftops of town. A peek at the church's interior reveals its old box pews, a turn-of-the-20th-century organ, and a trompe-l'oeil ceiling done by an unknown Italian painter in 1850 and since restored. The Old North Vestry in the rear, the oldest house of worship on the island, was built circa 1725 about a mile north of its present site. The main church was built in 1834. ⊠62 Centre St. ☎508/228–0950 ⊕www.nantucketfcc.org ☜Tower tour $2.50 ☉Mid-June–mid-Oct., Mon.–Sat. 10–4, and Fri. and Sat. Daffodil and Memorial weekends; services Sun. 10 AM.

⑫ Greater Light. With its whimsical blend of necessity and creativity, Greater Light is an example of the summer homes of the artists who flocked to Nantucket in its early resort days. In the 1930s two unusual Quaker sisters from Philadelphia—actress Hanna and artist Gertrude Monaghan—converted a barn into what now looks like the lavish set for an old movie. The exotic decor includes Italian furniture, Native American artifacts and textiles, a wrought-iron balcony, bas-reliefs, and a coat of arms. The sisters also remodeled the private house next door, called Lesser Light, for their parents. ⊠8 Howard St. ☎No phone.

⑯ Hadwen House. The pair of magnificent white porticoed Greek Revival mansions on upper Main Street—commonly referred to as the Two Greeks—were built in 1845 and 1846 by wealthy factory owner William Hadwen, a Newport native who made his money in whale oil and candles. No. 94, built as a wedding gift for his adopted niece, was modeled on the Athenian Tower of the Winds, with Corinthian capitals on the entry columns, a domed-stair hall with statuary niches, and an oculus. The Hadwens' own domicile, at No. 96, is now a museum, and its contents reflect how the wealthy of the period lived. The house has been restored to its mid-19th-century origins, with classic Victorian gas chandeliers and furnishings, as well as reproduction wallpapers and window treatments. Inside, on a guided tour, you can see such architectural details as the grand circular staircase, fine plasterwork, and carved Italian-marble mantels. A second-floor gallery hosts changing exhibits. ⊠*96 Main St.* ☎*508/228–1894* ⊕*www.nha. org* ⊠*NHA Combination Pass or Historic Sites Pass only* ⊙*Mid-May–mid-Oct., Mon.–Sat. 10–5, Sun. noon–5.*

㉘ Jared Coffin House. Operated as an inn since the mid-19th century, the handsome landmark also houses a restaurant and pub. Coffin, a wealthy merchant, built this brick house with Ionic portico, parapet, hip roof, and cupola—the only three-story structure on the island at the time—for his wife, who wanted to live closer to town. They moved here in 1845 from Moors End on Pleasant Street, but (so the story goes) nothing would please Mrs. Coffin, and within two years they left the island altogether for Boston. ⊠*29 Broad St.* ☎*508/228–2400 or 800/248–2405* ⊕*www.jaredcoffinhouse.com.*

㉙ John Wendell Barrett House. One of Nantucket's grand Main Street homes, the Barrett House was built in 1820 in early Greek Revival style. Legend has it that Lydia Mitchell Barrett stood on the steps and refused to budge when men tried to evacuate her so they could blow up the house to stop the spread of the Great Fire. Luckily, a shift in the wind settled the showdown. ⊠*72 Main St.*

㉛ Lily Pond Park. This 5-acre conservation area on the edge of town is a prime bird-watching spot. Its lawn and wetlands—there is a trail, but it can be muddy—foster abundant wildlife, including birds, ducks, and deer. You can pick blackberries, raspberries, and grapes in season wherever you find them. ⊠*N. Liberty St.*

Main Street. After the Great Fire of 1846 leveled all its wooden buildings, Main Street was widened to prevent future flames from hopping across the street. The cobblestone thoroughfare has a harmonious symmetry: the Pacific Club anchors its foot, and the Pacific National Bank, another redbrick building, squares off the head. The cobblestones were brought to the island as ballast in returning ships and laid to prevent the wheels of carts heavily laden with whale oil from sinking into the dirt. At the center of Lower Main is an old horse trough, today overflowing with flowers. From here the street gently rises; at the bank it narrows to its prefire width and leaves the commercial district for an area of mansions that escaped the blaze.

NEED A BREAK? You can breakfast or lunch inexpensively at several lunch counters, including **Congdon's Pharmacy** (⌧*47 Main St.* ☎*508/228–0020*) and the **Nantucket Pharmacy** (⌧*45 Main St.* ☎*508/228–0180*). **"The Strip,"** a hodgepodge of fun fast-food eateries on Broad Street near Steamboat Wharf, is another good option. Besides fresh-squeezed juices, the **Juice Bar** (⌧*12 Broad St.* ☎*508/228–5799*), open April–mid-October, serves homemade ice cream and frozen yogurt with waffle cones and toppings. Long lines signal that good things come to those who wait.

❼ The **Loines Observatory** (⌧*59 Milk St. Ext.* ☎*508/228–9273* ⊕*www.mmo.org* ⌦*$10*) is open for regular viewing sessions year-round. A new telescope was installed in April 2007 .

Maria Mitchell Association (MMA). Established in 1902 by Vassar students and astronomer Maria Mitchell's family, the association administers several historic properties in Nantucket Town.

㉕ The **Maria Mitchell Aquarium** (⌧*28 Washington St., near Commercial Wharf* ☎*508/228–5387* ⊕*www.mmo.org* ⌦*$4 or MMA pass*) is housed in the former Nantucket Railroad ticket office. It's a favorite stop for families with children, who like to touch the marine creatures on display in several touch tanks.

❾ The **Maria Mitchell Association Science Library** (⌧*2 Vestal St.* ☎*508/228–9219* ⊕*www.mmo.org*), which has more than 10,000 books, periodicals, and pamphlets on scientific topics and Nantucket history, can be used by scholars and visitors for research, by appointment only.

❽ The **Mitchell House** (⌧*1 Vestal St.* ☎*508/228–2896* ⊕*www. mmo.org* ⌦*$5 or MMA pass*) was Maria Mitchell's birthplace and is a typical Quaker house from the late 18th century. It became a historical museum in 1902.

❻ The **Natural Science Museum in Hinchman House** (⌧*7 Milk St.* ☎*508/228–0898* ⊕*www.mmo.org* ⌦*$5 or MMA pass*) is focused on local flora and fauna, including several live specimens.

❿ The **Vestal Street Observatory** (✉*3 Vestal St.* ☎*508/228–9273* ⊕*www.mmo.org* ⊿*$5 or MMA pass*)has a scale model of the solar system and a sundial outdoors, as well as an indoor astronomy exhibit. Public programs are held in the summer.

The MMA Museum Pass is a combination admission ticket to the Mitchell House, the Hinchman House, the Vestal Street Observatory, and the Maria Mitchell Aquarium. In summer the association conducts inexpensive classes for adults and children on astronomy, natural science, and Nantucket history. ✉*4 Vestal St.* ☎*508/228–9198* ⊕*www. mmo.org* ⊿ *$10 for MMA Pass.*

❹ Moors' End. Built between 1829 and 1834, this handsome Federal brick house is where merchant Jared Coffin lived before moving to what is now the Jared Coffin House—the proximity to the fumes from the Starbuck refinery was one of Mrs. Coffin's complaints. It's a private home, so you won't be able to see Stanley Rowland's vast murals of the whaling era on the walls or the scrawled notes about shipwreck sightings in the cupola, but keep an eye out for pictures in any number of coffee-table books about Nantucket. Beside the home is the largest walled garden on Nantucket; like the house, it's not open to the public. ✉*19 Pleasant St.*

㉗ Nantucket Atheneum. Nantucket's town library is a great
☺ white Greek Revival building, with a windowless facade
★ and fluted Ionic columns. Completed in 1847 to replace a structure lost to the 1846 fire, it's one of the oldest libraries in continuous service in the United States. Astronomer Maria Mitchell was its first librarian. Opening ceremonies included a dedication by Ralph Waldo Emerson, who—along with Daniel Webster, Henry David Thoreau, Frederick Douglass, Lucretia Mott, and John James Audubon—later delivered lectures in the library's second-floor Great Hall. During the 19th century the hall was the center of island culture—a role it fulfills to this day. The adjoining Atheneum Park is a great place to relax for a while, and the spacious Weezie Library for Children hosts readings and activities—a welcome respite for a rainy day. ✉*1 India St.* ☎*508/228–1110* ⊕*www.nantucketath-eneum.org* ☉*Late May–early Sept., Mon., Wed., Fri., and Sat. 9:30–5, Tues. and Thurs. 9:30–8; early Sept.–late May, Tues. and Thurs. 9:30–8, Wed., Fri., and Sat. 9:30–5.*

⓫ **Old Gaol.** It's tough to escape the law when you live on an island. Scofflaws ended up here, in an 1806 jailhouse in use until 1933. Shingles mask the building's construction of massive square timbers, plainly visible inside. Walls, ceilings, and floors are bolted with iron. The furnishings consist of rough plank bunks and open privies, but toward the end of the jail's useful existence things got a bit lax: prisoners were allowed out at night to sleep in their own beds. ✉ *15R Vestal St.* ☎ *508/228–1894* ⊕ *www.nha.org* 🎫 *NHA History Ticket only* ◷ *Late May–early Sept., daily 10–5.*

❷ **Old Mill.** Several windmills sat on Nantucket hills in the 1700s, but only this 1746 Dutch-style octagonal one, built with lumber from shipwrecks, remains. The Douglas fir pivot pole used to turn the cap and sails into the wind is a replacement of the original pole, a ship's foremast. The mill's wooden gears work on wind power, and when the wind is strong enough, corn is ground into meal that is sold here. An NHA interpreter is on hand to lead tours and answer questions. ✉ *50 Prospect St., at S. Mill St.* ☎ *508/228–1894* ⊕ *www.nha.org* 🎫 *NHA History Ticket only* ◷ *Late May–early Sept., daily 10–5.*

❸⓪ **Oldest House.** History and architecture buffs should be sure to get a look at this hilltop house, also called the Jethro Coffin House, built in 1686 as a wedding gift for Jethro and Mary Gardner Coffin. The most striking feature of the saltbox is the massive central brick chimney with a brick horseshoe adornment said to ward away witches. Other highlights are the enormous hearths and diamond-pane leaded-glass windows. Cutaway panels show 17th-century construction techniques. An NHA interpreter will tell you about the home's history and the interior's sparse furnishings, including an antique loom. ✉ *Sunset Hill, a 10- to 15-min walk along Centre St. from Main St.* ☎ *508/228–1894* ⊕ *www.nha.org* 🎫 *NHA Combination Pass or Historic Sites Pass* ◷ *Mid-May–mid-Oct., Mon.–Sat. 10–5, Sun. noon–5.*

❷④ **Pacific Club.** The building still houses the elite club of Pacific whaling masters for which it's named. However, since the last whaling ship was seen here in 1870, the club now admits whalers' descendants, who gather to enjoy the odd cribbage game or to swap tales. The building first served in 1772 as the counting house of William Rotch, owner of the *Dartmouth* and the *Beaver,* two of the three ships that hosted a famous tea party in Boston. The club is not open to the public, but a gallery occupies the main floor. ⊠*Main and S. Water Sts.*.

㉒ Pacific National Bank. Like the Pacific Club (a social club that counts whalers' descendants among its members) it faces, the bank, dating to 1818 and still in use today, is a monument to the far-flung voyages of the Nantucket whaling ships it financed. Inside, above old-style teller cages, are 1954 murals of scenes from the whaling days. Note the **Meridian Stone** on the south side of the building and to the left—it's about 3 feet high and pointed on top. Placed here in the 1830s by astronomers Maria Mitchell and her father, William, it marks the town's precise meridian—an important point to early navigators. ⊠*61 Main St.*

⑱ Quaker Meeting House. Built around 1838 as a Friends school, the Meeting House is now a year-round place of worship. A small room of quiet simplicity, with antique-glass 12-over-12 windows and unadorned wood benches, it's in keeping with the Quaker tenets that the divine spirit is within each person and that no one requires an intermediary (or elaborate church) to worship God. The adjoining **Fair Street Museum** was built in 1904 of poured concrete. Though it may seem a bit plain-Jane now, at the time its cost of $8,300 was high and its structure technically advanced. With the memory of Nantucket's Great Fire still fresh, planners wanted to safeguard their historical artifacts from that fate. Today the museum presents rotating NHA exhibits. ⊠*1 Fair St.* ☎*508/228–1655 or 508/228–1894* ⊕*www.nha.org* ☞*$6 or NHA History Ticket* ⊙*Services Sun. at 10 AM. Museum, late May–early Sept., daily 10–5; early Sept.–late May, Mon.–Sat. 10–5, Sun. noon–5.*

⑰ St. Paul's Episcopal Church. On a hot day, peek into the massive granite structure dating to 1901 and adorned at the front and back by beautiful Tiffany windows. The interior is cool and white, with dark exposed beams, and offers a quiet sanctuary from the summer crowds and the heat. ⊠*20 Fair St.* ☎*508/228–0916* ⊕*www.stpaulschurchnantucket. org* ⊙*Services Sun. at 8 AM and 10 AM.*

⑮ "Three Bricks." Many of the mansions of the golden age of
★ whaling were built on Upper Main Street. These well-known identical redbrick homes, with columned Greek Revival porches at their front entrances, were built between 1836 and 1838 by whaling merchant Joseph Starbuck for his three sons. They are not open to the public. ⊠*93–97 Main St.*

⑲ Unitarian Universalist Church. The 1809 church, also known as South Church, has a gold-dome spire that soars above town, just as the First Congregational Church's slender white steeple does. Also like First Congregational, South Church has a trompe-l'oeil ceiling painting, this one simulating an intricately detailed dome and painted by Swiss artist Carl Wendte in 1844. Here, however, illusion is taken to greater lengths: the curved chancel and paneled walls you see are also creations in paint. The 1831 mahogany-cased Goodrich organ in the loft is played at services and concerts. In the octagonal belfry of the tower, which houses the town clock, is a bell cast in Portugal that has been ringing out the noon hour ever since it was hung in 1830. ✉ *11 Orange St.* ☎ *508/228–5466* ⊕ *www.unitarianchurch nantucket.org* ⊙ *Services Sun. at 10:45* AM.

㉓ United Methodist Church. Another miraculous survivor of the Great Fire of 1846, this 1823 building was treated to a grand Doric-columned facade in 1840. Badly deteriorating by 1999, it was declared an endangered historic treasure and paid a visit by then–First Lady Hillary Clinton. Now undergoing a major restoration effort, it houses a small congregation, as well as two small theater spaces. Organ aficionados may want to have a look at the 1831 Appleton—one of only four extant. ✉ *2 Centre St.* ☎ *508/228–1882* ⊙ *Services Sun. at 10* AM.

③ ★ Fodor'sChoice Whaling Museum. Immersing you in Nantucket's whaling past with exhibits that include a fully rigged whaleboat and a skeleton of a 46-foot sperm whale, the museum—a complex that includes a restored 1846 spermaceti candle factory—is a must-see. The museum received a $14 million expansion and refurbishment in 2005. Items on view in the handsome galleries include harpoons and other whale-hunting implements; portraits of whaling captains and their wives (a few of whom went whaling as well); the South Seas curiosities they brought home; a large collection of sailors' crafts, a full-size tryworks once used to process whale oil aboard ship; and the original 16-foot-high 1850 lens from Sankaty Head Lighthouse. The Children's Discovery Room provides interactive learning opportunities. Be sure to climb—or take the elevator—up to the observation deck for a view of the harbor. ✉ *13–15 Broad St.* ☎ *508/228–1894* 🎫 *$15 or NHA Combination Pass* ⊙ *Jan.–mid-Apr., Fri.–Sun. 11–4; mid-Apr.–mid-May and mid-Oct.–mid-Dec., Thurs.–Mon. 11–4; mid-May–mid-Oct., Mon.–Wed., Fri.–Sun. 10–5, Thurs. 10–8.*

WHERE TO EAT

$$$$ ✕Òran Mór. In 2004 chef-owner Christopher Freeman
★ abandoned the cushy confines of Topper's at the Wauwinet
to strike out on his own at this tasteful little restaurant—a
trio of butter-yellow rooms accessed via a copper-encased
stairway. Initially, Freeman may have erred on the side of
nouvelle-cuisine minginess (a Topper's carryover, perhaps),
but now that he's firmly ensconced, the innate generosity of
a born chef is beginning to emerge. The artistry was there
all along and now shines in exuberant dishes such as cloud-
light lemon-garlic gnocchi, Peking duck breast with baby
bok choy and roast-plum chutney, and mascarpone cheesecake brûlée. Decades ago, this space was a New American
trendsetter known as the Second Story: Freeman does its
legacy proud. ✉*2 S. Beach St.* ☎*508/228–8655* ⊕*www.
oranmorbistro.com* ⊟*AE, MC, V* ⊘*No lunch.*

$$$$ ✕the pearl. This ultracool space—a sophisticated upstairs
★ cousin to the Boarding House—is seriously chic, with a
white onyx bar lighted in a Curaçao blue and, behind an
aquarium divider, cushy white-leather banquettes. These—
plus the garden porch, where tasting dinners can be prear-
ranged—are the power seats. However, everyone is well
served by Seth Raynor's enthusiasm for the bold flavors of
Asian cuisine, especially in its street-wise guise. You may
have a tough time choosing between the lobster salad with
fresh-shaved hearts of palm and the signature wok-fried
lobster with lo mein and grilled lime—so do yourself a
favor and order both. Raynor also pulls off a stellar Japanese variation on steak fries (the latter come dusted with
tasty choy shichimi). ✉*12 Federal St.* ☎*508/228–9701*
⊕*www.boardinghouse-pearl.com* ⊟*AE, MC, V* ⊘*Closed
Jan.–Apr. No lunch.*

$$$$ ✕21 Federal. An avatar of the New American culinary
★ revolution since 1985, 21 Federal retains its creative edge,
thanks to the ever-avant menus of chef Russell Jaehnig.
Nothing is too outré, mind you, in this handsome 1847
Greek Revival house with sconce-lighted, dove-gray interiors—except perhaps the boisterous young crowd (the bar
scene is quite popular). The cuisine, however, has a spark
to match the spirited clientele: try the seared sea scallops
matched with mango, avocado puree, and ancho chilies, or
tender Kobe beef cheek atop white truffle polenta with caramelized fennel. Pastry chef Benjamin Woodbury has come
up with the showiest—and tastiest—dessert on-island:

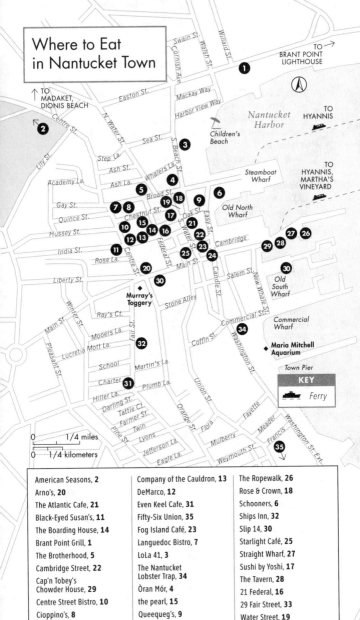

Where to Eat in Nantucket Town

TO BRANT POINT LIGHTHOUSE

↑ TO MADAKET, DIONIS BEACH

TO HYANNIS

TO HYANNIS, MARTHA'S VINEYARD

Nantucket Harbor

Children's Beach

Steamboat Wharf

Old North Wharf

Old South Wharf

Commercial Wharf

Murray's Toggery

Maria Mitchell Aquarium

Town Pier

KEY
🛳 Ferry

0 — 1/4 miles
0 — 1/4 kilometers

Street names: Swain St., Willard St., Cornish Ave., Walsh St., Easton St., Mackay Way, Harbor View Way, Centre St., N. Water St., Lily St., Sea St., S. Beach St., Step La., Ash St., Whalers La., Ash La., Academy La., Broad St., Gay St., Chestnut St., Oak St., Quince St., Easy St., Hussey St., Water St., Cambridge, India St., Federal St., Rose La., Salem St., New Whale St., Liberty St., Centre St., Main St., Caddie St., Stone Alley, Commercial St., Ray's Ct., Mooers La., Coffin St., Washington St., Lucretia Mott La., Martin's La., Winter St., School, Charter, Plumb La., Main St., Pleasant St., Hiller La., Darling St., Tattle Ct., Farmer St., Orange St., Union St., Pine St., Twin, Lyons, Jefferson La., Flora, Mulberry, Fayette, Meader, Weymouth St., Eagle La., Francis, Washington St. Ext.

coconut blancmange "oysters" nestled in white choco-
late shells, with dollops of passionfruit mignonette. ⊠*21
Federal St.* ☎*508/228–2121* ⊕*www.21federal.com* ⊟*AE,
MC, V* ⊗*Closed mid-Oct.–late Nov. and mid-Dec.–mid-
May. No lunch.*

$$$$ ╳**Water Street.** Two stylish young couples initiated this
chic eatery with cinnamon walls and handsome leather
high-back chairs. The locally provisioned, all-organic cuisine calls on micro-diced taste explosions—wild blueberry
preserves and sherry gastric spark the seared foie gras, and
charred-tomato gazpacho underlies the fresh-caught local-
striped bass. The vanilla-laced Bartlett Farm corn soup,
which packs a bonus chunk of crab tempura, is nonpareil,
and the closing "Study in Chocolate" is deeply satisfying.
⊠*21 S. Water St.* ☎*508/228–0189* ⊕*www.waterstreet
nantucket.com* ⊟*D, MC, V* ⊗*Closed Jan.–Mar.*

★ **Fodor'sChoice** ╳**American Seasons.** Picture a farmhouse gone
$$$–$$$$ sexy: that's the mood—wholesome yet seductive—at
this candlelighted hideaway, where inspired young chef
Michael LaScola marshals local bounty to concoct a culi-
nary Trip-Tik that ranges across the countryside, from the
Pacific Coast to New England, by way of the Wild West
and Down South. From his signature foie gras crème brûlée
(served with a plum-ginger compote and parsnip fries) to
roast duck breast with corn-bread pudding, and onward
to blood-orange creme brûlée, expect spectacular pan-
regional pyrotechnics. ⊠*80 Centre St.* ☎*508/228–7111*
⊟*AE, MC, V* ⊗*Closed Jan.–mid-Apr. No lunch.*

$$$–$$$$ ╳**Black-Eyed Susan's.** From a passing glance, you'd never
★ peg this seemingly humble storefront as one of Nantuck-
et's chic eateries—but as the invariable lines attest, it is.
The luncheonette setup is offset by improbably fancy glass
chandeliers, and foodies lay claim to the stools to observe
chef Jeff Worster's often pyromaniacal "open kitchen."
The dinner menu, which changes every few weeks, ven-
tures boldly around the world. The breakfasts (served until
1 PM) include such eye-openers as hearty Pennsylvania
Dutch pancakes fortified with Jarlsberg cheese. ⊠*10 India
St.* ☎*508/325–0308* ⊟*No credit cards* ⌸*BYOB* ⊗*Closed
Nov.–Mar. No dinner Sun. No lunch.*

$$$–$$$$ ╳**The Boarding House.** Beyond the throngs of twentysome-
things noisily mingling at the bar, you'll encounter a culi-
nary oasis, a vaulted semisubterranean space reminiscent
of a private wine cellar, with leather banquettes circling

antique-gold walls. Here, under the watchful eye of star chef-owner Seth Raynor, chef de cuisine Erin Zircher showcases her skill with Mediterranean market cuisine. Comfort is the universal watchword: it's implicit in the creamy Spanish-style almond soup bejeweled with roasted grapes and seared bay scallops, and in the signature dessert, warm dark-chocolate chocolate-chip cookies (like minimolten cakes) served with a pair of "mini malted-milk shakes." Come summer, you can sample from the menu at the sidewalk café—provided you succeed in snagging a table. ☒*12 Federal St.* ☎*508/228-9622* ⊕*www.boardinghouse-pearl. com* ⊟*AE, MC, V* ☉*Closed Jan.–Mar.*

$$$–$$$$ ✕**Brant Point Grill.** With its beautiful broad lawn set harborside, the Brant Point Grill—in-house restaurant for the elegant White Elephant hotel—has ventured beyond its à la carte haute steak-house menu with some protein-heavy variations—such as Kobe-beef meatballs, and slow-cooked pork shank with lemon spaetzle—that can weigh in on the heavy side as summer fare. Always appealing, though, is the straightforward salmon grilled on a firecone set up right outside, and the spritely salads, such as mesclun with a grilled orange-cranberry vinaigrette, are reliably refreshing. Desserts like the Guinness ice-cream mud pie are sure-fire resolution-destroyers, as is the Sunday brunch, featuring a make-your-own Bloody Mary station. ☒*50 Easton St.* ☎*508/325-1320 or 800/445-6574* ⊕*www.whiteelephanthotel.com* ⊟*AE, D, DC, MC, V* ☉*Closed Jan.–Mar.*

$$$–$$$$ ✕**The Club Car.** A longtime favorite among the moneyed set, this boxy dining room—its adjoining piano bar is an actual railroad car from the dismantled Sconset narrow-gauge—has never quite shaken its Continental origins (read occasionally salty and heavy sauces). Richness, however, has its own rewards, as in a plump double-cut slab of swordfish rolled in moisture-retaining crushed almonds and walnuts, topped with pecan butter. As for the Opera Cake—a kind of stand-up tiramisu—tradition never tasted so good. ☒*1 Main St.* ☎*508/228-1101* ⊕*www.theclubcar.com* ⊟*AE, MC, V* ☉*Closed mid-Dec.–mid-May. No lunch.*

$$$–$$$$ ✕**Company of the Cauldron.** This tiny dining room, a sconce-
★ lighted haven of architectural salvage, is served by an even smaller kitchen, from which chef-owner All Kovalencik issues only one menu per evening. Fans gladly forgo multiple choice when the chef's choice is invariably so dead-on. Rundowns of the weekly roster are available over the

2

phone or online, and a typically tantalizing lineup might start with seared scallops with a grilled fennel bulb and citrus coulis, Cisco Stout–marinated beef fillet with potato mille-feuille, and peanut butter pain perdu with Concord grape sherbet (a playful nod to PB&J). Given the close quarters, expect to come away not only sated but better acquainted with your near neighbors—and in love with Mary Keller's celestial harp. ⊠ *7 India St.* ☎*508/228–4016* ⊕*www.companyofthecauldron.com* ⌂*Reservations essential* ═*MC, V* ⊙*Closed Jan.–Mar. No lunch.*

$$$–$$$$ ✕**DeMarco.** Northern Italian cuisine debuted on-island at this cored-out clapboard house in 1980, slightly ahead of the wave. The delights endure: "badly cut" home-made pasta, for instance, in a sauce of wild mushrooms, prosciutto, and fresh sage, or luscious lobster cannelloni enrobed in a corn zabaglione. Braised lamb shank comes nestled in Parmesan polenta custard, and the panna cotta gets a bit of added zip from a rhubarb compote. The prevailing aesthetic may be rustic, but the results read as rare delicacies in these parts. ⊠ *9 India St.* ☎*508/228–1836* ⊕*www.demarcorestaurant.com* ═*AE, D, MC, V* ⊙*Closed Mid-Oct.–Apr. No lunch.*

$$$–$$$$ ✕**Fifty-Six Union.** You can tell there's a playful spirit at work here, just from the overdressed mannequin usually propped up at a hefty granite café table out front. Venture inside, though, and you can find a city-sophisticated space, with a civilized grown-up bar. Inside or out (the lovely garden out back harbors a chef's table), Peter Jannelle's cuisine delivers global pizzazz. You'll want to make a habit of the truffle-asiago frites, not to mention the mussels in mild Thai curry broth, and the Javanese spicy fried rice. ⊠ *56 Union St.* ☎*508/228–6135* ═*AE, MC, V* ⊙*No lunch.*

$$$–$$$$ ✕**Languedoc Bistro.** The only thing not exquisitely Gallic about this auberge-style restaurant, founded in 1975, is the portioning: American appetites will be satisfied—and then some—by the roasted rare Kobe rib eye, not to mention the oven-roasted lobster swimming in creamy polenta and festooned with parsnip "ribbons." Dining moods are divided into two modes: you can opt for the fairly formal upstairs rooms or the bistro-style conviviality of the cellar. In season the patio is a lovely place to toy with a salad—or to tackle a decadent, over-generous dessert. ⊠ *24 Broad St.* ☎*508/228–2552* ⊕*www.lelanguedoc.com* ═*AE, MC, V* ⊙*Closed Jan.–mid-Apr.*

$$$–$$$$ ✕ **The Ropewalk.** It's time to revise that tired old axiom of coastal living, that you can never find good food right on the water. Here at the very end of Straight Wharf (go any farther and you'll be boarding someone's yacht), the setting and cooking keep pace. Preparations are fairly straightforward but with some inventive—often Asian-inspired—spins, such as tempura cod with toasted coconut-ginger rice, and braised North Atlantic halibut with Japanese wild mushrooms and somen noodles steeped in mushroom tea. ⊠ *1 Straight Wharf* 🕾 *508/228–8886* ⊕ *www.theropewalk. com* ⊟ *AE, MC, V* ⊘ *Closed Nov.–Apr.*

★ **Fodor's**Choice ✕ **Straight Wharf.** This loftlike restaurant with
$$$–$$$$ harborside deck has enjoyed legendary status since the mid-1970s, when chef Marion Morash used to get a helping hand from culinary buddy Julia Child. The young couple who took over in 2006—Gabriel Frasca and Amanda Lydon—were fast-rising stars on the Boston restaurant scene, but their approach here is the antithesis of flashy. If anything, they have lent this venerable institution a more barefoot air, appropriate to the place and season. Hurricane lamps lend a soft glow to well-spaced tables lined with butcher paper; dish towels serve as napkins. Intense champions of local produce and catches, Frasca and Lydon concoct stellar dishes like lobster-stuffed zucchini flowers with saffron tomato vinaigrette, and line-caught swordfish in a vaguely Morroccan melange of golden raisins, pine nuts, and mint. Everything from cuisine to service entrances, and the price—for here—is right. If you'd like a preview, try the less costly café menu at the adjoining bar—provided you can get in. ⊠ *6 Harbor Sq., Straight Wharf* 🕾 *508/228–4499* ⊕ *www.straighwharfrestaurant.com* ⊟ *AE, MC, V* ⊘ *Closed mid-Oct.–mid-May.*

$$$–$$$$ ✕ **29 Fair Street.** This 1709 abode spent the past half century as a restaurant–rooming house, and now that the owners of 'Sconset's Summer House are running the show, it's a lot cheerier: the wood-panel interior has been spiffed with colorful silk pillows, and the menu has morphed into sunny Mediterranean staples. Fear not, fans of the beef Wellington and breakfast popovers for which the former Woodbox was long famed: they remain on the menu—alongside such welcome innovations such as lobster wrapped in kataif (angel-hair filo). The desserts are a Francophile's dream come true. ⊠ *29 Fair St.* 🕾 *508/228–7800* ⊟ *AE, MC, V* ⊘ *Closed Mon. and Jan.–Apr. No lunch.*

$$–$$$$ ✕**LoLa 41.** A hopping bar scene—LoLa 41 became *the* place to hang the minute it opened in '06—somewhat impedes the culinary experience here, but an evolving menu means that chefs at this trendy Galley Beach offshoot come up with compelling new dishes every few weeks. Just one bite, and you'll be hooked on the calamari doused with ultra-spicy Korean clay-pot-aged *kochujang* (a chili bean paste), not to mention the "indulgent mac & cheese" made with four artisanal Northern California varieties. ⊠*15 S. Beach St.* ☎*508/325–4001* ═*MC, V.*

$$–$$$$ ✕**Ships Inn.** Tucked beneath Captain Obed Starbuck's handsome 1831 mansion, this peach-tinted, candlelighted restaurant is a light and lovely haven wherein French cuisine meets a California sensibility and both cultures are the richer for it. If you want to eat healthy, you can—but why not sin a little and sup on warm cauliflower soup with Vermont cheddar, or grilled Chatham sea scallops served with black truffle hollandaise? The grilled shrimp with Belgian endive (braised into sweet submission) is a guilt-free option—easily undone if you preorder the soufflé du jour. ⊠*13 Fair St.* ☎*508/228–0040* ⊕*www.shipsinnnantucket.com* ═*AE, D, MC, V* ⊘*Closed late Oct.–mid-Apr. No lunch.*

¢–$$$$ ✕**Sushi by Yoshi.** This little jewel box of a restaurant purveys the output of Yoshihisa Mabuchi, a welcome "washashore" originally from Japan. The sushi and sashimi, available in dozens of guises, are nonpareil: try a special concoction such as the Caterpillar, a veggie roll wrapped in avocado. Also available are classic dishes ranging from gyoza to udon, soba, and teriyaki and, for dessert, green-tea ice cream and banana tempura. ⊠*2 E. Chestnut St.* ☎*508/228–1801* ☎*508/228–5827* ═*No credit cards* ⑭*BYOB* ⊘*Closed Nov.–May.*

$$$ ✕**Slip 14.** With its picturesque setting at the end of a shell-lined lane flanked by galleries, Slip 14 is an ideal spot to while away a summer night: portions are large, prices are fair—and all is well with the world. Skip the dull lobster cake, but feast on the refreshing likes of yellowfin tuna ceviche with red grapes and jicama, and definitely succumb to any cobbler you encounter on the dessert list. ⊠*14 Old South Wharf* ☎*508/228–2033* ⊕*www.slip14.com* ═*AE, MC, V* ⊘*Closed Oct.–Apr.*

$$–$$$ ✕**Arno's.** Arno's, which has a prime location right on Main Street, presents lush breakfasts (some featuring lobster), hearty lunches, and fairly ambitious dinners, all with generous portions. (Warning: the salads could constitute meals in themselves.) Molly Dee's nostalgic canvases adorn the brick walls, and a wine bar—offering 41 options by the glass or flight—invites adult schmoozing. Expect some envious looks—from inside and outside—if you get the prime spot in the storefront window. ⊠*41 Main St.* ☎*508/228–7001* ⊕*www.arnos.net* ▤*AE, MC, V* ⊘*Closed mid-Jan.–Mar.*

$$–$$$ ✕**Centre Street Bistro.** Tiny—there are 20 seats indoors, and
★ as many out—and perfect, this gem of a bistro is a find that devoted locals almost wish they could keep to themselves. Chef-owners Tim and Ruth Pitts's sizzling cuisine is a match for the persimmon-orange color scheme of this cozy hideaway lined with cushioned banquettes and splashed with exuberant flower paintings. Portions—whether of the sesame-crusted shrimp atop red curry rice noodles, or the Angus beef tenderloin with goat cheese and white truffle oil—are so ample as to quell the heartiest of appetites. Desserts are as lavish (try the warm flourless chocolate cake wrapped in filo) as the prices are modest. ⊠*29 Centre St.* ☎*508/228–8470* ⊕*www.nantucketbistro.com* ▤*MC, V.*

$$–$$$ ✕**Cioppino's.** Tracy Root's elegant house-restaurant has been popular since day one (in 1990). An appetizer of cool, deconstructed lobster with lemony hollandaise is the perfect answer to an overwarm evening, and awfully well priced. Beyond the signature dish—a San Franciscan seafood stew—the menu is ambitious, marrying classic technique and contemporary taste. Desserts—especially the tangy house-made key lime pie—have their own following. ⊠*20 Broad St.* ☎*508/228–4622* ⊕*www.cioppinos. com* ▤*AE, D, DC, MC, V* ⊘*Closed Nov.–Apr. No lunch.*

$$–$$$ ✕**Even Keel Cafe.** This former ice-cream parlor, with its tin
☾ ceilings and pretty backyard patio, is no mere restaurant— it's the very heart of town, especially off-season, when, as a public service, patrons are treated to two-for-one entrées (price-gouging is not in owner Marshall Thompson's vocabulary). It's the first place to head for a fancy coffee or a creative meal. The lobster risotto, studded with Bartlett Farm corn, holds its own against contenders at the fanciest restaurants in town, and the grilled salmon salad with pomegranate ginger vinaigrette makes for an ideal midday meal. ⊠*40 Main St.* ☎*508/228–1979* ⊕*www.evenkeel cafe.com* ▤*AE, MC, V.*

2

$$-$$$ ✕**Queequeg's.** More casual in mood than some of its neighbors but nonetheless dedicated to quality and creativity, this indoor-outdoor bistro straddles classical cuisine (pan-seared halibut with a mushroom beurre blanc) and fusiony experimentation (crispy quail with house-made pepper sauce and blue cheese–pecan slaw)—a good bet when you're part of a disparate party. ✉6 Oak St. ☎508/325–0992 ⊨MC, V.

$$-$$$ ✕**Starlight Café.** This tiny movie-theater anteroom and enclosed patio, spiffed up with cinematic artifacts, offers a casual menu—think mac 'n' cheese with lobster. It's ideal for a pre- or post-flick feed, and yes, you're allowed to take your drinks into the theater. Also, with a dinner reservation you can get a movie reservation—a great way to leapfrog the line. ✉1 N. Union St. ☎508/228–4479 ⊕www.starlight nantucket.com ⊨AE, D, MC, V.

$-$$$ ✕**The Brotherhood.** No, it's not really an 1840s whaling ☺ bar—though the atmospheric basement, which dates all the way back to 1972, presents a more convincing front than the open, family-friendly upper floors added in 2005. Upstairs or down, inside or out, you can dive into the same juicy burgers—incontrovertibly the best on-island—and signature curly fries. As a boon for late-night celebrants, the kitchen stays open until midnight in season. ✉23 Broad St. ☎508/228–2551 ⊕www.brother-hoodofthieves.com ⊨MC, V.

$-$$$ ✕**Cambridge Street.** This in-town storefront started out primarily as a bar—and the original room, painted midnight-blue and decorated with bizarre artifacts (such as a Medusa chandelier), is still a primo spot for spirited mixing. The open-grill international fusion cuisine proved so popular, though, that a quieter nook had to be added on. Even the most jaded of palates will thrill to this pan-Asian–barbecue–Middle Eastern mélange, where you might try shrimp pad thai one evening, and smoky beef brisket another. All ages and strata come here to be shaken *and* stirred and never, ever gouged. ✉12 Cambridge St. ☎508/228–7109 ⊨AE, D, DC, MC, V ⊙Closed mid-Jan.–Mar. No lunch.

$-$$$ ✕**Cap'n Tobey's Chowder House.** Kate and John O'Connor (who also own the Atlantic Cafe) operate what had been a retro-1950s dive for many years—it's seaside-moderne now, awash in halogen-light aqua tones. Late at night, it morphs into the closest thing on-island to a disco. Before the dancers get going, you can dine on such well-priced preparations as pistachio-crusted pan-seared tuna with caramelized shallots or more typical fried seafood and barbecue ribs. There's a late-night "munchie menu" available until 12:30 AM, in case all that dancing does make you hungry. ⊠*20 Straight Wharf* ☎*508/228–0836* ⊟*AE, D, DC, MC, V* ⊘*Closed Nov.–Apr.*

$-$$$ ✕**The Nantucket Lobster Trap.** You might not care much for the atmosphere at this fairly standard fish house with conventional offerings (bacon-wrapped scallops, stuffed quahogs, hefty lobsters, etc.). The ubiquity of TV screens gives it a sports-bar ambience—although no one seems to mind. Fussy types can always cart their feast to the beach: inquire about "Meals on Keels." ⊠*25 Washington St.* ☎*508/228–4200* ⊕*www.nantucketlobstertrap.com* ⊟*AE, MC, V* ⊘*Closed mid-Oct.–early May. No lunch.*

$-$$$ ✕**Schooners.** The theme is definitely nautical, but smartly so: flags strung from the rafters and navy awnings over the sidewalk café seem right at home on Steamboat Wharf. The menu is fairly pro forma (rings, wings, steamers, fajitas, shore dinners), but the pricing is nice, considering what they could get away with. ⊠*31 Easy St.* ☎*508/228–5824* ⊕*www.schoonersnantucket.com* ⊟*AE, MC, V* ⊘*Closed mid-Oct.–Mar.*

$-$$ ✕**The Atlantic Cafe.** Long popular with visitors and locals alike, the "AC" has a gifted kitchen staff, who grace the rather predictable crowd-pleasers (barbecue pork ribs, London broil, baked scrod) with a bit of culinary finesse. The nautical flotsam that represents the bulk of the decor is not some decorator's scheme but vestiges of the real thing. ⊠*15 S. Water St.* ☎*508/228–0570* ⊕*www.atlanticcafe. com* ⊟*AE, D, DC, MC, V.*

$-$$ ✕**Fog Island Café.** Cherished year-round for its exceptional breakfasts, Fog Island is just as fine a spot for lunch—or, in season, a charitably priced dinner. The storefront space is cheerily decked out in a fresh country style (echoed in the friendly service), and chef-owners Mark and Anne Dawson—both Culinary Institute of America grads—seem determined to provide the best possible value to transients and natives alike. Consider starting the day with pesto scrambled eggs and ending it with sesame-crusted tuna with Thai noodles. ⊠*7 S. Water St.* ☎*508/228–1818* ⊕*www.fogisland.com* ⊟*MC, V.*

$–$$ ✕**Rose & Crown.** Crayon-friendly paper tablecloths and
🕐 a children's menu cater to a family audience early in the
evening; later, DJs and live bands along with signature
cocktails stoke the post-collegiate crowd. There's nothing
special about the menu (who could foresee the day when
ahi tuna atop Szechuan noodles would seem ordinary?),
but you can amuse yourself, while waiting, by studying the
old signs hung about this former carriage livery. ✉*23 S.
Water St.* ☎*508/228–2595* ⊕*www.theroseandcrown.com*
🍴*AE, MC, V* ⊗*Closed Jan.–Mar.*

$–$$ ✕**The Tavern.** This is the two-tiered restaurant with deck you
can't help noticing just off Straight Wharf. Its bar has colo-
nized the bandstand in the middle of the cobblestone square,
and the whole place is almost always mobbed—partly thanks
to a middle-of-the-road menu that stresses seafood (mostly
fried or broiled), such as sea scallops Provençal and herb-
garlic shrimp. ✉*1 Harbor Sq., Straight Wharf* ☎*508/228–
1266* ⊕*www.nantuckettavern.com* 🍴*AE, MC, V* ⊗*Closed
mid-Oct.–mid-May.*

WHERE TO EAT ON THE NANTUCKET TOWN OUTSKIRTS

See ⇨*Where to Eat Outside Nantucket Town* map for these
properties.

$$$$ ✕**Galley Beach.** A beloved institution since 1958, this modest cottage plunked right on the Cliffside Beach Club's
swath of sand has managed to stay fresh and luxe thanks
to three generations of restaurateurs who know how to
spot and foster talent in the kitchen. These days, that's W.
Scott Osif, whose resume spans Philadelphia's Le Bec Fin
and New York's City Hall. The menu mostly sticks to the
safe side (a peril of catering to the moneyed crowd), but
Osif occasionally kicks loose with dishes like caramelized
sea scallops with uni-muscat sauce. Everything—even the
staid options—is very, very good. The deck, with its gay
blue-and-white awning ringed with red geraniums, takes
in a 180-degree beach view; it's perfectly oriented to capture what photographers call "the golden moment." ✉*54
Jefferson Ave.* ☎*508/228–9641* 🍴*AE, MC, V* ⊗*Closed
mid-Oct.–mid-May.*

★ Fodor'sChoice ✕**Cinco.** With this eclectic tapas oasis, affable
$$$–$$$$ owner Michael Sturgis has made mid-island a true din-
ing destination. The festive mood is irresistible: it starts
with the setting (a candlelighted patio leading to intimate
rooms painted in dark, sexy colors) and culminates in a

parade of thrilling small plates meant for sharing. Don't be surprised if you find yourself getting possessive over the grilled lamb chops sauced with lime "mojo," say, or the bay scallops tossed with pear brown butter—just order more for the table. Chef Jean-Luc Matecat tinkers with the menu daily, and keeps a bar menu going to 1 AM—ideal for those who like to observe a Spanish dinner hour. ⊠5 Amelia Dr. ☎508/325–5151 ⊕www.cinco5.com ⊟AE, MC, V ⊙Closed Jan.–Mar. No lunch.

$$–$$$$ ✕**The SeaGrille.** Though it may lack the flashy profile of other top island restaurants, this mid-island eatery deserves its popularity. The lobster bisque alone, even without the bonus of a dill-flecked pastry bonnet, warrants a following, as does the free-form seafood ravioli. Off-season, the dining room, with its murals of wharf and street scenes, is a peaceful haven. When summer arrives, so do the faithful crowds. ⊠45 Sparks Ave. ☎508/325–5700 ⊕www.theseagrille.com ⊟AE, MC, V.

$$–$$$$ ✕**Sfoglia.** Culinary Institute of America grads Ron and Colleen Suhanosky appointed their celery-tinted trattoria with mismatched tables (including some enamel-top honeys from the '40s), chairs, crockery—even silverware. You can feast on home-style Italian dishes such as gnocchi with pecorini romano, or chicken al mattone (cooked under a brick). Desserts—Colleen's province—include rustic seasonal tarts and seductive semifreddos. Sfoglia's New York branch on the Upper East Side has earned solid foodie kudos. ⊠130 Pleasant St. ☎508/325–4500 ⊕www.sfogliarestaurant.com ⊟No credit cards ⊙Closed Sun.

$–$$$ ✕**The Hen House.** Another mid-island destination for the non-trust-funded, this unassuming restaurant started out as a breakfast joint catering to the island's large Irish summer workforce—you can still get rashers with your eggs or buttermilk pancakes—and soon turned into a source of three square meals, mostly of the stick-to-your-ribs school (baby back ribs, grilled sirloin, etc.). In season, you can get takeout 'til all hours—well, until 2 AM, which is way late, island time. ⊠1 Chin's Way ☎508/228–2639 ☖BYOB ⊟MC, V.

$–$$$ ✕**Kitty Murtaugh's.** This mid-island pub does its best to replicate its Irish forebears, with cottage pie, bangers and mash, bacon and cabbage, and more. Steaks are a specialty (they rate their own menu heading, "The Butcher Shop"), and of course the fish-and-chips gets a Guinness batter. Much of the seasonal workforce hails from the Auld Sod, and now they need never feel homesick. ⊠*4 West Creek Rd.* ☎*508/325–0781* ▤*MC, V.*

¢ ✕**The Downyflake.** Locals flock here for bountiful breakfasts—featuring much sought-after homemade doughnuts—and well-priced lunches, from codfish cakes to burgers. ⊠*18 Sparks Ave.* ☎*508/228–4533* ▤*No credit cards* ⊘*Closed Jan.–Mar. No dinner.*

WHERE TO STAY

$$$$ ⌂**The Beachside at Nantucket.** Nantucket has only one "motel" ↻ in the classic rooms-around-a-pool configuration, and it's a honey—not at all out of place amid its tony neighbors. Between the town and Jetties Beach (both are within a bracing 10-minute walk), the complex ascends to two stories; rooms—decor is of the cheery wicker-and-florals school—have little pool-view terraces separated by whitewashed latticework. Families naturally flock here, but business travelers are equally well served. **Pros:** Kids have company, near the beach, pretty rooms. **Cons:** Kids rule, sounds carry from the pool, location not actually beachside. ⊠*30 N. Beach St., 02554* ☎*508/228–2241 or 800/322–4433* ▤*508/228–8901* ⊕*www.thebeachside.com* ➳*87 rooms, 3 suites* ⌂*In-room: refrigerator, Wi-Fi. In-hotel: pool, some pets allowed* ▤*AE, D, DC, MC, V* ⊘*Closed early Dec.–late Apr.* ⦿*CP.*

$$$$ ⌂**The Cottages at the Boat Basin.** These weathered-shingle ↻ cottages sit on South Wharf, amid the yachts—you could reserve a mooring and bring your own boat. Cottages range from studios to three bedrooms, and each has attractive modern decor with a nautical flavor: white walls, navy blue rugs, and light-wood floors and furniture. All have water views, though they're not always equal—some cottages have picture windows plus a little garden terrace. **Pros:** Right on the water, marina access, center of town. **Cons:** Tourist central, attendant noise, occasional foghorns. ⊠*New Whale St., Box 1139, 02554* ☎*508/325–1499 or 866/838–9253* ▤*508/228–7639* ⊕*www.thecottagesnantucket.com* ➳*23 cottages* ⌂*In-room: kitchen, DVD, Wi-Fi. In-hotel: concierge, some pets allowed* ▤*AE, D, DC, MC, V* ⊘*Closed late Oct.–mid-May* ⦿*BP.*

$$$$ ⌂**Harbor House Village.** An 1886 grand hotel forms the core ↻ of this family-oriented complex, where nicely landscaped

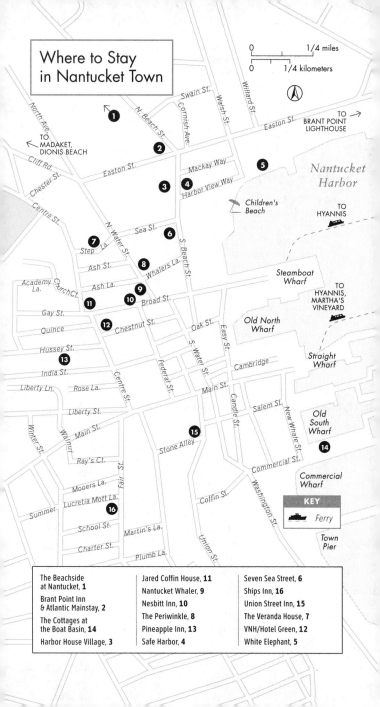

Where to Stay in Nantucket Town

0   1/4 miles
0   1/4 kilometers

Swain St.
N. Beach St.
Cornish Ave.
Walsh St.
Willard St.
Easton St.
TO BRANT POINT LIGHTHOUSE

North Ave.
TO MADAKET, DIONIS BEACH
Cliff Rd.
Chester St.
Centre St.
Easton St.
Mackay Way
Harbor View Way

Nantucket Harbor

Children's Beach
TO HYANNIS

N. Water St.
Sea St.
Step La.
Ash St.
Whalers La.
S. Beach St.

Steamboat Wharf
TO HYANNIS, MARTHA'S VINEYARD

Academy La.
Church Ct.
Ash La.
Broad St.
Gay St.
Quince
Chestnut St.
Oak St.
Easy St.
Old North Wharf

Straight Wharf

Hussey St.
India St.
Liberty Ln.
Rose La.
Centre St.
Federal St.
S. Water St.
Cambridge
Main St.
Candle St.
Salem St.
New Whale St.
Old South Wharf

Liberty St.
Winter St.
Walnut
Main St.
Ray's Ct.
Stone Alley
Commercial St.
Washington St.
Commercial Wharf

Mooers La.
Lucretia Mott La.
Summer
School St.
Fair St.
Coffin St.
Town Pier

Charter St.
Martin's La.
Plumb La.
Union St.

KEY
🚢 Ferry

The Beachside at Nantucket, **1**

Brant Point Inn & Atlantic Mainstay, **2**

The Cottages at the Boat Basin, **14**

Harbor House Village, **3**

Jared Coffin House, **11**

Nantucket Whaler, **9**

Nesbitt Inn, **10**

The Periwinkle, **8**

Pineapple Inn, **13**

Safe Harbor, **4**

Seven Sea Street, **6**

Ships Inn, **16**

Union Street Inn, **15**

The Veranda House, **7**

VNH/Hotel Green, **12**

White Elephant, **5**

brick walkways lead to a half-dozen town houses and an outdoor heated pool. Rooms are decorated in a pale-pine-and-wicker motif, in a summery color scheme of white, sunny yellow, and hydrangea blue; many come with private balconies. Owner Stephen Karp installed his favorite Chinese chefs in Harbor Wok, open in season. Babysitters are on call in season, and children's programs are offered from mid-June to Labor Day. Dogs get a special welcome at the "Woof Hotel," a dozen rooms dedicated to canine comfort—with dog beds, treats, and even a "Yappy Hour" for socializing. **Pros:** Child- and pet-friendly, in town, close to Children's Beach. **Cons:** Geared more to families than romance, can be impersonal, some rooms near busy street. ⊠*S. Beach St., Box 1139, 02554* ☎*508/228–1500 or 866/325–9300* ☒*508/228–7639* ⊕*www.harborhouse village.com* ⇆*104 rooms* ⌂*In-room: Wi-Fi. In-hotel: restaurant, bar, pool concierge, children's programs (ages 3– 13), ferry shuttle, some pets allowed, no elevator* ☰*AE, D, DC, MC, V* ⊗*Closed late Oct.–late Apr.* ⏀*CP.*

$$$$ 🖫**Jared Coffin House.** The largest house in town when it was built in 1845, this three-story brick manse is still plenty impressive. The antiques-filled parlors are a study in timeless good taste. The inn's umbrella extends to two other nearby buildings, the handsomest of which is the 1842 Greek Revival Harrison Gray House. Rooms vary greatly in terms of size and grandeur (the inn even has some very affordable singles). **Pros:** Elegant parlors, knowledgeable concierge, old-money aura. **Cons:** Lack of dining, some tiny rooms, street noise for those in front. ⊠*29 Broad St., Box 1580, 02554* ☎*508/228–2405 or 800/248–2405* ⊕*www.jaredcoffinhouse.com* ⇆*43 rooms* ⌂*In-room: no a/c (some), Wi-Fi. In-hotel: concierge* ☰*AE, D, DC, MC, V* ⊗*Closed early Dec.–mid-May* ⏀*BP.*

$$$$ 🖫**Nantucket Whaler.** Let's not mince words: the suites ★ carved out of this 1850 Greek Revival house are gorgeous. Neither Calliope Ligelis nor Randi Ott, the New Yorkers who rescued the place in 1999, had any design experience, but they approached the project as if preparing to welcome friends. Each suite has a private entrance and the wherewithal to whip up a meal. The spacious bedrooms are lavished with flowers, well-chosen antiques, and fine linens, including plush robes. Couples who have come to explore not so much the island as each other will scarcely have to come up for air. **Pros:** Pretty rooms, well decked out, romantic. **Cons:** No real reception area, lacks

a common room, the usual in-town noise. ⊠*8 N. Water St., Box 1337, 02554* ☎*508/228–6597 or 888/808–6597* 🖷*508/228–6291* ⊕*www.nantucketwhaler.com* ⌕*12 suites* ⌂*In-room: DVD, Wi-Fi. In-hotel: no kids under 11, refrigerator* ⊟*AE, MC, V* ⊘*Closed Jan. and Feb.*

$$$$ ★ **Fodor's**Choice ☎**Union Street Inn.** Ken Withrow worked in the hotel business, Deborah Withrow in high-end retail display, and guests get the best of both worlds. This 1770 house, a stone's throw from the bustle of Main Street, has been respectfully yet lavishly restored. Guests are treated to Frette linens, plump duvets, and lush robes (the better to lounge around in, my dear), as well as a full gourmet breakfast served on the tree-shaded garden patio. **Pros:** Pampering by pros, sensual pleasures, conducive to romance. **Cons:** No nearby beach, bustle of town, some small rooms (disclosed on Web site). ⊠*7 Union St., 02554* ☎*508/228–9222 or 800/225–5116* 🖷*508/325–0848* ⊕*www.unioninn. com* ⌕*12 rooms* ⌂*In-room: Wi-Fi. In-hotel: no kids under 12* ⊟*AE, MC, V* ⊺⊙*BP.*

$$$$ ☎**The Veranda House.** A fixture since the early 1880s, the
★ former Overlook, whose tiers of balconies take in a sweeping harbor vista, has been treated to a trendy "retro-chic" overhaul. The exterior may look unchanged, but the rooms got a makeover that introduced Frette linens, Simon Pearce lamps, Italian-tile rainfall showers, and the like. The buffet breakfasts are equally lush, featuring frittatas and stuffed French toast. **Pros:** Central but quiet location, harbor views, impeccable condition. **Cons:** Children's is the only close beach, decor a bit austere, pricey (though not for Nantucket). ⊠*3 Step La., Box 1112, 02554* ☎*508/228–0695* ⊕*www.theverandahouse.com* ⌕*17 rooms, 1 suite* ⌂*In-room: DVD, Wi-Fi. In-hotel: concierge, no kids under 10* ⊟*AE, D, MC, V* ⊘*Closed early Dec.–mid-May* ⊺⊙*BP.*

$$$$ ☎**VNH–Vanessa Noel Hotel and Hotel Green.** Minimalist chic has waltzed in the door—in a sweet pair of kitty heels. Opened in 2002 by native New Yorker and island-summerer shoe designer Vanessa Noel, VNH is a living catalog of trendy decor: each of the eight rooms (some admittedly as small as shoeboxes) boasts Armani Casa bedside tables, Philippe Starck bathroom fixtures, Mascioni linens, and Bulgari toiletries. Though the concept might seem a bit at odds with the island aesthetic, you'd be hard pressed to name a hotel with these touches outside a metropolis. Organo-purists will want to check out Noel's 2006 addition a few doors

2

down: the 10-room Hotel Green—distinguished by its grass windowboxes—has milk-painted walls, hemp shower curtains (the water is dechlorinated), and Ayurvedic body products. Rooms in the latter are slightly less pricey, as well as open to children. Both inns share an outdoor breakfast café. **Pros:** Centrally located, trendy, glamour quotient. **Cons:** Street noise, size of rooms, preciousness factor. ⊠*5 Chestnut St., at Centre St., 02554* ☎*508/228–5300* ⊕*www. vanessanoelhotel.com* ☞*18 rooms* ⌂*In-room: refrigerator. In-hotel: bar, no kids* ☰*AE, D, MC, V.*

$$$$ ⌑**White Elephant.** The White Elephant, a 1920s behemoth right on Nantucket Harbor, seems determined to keep raising the bar in service and style. The complex—a main building plus a cluster of cottages with breezy country-chic decor—hugs the harbor, leaving just enough room for a sweep of emerald lawn and the veranda of the hotel's in-house restaurant, the Brant Point Grill, where jazz combos entertain in season. Prices are lofty but, for the echelon it attracts, not all that extreme. **Pros:** Right on harbor, elegant, built-in entertainment. **Cons:** Can be snooty, Children's the only nearby beach, expensive. ⊠*Easton St., Box 1139, 02554* ☎*508/228–2500 or 800/445–6574* ☒*508/325–1195* ⊕*www.whiteelephanthotel.com* ☞*21 rooms, 31 suites, 11 cottages* ⌂*In-room: safe, refrigerator, DVD, dial-up, Ethernet. In-hotel: restaurant, room service, bar, laundry service, concierge, ferry shuttle* ☰*AE, D, DC, MC, V* ⊘*Closed Jan.–Mar.* ⍓*BP.*

$$$–$$$$ ⌑**Pineapple Inn.** No expense was spared in retrofitting this
★ 1838 Greek Revival captain's house for its new role as pamperer. It's decorated with impeccable taste, with down quilts and marble-finished baths. Breakfast is served in a formal dining room or beside the garden fountain. Whaling captains displayed a pineapple on their stoops upon completion of a successful journey, signaling the neighbors to come celebrate; here that spirit prevails daily. **Pros:** True Nantucket elegance, quiet location, cushy quarters. **Cons:** Some small rooms (Web site warns), no nearby beach, communal breakfast setup (not everyone's cup of cappuccino). ⊠*10 Hussey St., 02554* ☎*508/228–9992* ☒*508/325–6051* ⊕*www.pineappleinn.com* ☞*12 rooms* ⌂*In-room: Wi-Fi* ☰*AE, MC, V* ⊘*Closed mid-Dec.–late Apr.* ⍓*CP.*

$$$–$$$$ ⌑**Seven Sea Street.** If this red-oak post-and-beam B&B looks awfully well preserved, that's because it was custom-built

in 1987. Decked out in Early American style (decorative stenciling, fishnet-canopy beds, braided rugs), it offers the ambience of antiquity without all the creaky drawbacks. The Deluxe Suite, with its cathedral ceiling, full kitchen, gas fireplace, and harbor view, warrants a leisurely stay. Two satellite buildings up your odds of booking a room. **Pros:** On a quiet side street, central location, handsome decor. **Cons:** Some rooms smallish, some darkish, Children's the only nearby beach. ⊠ *7 Sea St., 02554* ☎ *508/228–3577 or 800/651–9262* 🖷 *508/228–3578* ⊕ *www.sevenseastreetinn. com* ↪ *13 rooms, 2 suites* 🛈 *In-room: refrigerator, VCR, Wi-Fi. In-hotel: some pets allowed, no kids under 5* ═ *AE, D, MC, V* ⦿ *CP.*

$$–$$$$ 🖬 **The Periwinkle.** Sara Shlosser-O'Reilly's B&B has spark—and a variety of rooms ranging from affordable singles to nice-size quarters with canopied king-size beds and harbor views. In one especially pretty setting the blue-ribbon pattern of the wallpaper matches the cushions and canopy: it's like living in a nicely wrapped gift. **Pros:** Central location, heavenly baking aromas, garden for lounging. **Cons:** Usual town noises, Children's the only nearby beach, tiny breakfast room (opt for the garden). ⊠ *7–9 N. Water St., Box 1436, 02554* ☎ *508/228–9267 or 800/837–2921* 🖷 *508/325–0245* ⊕ *www.theperiwinkle.com* ↪ *16 rooms, 1 cottage* 🛈 *In-room: refrigerators, DVD (some), VCRs (some), Wi-Fi* ═ *D, MC, V* ⦿ *CP.*

$$$ 🖬 **Safe Harbor.** The name is apt: children *and* pets are wel-
☾ come at this homey B&B with an enviable location mere steps from Children's Beach. Some of the rooms harboring American and Oriental antiques have water views; some have private decks. Everyone's welcome to sit on the wide front porch and enjoy the ocean breezes. **Pros:** Family-friendly, laid-back, well cared for. **Cons:** Noise can carry from Children's Beach, boat-launch traffic, occasional foghorns. ⊠ *2 Harbor View Way, 02554* ☎🖷 *508/228–3222 or 800/651–9262* ⊕ *www.beesknees.net/safeharbor* ↪ *5 rooms* 🛈 *In-room: Wi-Fi. In-hotel: some pets allowed* ═ *AE, MC, V* ⦿ *CP.*

$$–$$$ 🖬 **Brant Point Inn & Atlantic Mainstay.** You can't beat the edge-of-town location (Jetties Beach is a five-minute walk), especially given the modest rates that prevail at this pair of handsome post-and-beam guesthouses. Innkeeper Thea Kaizer grew up in a Nantucket inn; her husband, Peter, leads fishing charters, and should you catch something,

Navigating the Rental Market

If you're going to be staying for a week or more, you might want to consider renting a cottage or house—an arrangement that gives you a chance to settle in and get a real taste of island living. Many visitors, especially those with children, find renting more relaxing than staying in a hotel or an inn. With your own kitchen, you can save money by eating in; plus you can enjoy such homey summer pleasures as barbecues. Though decor can vary from chichi to weather-worn, most cottages come equipped with all you'll need to ensure a comfortable stay. Steer clear of a house without linens; it's a sign of bad things to come. The better houses come fully accoutered: not just with basics but with luxury touches like cable or satellite TV, a CD player, gourmet kitchen implements, beach chairs, and bikes.

Finding a great cottage or house can be tough, however, especially since so many are rented a year or more in advance by returning guests. The time to start your search is a summer ahead, though you can occasionally find a property as late as spring. A good way to shop is to stop in and visit Realtors when you happen to be in town. Be prepared for a bit of sticker shock,

though. Prices are generally about twice what you'd have to pay on Cape Cod or even the Vineyard. In summer very rustic (read shabby) rentals start at about $1,200 a week and can run to many times that ($3,500 and up) for multibedroom or waterfront properties.

Information Country Village Rentals (✉10 Straight Wharf ☎508/228–8840 or 800/599–7368 ⊕www.cvrandr. com) knows its clientele, who like to flit to sweet spots like Stowe and St. Bart's.

Lucille Jordan Real Estate (✉8 Federal St. ☎508/228–4449 ⊕www.jordanre.com) has a broad rental inventory; check the photos lining the storefront windows.

The **Maury People** (✉35–37 Main St. ☎508/228–1881 🖷508/228–1481 ⊕www. maurypeople.com), associated with Sotheby's, has more than 1,000 private homes in its rental inventory, including historic and beach homes; service is not only knowledgeable but personable.

Preferred Properties (✉76 Easton St. ☎508/228–2320 or 800/338–7715 🖷508/228–8464 ⊕www.preferredpropertiesre.com) is a Christie's affiliate whose offerings range "from cottages in the sand to castles on the cliff."

he'll expedite it to the restaurant of your choice. **Pros:** Friendly native owners, comfy-casual, near town and beaches. **Cons:** Lack of a/c (though unneeded), too casual for some tastes, on busy road. ⊠*6 N. Beach St., 02554* ☎*508/228–5442* 🖷*508/228–8498* ⊕*www.brantpointinn. com* ⤶*17 rooms, 2 suites* ⬧*In-room: no a/c, refrigerator* ⊟*AE, MC, V* ⦿⎮*CP.*

$$–$$$ ⊤**Ships Inn.** This 1831 home exudes history: it was built
★   for whaling captain Obed Starbuck on the site of the birth-place of abolitionist Lucretia Mott. Guest rooms, named for the ships Starbuck commanded, are furnished with period antiques and pretty wall coverings. The basement has a restaurant of the same name (delighted murmurings waft up); it generates a wonderful Continental breakfast and afternoon tea. **Pros:** Large rooms, handsome decor, fine in-house restaurant. **Cons:** Front rooms face street, noise from exuberant exiting diners, uphill from ferries. ⊠*13 Fair St., 02554* ☎*508/228–0040 or 888/872–4052* ⊕*www.shipsinnnantucket.com* ⤶*13 rooms, 11 with bath* ⬧*In-room: refrigerator. In-hotel: restaurant, no kids under 8* ⊟*AE, D, MC, V* ⊘*Closed Jan.–Apr.* ⦿⎮*CP.*

$–$$ ⊤**Nesbitt Inn.** The last real deal left in town, this homey Victorian has been in the same family since 1914. Fourth-generation proprietors Joanne and Steve Marcoux are so nice, and the rates so reasonable, you're willing to overlook the shared baths and gently worn furnishings. Here you can find the authentic, pre-glitz Nantucket. **Pros:** Friendly native owners, no pretense, the true Nantucket. **Cons:** Noisy street, small rooms, shabby (but clean). ⊠*21 Broad St., Box 1019, 02554* ☎*508/228–0156* 🖷*508/228–2446* ⤶*12 rooms share 3 baths, 1 room with private bath, 2 cottages* ⊟*MC, V* ⦿⎮*CP.*

WHERE TO STAY ON THE NANTUCKET TOWN OUTSKIRTS
See ⇨ *Where to Stay Outside Nantucket Town* map for these properties.

$$$$ ⊤**Cliffside Beach Club.** Which way to the beach? You're on
☾   it: this snazzily updated 1920s beach club stakes its claim
★   with a flotilla of colorful umbrellas—somewhat miffing natives, who consider sand rights anathema. Local politics aside, this is one prime chunk of gentle bay beach, and the complex makes the most of its site, with a gorgeous cathedral-ceiling lobby decorated with hanging quilts and rooms of every size and shape enhanced by island-made modern

furnishings. Best of all, you can traipse across the sand to Galley Beach, one of the best restaurants around. **Pros:** Right on beach, two pools, good restaurant. **Cons:** Questionable private-beach karma, over-entitled guests, high prices. ⊠ *46 Jefferson Ave., Box 449, 02554* ☎ *508/228–0618 or 800/932–9645* ⊕ *www.cliffsidebeach.com* ⤸ *26 rooms, 3 suites, 2 apartments, 1 cottage* ⌂ *In-room: safe, kitchen (some), refrigerator, DVD (some), VCR (some), no TV (some), Wi-Fi. In-hotel: restaurant, pools, gym, beachfront* ☰ *AE* ⊘ *Closed mid-Oct.–May* ⍥ *CP.*

¢–$$ 🏨 **Robert B. Johnson Memorial Hostel.** One of the country's most picturesque hostels, this 49-bed Hostelling International facility occupies a former 1873 lifesaving station—known as "The Star of the Sea"—right on Surfside Beach, a 3-mi ride from town on the bike path. Dorm rooms (the three private rooms book quickly) are divided into men's, women's, and coed; the common areas include a kitchen. There's no lockout (customary at many urban hostels) and—huzzah—no curfew. Reservations are always a good idea, and essential come summer. **Pros:** Super-cheap, right on island's best beach, good company. **Cons:** Little privacy, no frills, a long haul (3-mi public shuttle or bike ride) from town. ⊠ *31 Western Ave., 02554* ☎ *508/228–0433* ⊕ *www.usahostels.org* ⤸ *49 dorm-style beds* ⌂ *In room: no a/c, no phone, no TV. In-hotel: beachfront, Wi-Fi* ☰ *MC, V* ⊘ *Closed mid-Oct.–early May.*

NIGHTLIFE & THE ARTS

The phrase "Nantucket nightlife" verges on an oxymoron—and during the off-season, it's virtually a nonentity. If it's glitz and nonstop action you're after, better stick to the mainland. On the other hand, if you like live music, you will never go lacking—at least in season.

For listings of events, see the *Inquirer and Mirror* (⊕ *www. ack.net*), the *Nantucket Independent* (⊕ *www.nantucket independent.com*), and (in season) *Yesterday's Island* (⊕ *www.yesterdaysisland.com*); the latter two are distributed free. Posters around town announce coming attractions: check the board outside the Hub, a newsstand at the corner of Federal and Main streets.

FILM

The **Nantucket Film Festival** (☎*508/325–6274 or 212/642–6339* ⊕*www.nantucketfilmfestival.org*), held each June, emphasizes the importance of strong scripts. The final playlist—about two dozen short and feature-length films—always includes a few world premieres, and many selections have gone on to considerable commercial success. Shows tend to sell out, so it's best to buy online, well ahead. Informal daily coffee-klatch discussions with directors provide the inside scoop.

The **Dreamland Theatre** (⊠*17 S. Water St.* ☎*508/228–5356*) is housed in a pleasantly ramshackle old ark of a building, which used to be a Quaker meetinghouse, then a straw factory, and, finally, an entertainment hall. After a two-year hiatus, new owners have turned it back into a summer cinema (open mid-May–mid-September) running first-run mainstream movies and the occasional rainy-day matinee.

The **Starlight Theatre** (⊠*1 N. Union St.* ☎*508/228–4435* ⊕*www.starlightnantucket.com*) is a small screening room appended to a café of the same name. It presents two shows nightly in season, plus sporadic matinees.

FINE ARTS & CRAFTS

The **Artists Association of Nantucket** (⊠*Gardner Perry La.* ☎*508/228–0722* ⊕*www.nantucketarts.org*), founded in 1945, leads classes year-round in various media, often presented by some of the island's most noteworthy artists. The association's **gallery** (⊠*19 Washington St.* ☎*508/228–0294*) hosts juried shows.

The **Nantucket Island School of Design and the Arts** (⊠*23 Wauwinet Rd.* ☎*508/228–9248* ⊕*www.nisda.org*), affiliated with the Massachusetts College of Art in Boston, teaches fine-art classes in many media; it also hosts shows, lectures, and events.

Nantucket Lightship Basket Museum (⊠*49 Union St.* ☎*508/228–1177*) mounts demos Friday and Saturday in summer.

MUSIC

The **Boston Pops** put on a blow-out concert on Jetties Beach in mid-August to benefit the Nantucket Cottage Hospital (☎*508/825–8250* ⊕*www.nantuckethospital.org*).

The **Nantucket Arts Council** (⊠*Box 554, 02554* ☎*508/228–8588* ⊕*www.nantucketartscouncil.org*) sponsors a music series (jazz, country, classical) September to June.

The **Nantucket School of Music** (⊠*11 Centre St.* ☎*508/228–3352* ⊕*www.ackmusic.com*) arranges year-round choral and instrumental instruction and sponsors and puts on concerts; choristers are always welcome.

Nantucket Musical Arts Society (☎*508/228–1287*) mounts concerts by internationally acclaimed musicians Tuesday evenings at 8:30 July through August. The concerts are mostly classical but sometimes venture into jazz.

The **Nantucket Park & Recreation Commission** (⊠*Children's Beach bandstand, off Harbor View Way* ☎*508/228–7213*) hosts free jazz/pop/classical concerts (and the occasional theater production) from July 4 to Labor Day. Programs begin at 6 PM. Bring blankets, chairs, and bug repellent.

The **Noonday Concert Series** (⊠*Unitarian Universalist Church, 11 Orange St.* ☎*508/228–5466*), Thursday at noon in July and August, brings in visiting performers and also showcases outstanding local musicians. Concerts range from bluegrass to classical.

BARS & CLUBS

American Seasons (⊠*80 Centre St.* ☎*508/228–7111*) has an intimate patio bar serving tapas.

The **Bamboo Pub** (⊠*3 Chins Way* ☎*508/228–0200*) draws a youngish, fairly rambunctious crowd year-round with such specialty drinks as the potent Red Bull Purple Haze splashed with Chambord and Absolut Mandarin. There's a pool table upstairs.

At the White Elephant's **Brant Point Grill** (⊠*50 Easton St.* ☎*508/325–1320 or 800/445–6574* ⊕*www.brantpoint-grill.com*), the setting is country-elegant—Windsor chairs, varnished woodwork with hunter-green trim—and the patrons are patently moneyed, since many are hotel guests. A pianist or jazz-standards band provides atmosphere (and takes requests).

The **Chicken Box** (*The Box* ⊠*14 Dave St., off Lower Orange St.* ☎*508/228–9717*) rocks! Live music—including some big-name bands—plays six nights a week in season, and weekends throughout the year. On the off nights, you can always play pool, foosball, or darts.

Cioppino's (⊠*20 Broad St.* ☎*508/228–4622*) has a winning wine list; owner Tracy Root used to be the maître d' at Chanticleer. A small bar within the elegant house welcomes all comers, especially aficionados of fine port; late-nighters can find succor in the garden patio.

The under-21 crowd tends to cluster along "The Strip," a series of fast-food joints extending along Broad Street toward Steamboat Wharf. By far the biggest draw, for loiterers of all ages, is the **Juice Bar** (⊠*12 Broad St.* ☎*508/228–5799*), which, despite its name, is famed primarily for its fabulous homemade ice cream.

The **Muse** (⊠*44 Surfside Rd.* ☎*508/228–6873* ⊕*www. museack.com*) is *the* place to catch big-name acts year-round. DJs spin between sets and on nights when there's no live act. The barnlike Muse accommodates some 370 people, who also have the option of playing pool or Ping-Pong or scarfing pies produced on-site at **Muse Pizza** (☎*508/228–1471*).

Refined sorts find their way upstairs to the tiny bar at **Òran Mór** (⊠*2 S. Beach St.* ☎*508/228–8655*) to sip fine wines and shots of single-malt Scotch: one such elixir inspired the restaurant's name.

★ You don't have to be fabulous to fit in at **the pearl** (⊠*12 Federal St.* ☎*508/228–9701*), but it wouldn't hurt. Patrons tend to be as chic as the white onyx bar itself, whose blue lighting lends a mysterious glow to all assembled.

Rose and Crown (⊠*23 S. Water St.* ☎*508/228–2595*) is a family-friendly restaurant that morphs into a pub popular with the barely post-collegiate crowd. DJs keep the dance floor moving, as do various frozen drinks and the redoubtable Goombay Smash; occasional karaoke nights are similarly fueled.

The café tables of the **Tavern** (⊠*1 Harbor Sq., Straight Wharf* ☎*508/228–1266*) spill out onto a Straight Wharf plaza, at the center of which stands the Gazebo, the island's closest analog to a singles bar. You can stroll around and scan the throng before committing to joining the crush.

The formal interiors of **21 Federal** (⊠*21 Federal St.* ☎*508/228–2121*) make a surprisingly conducive setting for well-heeled camaraderie. The specialty drink is the Bermudian Dark and Stormy.

Michelangelo on the Beach

CLOSE UP

Buddhas, dragons, mermaids, and, of course, whales inhabit Jetties Beach during the annual Sandcastle & Sculpture Day in August. Creative concoctions, often with maritime themes, emerge from the sand: porpoises, submarines, spaceships, flowers, and the famous lightship baskets are carefully and creatively crafted out of sand, shells, seaweed, and even beach litter (you may even see a castle or two). Anyone can stake out a patch of sand. There are prizes in several age groups and categories, so grab a shovel, bucket, turkey baster (a secret weapon for blowing sand), rake, and sunscreen and join the fun. Registration forms are available at the chamber office, 48 Main Street.

READINGS & TALKS

The **Nantucket Atheneum** (✉*1 India St.* ☎*508/228–1110* ⊕*www.nantucketatheneum.org*) hosts a dazzling roster of writers and speakers year-round. Except for a few big-name fund-raisers in summer, all events are free.

The **Nantucket Historical Association** (✉*15 Broad St.* ☎*508/228–1894* ⊕*www.nha.org*) hosts evening talks on a variety of topics touching on local history.

THEATER

Theatre Workshop of Nantucket (✉*Methodist Church, 2 Centre St.* ☎*508/228–4305* ⊕*www.theatreworkshop.com*), a semi-professional community theater since 1956, stages plays, musicals, and readings year-round.

SPORTS & THE OUTDOORS

BEACHES

☼ A calm area by the harbor, **Children's Beach** (off Harbor View Way) is an easy walk north from the center of town and a perfect spot for small children. The beach has a grassy park with benches, a playground, lifeguards, a café, picnic tables, showers, and restrooms. Tie-dyeing classes are offered Friday at noon mid-July through August.

Cisco (✉*Hummock Pond Rd., South Shore*) has heavy surf, lifeguards, but no food or restrooms. It's not easy to get to or from Nantucket Town, though: it's 4 mi from town, and there are no bike trails to it, so you'll have to ride in the road, walk, drive, or take a taxi. Also, the dunes are severely eroded, so getting down onto the beach can be difficult. Still, the waves make it a popular spot for body- and boardsurfers.

Dionis Beach (⊠*Eel Point Rd.*) is, at its entrance, a narrow strip of sand that turns into a wider, more private strand with high dunes and fewer children. The beach has a rocky bottom and calm, rolling waters; there are lifeguards on duty and restrooms. Take the Madaket Bike Path to Eel Point Road, about 3 mi west of town.

★ A short bike- or shuttle-bus ride from town, **Jetties Beach** (Bathing Beach Rd., 1½ mi northwest of Straight Wharf) is a most popular family beach because of its calm surf, lifeguards, bathhouse, restrooms, and snack bar. It's a good place to try out water toys: kayaks, sailboards, and day sailers are rented in summer. On shore it's a lively scene with playground and volleyball nets on the beach and adja- cent tennis courts. There's a boardwalk to the beach and you can watch the ferries pass.

Madaket Beach (⊠*Off Madaket Rd., Madaket*) is reached by shuttle bus from Nantucket Town or the Madaket Bike Path (5 mi from Upper Main Street) and has lifeguards, but no restrooms. It's known for challenging surf (beware the rip currents) and unbeatable sunsets.

★ Fodor'sChoice **Surfside Beach** (⊠*Surfside Rd., South Shore*), accessible via the Surfside Bike Path (3 mi) or shuttle bus, is the island's most popular surf beach, with lifeguards, rest- rooms, a snack bar, and a wide strand of sand. It pulls in college students as well as families and is great for kite fly- ing and surf casting.

BICYCLING

The best way to tour Nantucket is by bicycle. Nearly 28 mi of paved bike paths wind through all types of terrain from one end of the island to the other; it's possible to bike around the entire island in a day. Most paths start within ½ mi of town, and all are well marked. Several lead to beaches. And if you're without your wheels, it's easy enough to rent some. The paths are also perfect for run- ners and bladers—but not mopeds, which are forbidden. Note that Nantucket now requires all bike riders—includ- ing adults—to wear a helmet.

The easy 3-mi **Surfside Bike Path** leads to Surfside, the island's premier ocean beach. A drinking fountain and rest stop are placed at about the halfway point.

Milestone Bike Path, a straight shot linking Nantucket Town and Sconset, is probably the most monotonous of the paths but can still be quite pleasant. It's about 7 mi—paired with the scenic Polpis Path, it becomes a 16-mi island loop.

At 1.2 mi, the **Cliff Road Path,** on the north shore, is one of the easiest bike paths, but it's still quite scenic, with gentle hills. It intersects with the Eel Point and Madaket paths.

The **Eel Point/Dionis Beach Path** starts at the junction of Eel Point Road and Madaket Road and links the Cliff Road and Madaket bike paths to Dionis Beach. It's less than a mile long.

The **Madaket Path** starts at the intersection of Quaker and Upper Main Street and follows Madaket Road out to Madaket Beach, on the island's west end and about 6 mi from the edge of Nantucket Town. About one-third of the way you could turn off onto Cliff Road Path or the Eel Point/Dionis Beach Path.

Young's Bicycle Shop (✉ *6 Broad St., Steamboat Wharf* ☎ *508/228–1151* ⊕ *www.youngsbicycleshop.com*), established in 1931, rents bicycles, including tandems and children's equipment; weekly rates are available. The knowledgeable third-generation Young family and staff will send you off with everything you need—an excellent touring map, a helmet, and a quaint little Portuguese basket for your handlebars.

BIRD-WATCHING

Hundreds of species flock to the island's moors, meadows, and marshes in the course of a year. Birds that are rare in other parts of New England thrive here, because of the lack of predators and the abundance of wide-open, undeveloped space. Almost anywhere outside of town you're sure to see interesting birdlife, not just in migratory season but year-round. Set up your spotting scope near the salt marsh at Eel Point any time of year and you're bound to see shorebirds feeding—low tide is the best time. Endangered piping plovers and least terns nest on the ocean side in spring. Folger's Marsh about 3 mi east of town and the Harbor Flats at the end of Washington Street on the eastern edge of town are also good shorebird-watching sites. Inland, a walk through Sanford Farm from Madaket Road to the south shore, traversing upland, forest, heath, and shore habitats, will bring you in range of Savannah sparrows, yellow warblers, osprey, and red-tailed hawks, the island's most common raptor. Be on the lookout for the protected Northern harrier. For woodland species, check out the trails through Windswept Cranberry Bog or the Masquetuck Reservation near Polpis Harbor.

Eco Guides: Strong Wings (⊠ *9 Nobadeer Farm Rd.* ☎ *508/228–1769* ⊕ *www.strongwings.org*) customizes environmentally savvy birding tours based on interest and group size and, depending on your preferred degree of difficulty, can include a hike, a bike ride, or a casual stroll.

The **Maria Mitchell Association** (*MMA* ⊠ *4 Vestal St.* ☎ *508/228–0898* ⊕ *www.mmo.org*) leads marine-ecology field trips and nature and bird walks weekly in spring and early summer and three times a week from June through Labor Day.

BOATING

During July and August, Nantucket is *the* place to study, close-up, some of the world's most splendid yachts—and the well-to-do people who own and sail them. Don't be surprised if you see yachts with piggyback motor launches, automobiles, and helicopters. Most of them spend a few days here, many from a tour that originated in the Mediterranean via the Caribbean. If you don't happen to own a floating palace, you can still hit the water—Nantucket has plenty of boat charters, rentals, and scenic cruises.

Nantucket Community Sailing (⊠ *4 Winter St.* ☎ *508/228–6600* ⊕ *www.nantucketcommunitysailing.org*) rents Sunfish sailboats, sailboards, and kayaks from Jetties Beach (Memorial Day–Labor Day); it also has youth and adult instructional sailing programs, as well as adaptive watersport clinics for athletes with disabilities. NCS's Outrigger Canoe Club—a Polynesian tradition—heads out three evenings a week (depending on interest) in season.

Sea Nantucket (⊠ *Washington St. Extension, ¼ mi southeast of Commercial Wharf* ☎ *508/228–7499*) rents kayaks and small sailboats by the hour or half day at the vest-pocket Francis Street Beach.

☾ The **Endeavor** (⊠ *Slip 1015, Straight Wharf* ☎ *508/228–5585*
★ ⊕ *www.endeavorsailing.com*), a charter replica Friendship sloop, makes four daily 1½-hour trips out to the jetties and into the sound. Private charters and special theme trips for children—"Pirate Adventure" and "Songs and Stories of the Sea"—are available.

Shearwater Excursions (☎*508/228–7037* ⊕*www.explore nantucket.com*) mount various seaborne ecotours aboard a 50-foot power catamaran. One option is a two-hour trip to view Muskeget Island's 2,500 resident gray seals; one-hour lobster cruises to nearby Tuckernuck Island are offered on a flexible schedule out of Madaket. Sunday is for whale-watching 15–30 mi southeast of Nantucket; Captain Blair Perkins guarantees a sighting, which means that if no mammals show up, you can go again for free. The Shearwater is also available for private evening charters.

FISHING

Surf fishing is very popular on Nantucket, especially in the late spring when bluefish are running (the best place to go after them is Great Point). Freshwater fishing is also an option at many area ponds.

Many of the fishing charters will gladly make detours to spot whales.

Captain Peter Kaizer, a former commercial fisherman, guarantees a good catch aboard the *Althea K* (☎*508/228–3471* ⊕*www.altheasportfishing.com*); he also offers whale-watching and charter cruises.

Captain Tom's Charters (✉*Public Landing, Madaket* ☎*508/228–4225* ⊕*www.captaintomscharters.com*) win consistent "best of" awards for Tom Mleczko's hands-on expertise. Choose among rips, bars, surf, open water, and flats (the latter for the added challenge of sight fishing with fly rods).

A permit is required for **shellfishing,** specifically foraging for littleneck and cherrystone clams, quahogs, scallops, oysters, steamers, and mussels. You can pick one up—along with tips on where and how to get the best catch—at the **Marine and Coastal Resources Department** (✉*34 Washington St.* ☎*508/228–7261* ⊕*www.nantucket-ma.gov*).

FITNESS CLUBS

Nantucket Health Club (✉*10 Young's Way* ☎*508/228–4750* ⊕*www.nantuckethealthclub.com*) has StairMasters, Lifecycles, treadmills, rowers, Airdyne bikes, New Generation Nautilus, and free weights; aerobics, Spinning, and yoga classes; and personal trainers. You can get a short-term pass that covers the machines, fitness classes, or both.

GOLF

Miacomet Golf Club (⊠ *12 W. Miacomet Ave.* ☎ *508/325–0333* ⊕ *www.miacometgolf.com*) is a public links-style course owned by the Land Bank and built over natural terrain—mostly coastal heathland. It has 18 very flat holes.

HIKING

Nantucket supports approximately 1,200 species of vegetation: that's a greater variety than is found in any other area of equivalent size in the United States. It has 82 mi of beaches, and though almost 97% of the shoreline is privately owned, it's a point of pride that almost all is open for public use. There are hardwood forests, salt marshes, cranberry bogs, squam swamps, freshwater ponds, and coastal heathlands, and, with Martha's Vineyard and nearby Tuckernuck Island, the island holds more than 90% of the acreage of sandplain grassland *worldwide*. The island is home to a huge number of deer; significant colonies of harbor seals, gray seals, and harbor porpoises; and turtles, frogs, rabbits, voles, and other reptiles and small field mammals. A lack of land-bound predators such as skunks and raccoons allows bird populations to thrive, and hundreds of species either live on the island or pass through on their annual migrations.

Nearly all of the 8,900 acres maintained by the **Nantucket Conservation Foundation** (⊠ *118 Cliff Rd.* ☎ *508/228–2884* ⊕ *www.nantucketconservation.com*) are open to the public; though only a few trails are marked, you can feel free to wander knowing that you can't get lost—if you keep going in one direction, you're bound to hit a road or a beach eventually. The foundation, open weekdays 8–5, puts out maps and informative brochures on the most popular hiking spots. Remember that these conservation areas are set aside to preserve and protect Nantucket's fragile ecosystems—tread carefully—and also be aware that ticks are a serious problem here. Dress accordingly and carry plenty of repellent.

A 5- to 10-minute bike ride from Nantucket Town on the way to Madaket, the **Sanford Farm, Ram Pasture, and the Woods** (⊠ *Madaket Rd., between Milford and Cliff Rds.*) comprises 300 acres that were saved from developers by the Nantucket Conservation Foundation in 1971. The southern edge of the property borders the ocean.

The **Tupancy Links** (⊠ *165 Cliff Rd., 1¼ mi west of town*) runs between the Cliff Road bike path and Nantucket

Petticoat Row

During the whaling era—a time, remember, when women were generally considered better seen than heard—a circumstance developed in Nantucket Town that was perhaps unique in the country: a large portion of Centre Street shops near Main Street were almost completely run by women merchants. It eventually became known as Petticoat Row, and it still exists today. Women have always played a strong role in Nantucket's history, partly because of the Quaker philosophy of sexual equality and partly because on whaling expeditions men could be gone for years at a time—and it was up to women to keep the town going. They became leaders in every arena, from religion to business.

Sound. It's a smaller property that passes mainly through grassland populated by plants like false heather, oxeye daisy, and Queen Anne's lace, and it provides wonderful views once you reach the overlook at the water's edge. The cliff is only 42 feet above sea level, but from it you can see great stretches of the island's north shore.

SURFING

The relatively mild breakers at Cisco Beach make picking up the sport easier than it might be in, say, Maui. **Nantucket Island Surf School** (☎508/560–1020 ⊕*www.surfack. com*) owner Gary Kohner and his crew can tell you everything you need to know to get up and cruising, from surfing etiquette to ocean safety. Group and private lessons and equipment and wet-suit rental are available.

TENNIS

The Jetties Beach Tennis Courts (☎508/325–5334), six contiguous asphalt courts overseen by the Park & Recreation department, charge a nominal fee 8 AM–6 PM in season and are much in demand, so reserve early in the day. Early- and latecomers play free, and off-season, you're golden: they leave the nets up year-round.

Nantucket Tennis and Swim Club (⊠*23 Nobadeer Farm Rd., near airport* ☎*508/228–3700* ⊕*www.nantuckettennis.com* ☉*Memorial Day–Columbus Day, daily 7 AM–9:30 PM*) has nine fast-dry clay courts, five lighted courts, and a pro shop. Lessons, rentals, clinics, and round-robins are available.

SHOPPING

The historic center of town doubles as the commercial district: shops are concentrated primarily in the grid formed by Main, Centre, Broad, and Easy streets, with a few shops trailing off along the periphery. The former boathouses of Straight Wharf and Old South Wharf, retrofitted as shops and galleries, attract well-heeled browsers as well. The necessities of island life—hardware, office supplies, etc.—tend to be clustered mid-island, where new stores offering nonessentials are gradually making inroads as well.

Most of Nantucket's shops are seasonal, opening in time for the Daffodil Festival in late April and closing soon after Christmas Stroll in early December; a hardy few stay open year-round and often offer rather astounding bargains off-season. On summer weekends, many shops stay open late (until 9 or 10). Most galleries hold their openings on Friday evenings.

ANTIQUES

Antiques Depot (⊠*14 Easy St.* ☎*508/228–1287*) has an intriguing mix of furniture, art, Persian rugs, and accessories, including decoys.

G. K. S. Bush (⊠*13 Old South Rd.* ☎*508/325–0300*) carries ultra-high-end American antique furniture, paintings, and decorative arts (winter headquarters are on New York's Upper East Side).

In business since 1974, **Lynda Willauer Antiques** (⊠*2 India St.* ☎*508/228–3631*) has amassed a stellar cache of American and English furniture, plus fine collectibles, including Chinese export porcelain and majolica; the shop winters in Greenwich, Connecticut.

★ **Nantucket Country** (⊠*38 Centre St.* ☎*508/228–8868* ⊕*www.nantucketcountryantiques.com*) has an especially rich inventory of quilts and flags; another specialty—in addition to maritime and "Nantucketiana"—is antique children's toys.

Nantucket House Antiques (⊠*2 S. Beach St.* ☎*508/228–4604* ⊕*www.nantuckethouse.com*) displays a wealth of well-chosen artifacts, in inspired aggregations; the owners are interior decorators.

Nina Hellman Marine Antiques & Americana (⊠*48 Centre St.* ☎*508/228–4677* ⊕*www.nauticalnantucket.com*) carries scrimshaw, whaling artifacts, ship models, instruments, and other marine antiques, plus folk art and Nantucket memorabilia. Charles Manghis, a contemporary scrimshaw artist, demonstrates and exhibits his craft here.

★ Fodor'sChoice **Rafael Osona Auctions** (⊠*American Legion Hall, 21 Washington St.* ☎*508/228–3942* ⊕*www.rafaelosonaauction.com*) holds auctions of fine antiques most Saturday mornings from Memorial Day weekend to early December; the items—furniture, decorative accessories, art, jewelry, and more—are previewable two days in advance.

Established in 1927, **Sylvia Antiques** (⊠*6 Ray's Ct.* ☎*508/228–0960* ⊕*www.sylviaantiques.com*) retains the richest stash of island-related antiquities.

Tonkin of Nantucket (⊠*33 Main St.* ☎*508/228–9697* ⊕*www.tonkin-of-nantucket.com*) has two floors of fine Continental antiques—including furniture, china, art, silver, and scientific instruments—as well as sailors' valentines and lightship baskets.

Wayne Pratt (⊠*28 Main St.* ☎*508/228–8788* ⊕*www.waynepratt.com*) specializes in American antiques and handcrafted reproductions. Items of special interest include Jose Reyes baskets and maritime antiques.

ART GALLERIES

The **Artists' Association of Nantucket** (⊠*19 Washington St.* ☎*508/228–0772* ⊕*www.nantucketarts.org*) is the best place to get an overview of the work being done on-island; many members have galleries of their own.

★ At **The Brigham Galleries** (⊠*54 Center St.* ☎*508/925–2525* ⊕*www.thebrighamgalleries.com*) Sara Boyce has an entire Federal-style house in which to showcase her excellent, at times playful taste; portrait commissions are a specialty.

The **Gallery at Four India** (⊠*4 India St.* ☎*508/228–8509* ⊕*www.galleryatfourindia.com*) is a quiet, spacious refuge, with highly sought-after American and marine paintings dating from the 1850s to 1940s, plus a small sampling of contemporary realism.

SVG Collection (⊠*8 Howard Court* ☎*508/228–2011* ⊕*www.sailorsvalentinegallery.com*) presents an international array of contemporary fine and folk art, plus the namesake keepsakes created by homesick mariners in the 19th century.

★ The **South Wharf Gallery** (✉3 *India St.* ☎*508/228–0406* ⊕*www.southwharfgallery.com*) has been showing top local work since 1978.

BOOKS

Nantucket Bookworks (✉25 *Broad St.* ☎*508/228–4000* ⊕*www.nantucketbookworks.com*) carries an extensive inventory, with an emphasis on literary works and Nantucket-specific titles, as well as children's books and gift items.

CANDY

Aunt Leah's Fudge (✉*Courtyard, Straight Wharf* ☎*508/228–1183 or 800/824–6330* ⊕*www.auntleahsfudge.com*) whips up—and ships—several dozen varieties, including Chocolate Cranberry Nut Supreme.

The aroma of chocolate confections being cooked up in the back room of **Sweet Inspirations** (✉26 *Centre St.* ☎*508/228–5814* ⊕*www.nantucketchocolatier.com*) will instantly dispel any notions of dieting. Cranberries and chocolate make a surprisingly seductive duo, especially in the form of cranberry cheesecake truffles.

CLOTHING

Watch your head as you step down into **Cordillera Imports** (✉18 *Broad St.* ☎*508/228–6140*). Offering casual clothing, sandals, accessories, and crafts from Third World countries, this semi-basement is one of the few shops non-trust-funded teenagers can afford to patronize.

★ **Eye of the Needle and Eye of the Needle Girls** (✉14–14A *Federal St.* ☎*508/228–1923 or 508/228–4449*) is a microcosm of urban fashion trends, playfully leavened.

Handblock (✉4 *S. Water St.* ☎*508/228–4500* ⊕*www.handblock.com*) stocks April Cornell clothing (for women and girls) and linens, along with countrified home furnishings.

Namesake-muse Audrey would have approved of **Hepburn** (✉3 *Salem St.* ☎*508/228–1458*), with its slim-profile, high-fashion dresses; the accessories are especially nice, including an intriguing array of silver.

She's back! The splashy resort wear so popular in the '60s is enshrined at the **Lilly Pulitzer Shop** (✉5 *S. Water St.* ☎*508/228–0569* ⊕*www.lillyshop.com*).

Nantucket Reds

Bermuda has its shorts, Fiji its sarongs. Nantucket's totemic clothing items are made of cotton dyed red so as to fade to a dull salmon shade. The reds were something of a secret code until they were singled out by *The Official Preppy Handbook* in 1980: "By their pink shirts ye shall know them" might be the watchwords for Nantucketers among the worldwide sailing community. Now reds are as site-specific as Martha's Vineyard's Black Dog line (attempting to compete, of late, with a satellite shop on Straight Wharf).

The principal purveyor of Nantucket reds is Murray's Toggery Shop on Main Street, which has catered to conservative dressers since the early 1900s. (Roland Macy worked here at his father's shop in the early 1800s before setting off to rewrite retailing history.) From baby togs to tote bags, you can find everything you could want here in the way of reds. But for that weathered look that sets them off so well, you'll have to get out on the water.

Mallory Alfano (⊠*32 Center St.* ☎*508/228–0569*) combs the international boutique market to stock her namesake store with exquisite, of-the-moment accessories.

Murray's Toggery Shop (⊠*62 Main St.* ☎*508/228–0437* ⊕*www.nantucketreds.com*) can claim credit for introducing the signature "Nantucket reds" *(⇨Nantucket Reds box)*—now available in a range of styles for men, women, and children.

Murray's Warehouse (⊠*7 New St.* ☎*508/228–3584* ⊕*www. nantucketreds.com*) offers discounts of up to 75% on surplus stock from Murray's Toggery Shop.

Something about the Nantucket lifestyle prompts hat hunger. **Peter Beaton** (⊠*16½ Federal St.* ☎*508/228–8456* ⊕*www.peterbeaton.com*) shows an international array of beauties, all customizable with special trim, along with a smattering of clothing.

Ralph Lauren (⊠*16 Main St.* ☎*508/228–9541* ⊕*www.polo. com*) supplanted the Looms—an island institution—in the spring of '04 and the sky didn't cave in, but locals are still not happy about the incursion of a chain.

Vanessa Noel (⌂*5 Chestnut St., at Centre St.* ☎*508/228–6030* ⊕*www.vanessanoel.com*) creates ultraglam shoes—they're expensive, to be sure, but fans gladly toe the line.

Island loyalties might be tested, but the **Vineyard Vines** (⌂*2 Harbor Sq.* ☎*800/892–4982* ⊕*www.vineyardvines.com*) line—from flip-flops to bathing trunks, not to mention the ties that started it all—is just so irresistibly preppy, resistance is futile.

★ **Fodor's**Choice The inviting windows of **Vis-a-Vis** (⌂*34 Main St.* ☎*508/228–5527* ⊕*www.visavisnantucket.com*) display relaxed-luxe women's fashions amid antique home furnishings, some of which, including hooked rugs, quilts, and collectibles, are also for sale.

CRAFTS

Claire Murray (⌂*11 S. Water St.* ☎*508/228–1913 or 800/252–4733* ⊕*www.clairemurray.com*) carries the designer's Nantucket-theme and other hand-hooked rugs and rug kits, quilts, and knitting and needlework kits; this little shop is where the empire got started.

Erica Wilson Needle Works (⌂*25 Main St.* ☎*508/228–9881*) embodies the enthusiasms of the famous British-born designer, an island resident since 1958. In addition to her own embroidery and needlepoint kits, the store carries winning clothing and accessories for women (look for Heidi Weddendorf's Nantucket knot jewelry), baby gifts, and appealing elements of home decor.

Since 1927 the **Four Winds Craft Guild** (⌂*6 Ray's Ct.* ☎*508/228–9623* ⊕*www.sylviaantiques.com*) has showcased local folk arts, including scrimshaw and lightship baskets (old and new), ship models, and duck decoys; the guild also offers a kit for making your own lightship basket. A satellite shop within the historic Pacific Club at 1 Main Street displays outstanding new work.

Made on Nantucket (⌂*44 Main St.* ☎*508/228–4487* ⊕*www.madeonnantucket.com*) represents the work of more than 80 local artisans, ranging from quilters to woodworkers. The owner also collects Bakelite and other vintage jewelry.

★ **Nantucket Looms** (⌂*16 Federal St.* ☎*508/228–1908* ⊕*www.nantucketlooms.com*) stocks luscious woven-on-the-premises textiles and chunky Susan Lister Locke jewelry, among other adornments for self and home.

DEPARTMENT STORES

Marine Home Center (✉*Lower Orange St.* ☎*508/228–0900* ⊕*www.marinehomecenter.com*) carries everything you could possibly need, from major appliances to baby clothes. Prices are unfortunately a bit inflated from mainland norms.

MARKETS

Annye's Whole Foods (✉*14 Amelia Dr.* ☎*508/228–4554* ⊕*www.annyeswholefoods.com*) has organic staples, including fresh produce and prepared meals to go.

★ **Bartlett's Ocean View Farm** (✉*Bartlett Farm Rd.* ☎*508/228–9403*) encompasses 100 acres overseen by eighth-generation Bartletts. Healthy, tasty prepared foods—within a mini-supermarket—add incentive to visit. If you're not up for the trek, a produce truck is parked on Main Street through the summer.

Sconset Market (✉*4 Main St.* ☎*508/228–9915*), though strictly seasonal, is well stocked with basics and gourmet comestibles alike.

GIFT SHOPS

Forget the fishing nets and buoys: Karen Fisher's **Coastal** (✉*12 Oak St.* ☎*508/228–4662*) redefines seaside decor with beautifully spare antique and contemporary pieces.

Diane Johnston (✉*35 Centre St.* ☎*508/228–4688*) blends select clothing (hand-knit sweaters, needlepoint slippers) with antique quilts, lush rugs (from kilims to contemporary creations), and whatever else strikes the owner's fancy; the mix is magical.

The **English Trunk Show Company** (✉*8 Washington St.* ☎*508/228–4199* ⊕*www.englishtrunkshowco.com*) assembles everything for the Anglophile, from tableware and linens to gardening tools; much of the stock is antique.

In addition to fresh blooms, **Flowers on Chestnut** (✉*1 Chestnut St.* ☎*508/228–6007* ⊕*www.flowersonchestnut.com*) carries appealing gifts, including books, baby presents, lamps, and picture frames.

Leslie Linsley Nantucket (✉*0 India St.* ☎*508/325–4900* ⊕*www.leslielinsley.com*), the project of a widely published crafts aficionado, carries supplies, tasteful souvenirs, and other decorative touches.

The **Lion's Paw** (✉0 Main St. ☎508/228–3837) is full of the sort of furnishings Nantucketers favor—fancy cottage-style.

An outreach program of the Nantucket Historical Association, the **Museum Shop** (✉11 Broad St., next to the Whaling Museum ☎508/228–5785 ⊕www.nha.org) sells island-related books, reproduction furniture and accessories, and toys.

Vanessa @ Seven Seas (✉46 Centre St. ☎508/228–8010 ⊕www.vanessanoel.com) gathers everything from handbags and jewelry to antique maps and furniture.

JEWELRY

Diana Kim England, Goldsmiths (✉56 Main St. ☎508/228–3766 or 800/343–1468 ⊕www.dianakimengland.com) has created an elegant contemporary line featuring unusual gems such as tourmaline, chalcedony, and tanzanite.

The **Golden Basket** (✉44 Main St. ☎508/228–4344 or 800/626–2758 ⊕www.thegoldenbasket.com) was founded in 1977 by designer Glenaan M. Elliott, who fashioned the first miniature lightship basket. Other popular motifs include starfish and shells.

Jola Jewelry Designs (✉29 Centre St. ☎508/325–6999) is a jewel box—the tiny, lovely atelier of Polish-born goldsmith Jolanta Gutnik, who creates "passionate statements" using unusual stones and rare pearls.

Trianon (✉50 Main St. ☎508/325–5806) carries contemporary work—including some pieces incorporating Nantucket shells and sand—as well as the mostly nature-motif Seaman Schepps line, established in 1904.

PHARMACIES

Congdon's (✉47 Main St. ☎508/228–0020) is an 1860 drugstore with much of its original woodwork intact.

Nantucket Pharmacy (✉45 Main St. ☎508/228–0180) looks lifted from the '50s.

TOYS

Carrying plenty of its namesake items in various sizes and shapes, the **Toy Boat** (✉41 Straight Wharf ☎508/228–4552 ⊕www.thetoyboat.com) also sells other high-quality toys for youngsters, including Nantucket mermaids, and children's books based on local themes (look for Joan Aiken's classic *Nightbirds on Nantucket*).

SIASCONSET & WAUWINET

★ *7 mi east of Nantucket Town.*

Siasconset began as a community of cod and halibut fishermen and shore whalers in the 17th century. But even then it was already becoming a summer resort: people from Nantucket Town would come here to escape the smell of whale oil burning in the refineries. In 1884 the Nantucket Railroad was extended to Sconset (as it's known locally), bringing more off-islanders. The writers and artists who came from Boston in the 1890s were soon followed by Broadway actors on holiday during the theaters' summer hiatus. Attracted by the village's beauty, remoteness, sandy ocean beach, and cheap lodgings—converted one-room fishing shacks, and cottages built to look like them—they spread the word, and before long Sconset became a thriving actors' colony.

Today a charming village of pretty streets with tiny rose-covered cottages and driveways of crushed white shells, Sconset is almost entirely a summer community (about 150 families live here through the winter), served by a post office, a general store, and two restaurants, as well as a unique liquor store–cum–informal lending library. Sconset makes a lovely day trip from Nantucket Town—try it on bike or shuttle bus, stopping to take a stroll in the village and continuing on to nearby beaches, bogs, and conservation areas.

Numbers in the text correspond to numbers in the margin and on the Siasconset, Polpis & Wauwinet map.

WHAT TO SEE

❶ **Altar Rock.** Altar Rock Road, a dirt track about 3 mi west of the Milestone Road Rotary on Polpis Road, leads to the island's highest point, Altar Rock, from which the view is spectacular. The hill overlooks open moor and bog land—technically called lowland heath—which is very rare in the United States. The entire area is laced with paths leading in every direction. Don't forget to keep track of the trails you travel to find your way back.

Milestone Bog. The 200-plus acres of cranberry bogs, surrounded by conservation land, is always a beautiful spot to visit, particularly in the fall. The sight of bright red berries and the moors' rich autumn colors is not to be missed. ⊠ *Off Milestone Rd., west of Siasconset.*

Siasconset, Polpis & Wauwinet

Altar Rock, **1**

Nantucket Life Saving Museum, **2**

Sankaty Head Lighthouse, **3**

Sesachacha Pond, **4**

Siasconset Casino, **5**

Wauwinet, **6**

Windswept Cranberry Bog, **7**

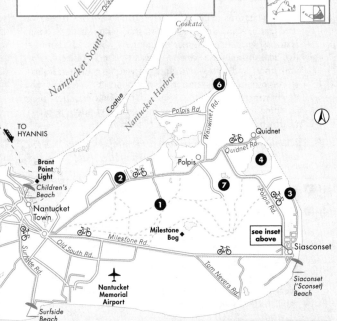

SIASCONSET

Sankaty Head Golf Club

Coffin St.

Burnell St.

The Chanticleer

King St.

New St.

Milestone Rd.

W. Main St.

Post Office Square

Lily St. Cottage Ave.
Evelyn St. Magnolia Ave.
Everett St. Pochick St.

Morey Ln.

Ocean Av.

McKinley Av.

Shell St.

Front St.

Codfish Park Ln.

Broadway

TO SANKATY HEAD LIGHTHOUSE

5

Siasconset ('Sconset) Beach

TO NANTUCKET TOWN

Coskata

Nantucket Sound

Coatue

Nantucket Harbor

Polpis Rd.

Wauwinet Rd.

6

TO HYANNIS

Brant Point Light

Children's Beach

Nantucket Town

Quidnet Rd.

Quidnet

Polpis

4

7

Polpis Rd.

2

3

1

Milestone Rd.

Milestone Bog

Old South Rd.

Surfside Rd.

Nantucket Memorial Airport

Surfside Beach

Tom Nevers Rd.

see inset above

Siasconset

Siasconset ('Sconset) Beach

KEY

🚲 Bike Trail

⛴ Ferry

- - - Unpaved road

0   2 miles

0   2 kilometers

② **Nantucket Life Saving Museum.** Items displayed in this re-creation of the 1874 Life Saving Service station that still stands on Surfside Beach (it's a hostel now), include original rescue equipment and boats, artifacts recovered from the *Andrea Doria* wreck, and photos and accounts of daring rescues. There are several rare pieces: for instance, one of four surviving surfboats and an equally well-preserved original beach cart. ⊠*158 Polpis Rd.* ☎*508/228–1885* ⊕*www. nantucketlifesavingmuseum.com* ⊠*$5* ⊙*Mid-June–mid-Oct., daily 9:30–4.*

③ **Sankaty Head Lighthouse.** The red-and-white-striped beacon overlooking the sea on one side and the Scottish-looking links of the private Sankaty Head Golf Club on the other is one of New England's many endangered lighthouses. It's not open to the public, but you can approach it, via a sea-shell gravel road. ⊠*Baxter Rd.*

NEED A BREAK? For a great picnic in Sconset, stop at **Claudette's** (⊠*Post Office Sq.* ☎*508/257–6622*) for a box lunch to go; or dig right in on the shady patio. It's open mid-May through mid-October.

④ **Sesachacha Pond.** This kettle pond (pronounced *Sah*-kah-cha) off Polpis Road is a good spot for bird-watching. It's circled by a walking path that leads to an Audubon wildlife area and is separated from the ocean by a narrow strand on its east side. It provides a good view of Sankaty Head Lighthouse.

⑤ **Siasconset Casino.** Despite its name, this property dating to 1899 has never been used for gambling—the meaning of "casino" was broader back when it was built—but was instead used from the beginning as a theater venue, particularly during the actors'-colony heyday, and as a gathering place. Some theater can still be seen here, but it's primarily a tennis club and informal cinema. ⊠*New St.* ☎*508/257–6661.*

⑥ **Wauwinet.** Now it's a hamlet of beach houses on the northeastern end of Nantucket. But early European settlers found the neck of sand above it to be the easiest way to get to the ocean for fishing. Instead of rowing around Great Point, fishermen would go to the head of the harbor and haul their dories over the narrow strip of sand and beach grass separating Nantucket Harbor from the ocean. Hence the name for that strip: the haulover.

❼ Windswept Cranberry Bog. Throughout the year, the 205-acre conservation area off Polpis Road is a beautiful tapestry of greens, reds, and golds—and a popular hangout for many bird species. The bog is especially vibrant in mid-October, when the cranberries are harvested. (Although the weekend after Columbus Day has historically been a harvesting holiday, a glut in the market has canceled the harvesting in recent years. Call the Chamber of Commerce for information.) A map is available from the **Nantucket Conservation Foundation** (✉118 Cliff Rd. ☎508/228–2884 ⊕www.nantucketconservation.com).

OFF THE BEATEN PATH ★Fodor's Choice **Coatue–Coskata–Great Point.** A trip to an unpopulated spit of sand, comprising three cooperatively managed wildlife refuges, is a great way to spend a day relaxing or pursuing a favorite activity, such as bird-watching or fishing. Coatue, the strip of sand enclosing Nantucket Harbor, is open for many kinds of recreation—shellfishing (permit required) for bay scallops, soft-shell clams, quahogs, and mussels; surf casting for bluefish and striped bass (spring through fall); picnicking; or just enjoying the crowdless expanse. Coskata's beaches, dunes, salt marshes, and stands of oak and cedar attract marsh hawks, egrets, oystercatchers, terns, herring gulls, plovers, and many other birds, particularly during spring and fall migration. A successful program has brought ospreys here to nest on posts set up in a field by Coskata Pond. You'll want to bring your field glasses.

Because of dangerous currents and riptides and the lack of lifeguards, swimming is strongly discouraged in the refuges, especially within 200 yards of the 70-foot stone tower of **Great Point Light.** Those currents, at the same time, are fascinating to watch at the Great Point tide rip. Seals and fishermen alike benefit from the unique feeding ground that it creates. The lighthouse is a 1986 re-creation of the light destroyed by a storm in 1984. The new light was built to withstand 20-foot waves and winds of up to 240 mph, and it was fitted with eight solar panels to power it.

You may enter the area only on foot or by four-wheel-drive vehicle, for which a **permit** (✉$100–$125 for a year ☎508/228–5646 ⊕www.thetrustees.org) is required. Rental vehicles usually come with permits—double-check with your rental agency. Permits are available at the **gatehouse at Wauwinet** (✉Wauwinet Rd. ☎508/228–0006) 8 AM–6 PM June to mid-October or off-season from a ranger patrolling the property. If you enter on foot, be aware that Great Point is a 5-mi walk from the entrance on soft, deep sand.

WHERE TO STAY & EAT

$$$$ ✕**Topper's.** The Wauwinet—a lavishly restored 19th-cen-
★ tury inn on Nantucket's northeastern shore—is where islanders and visitors alike go to experience utmost luxury. Many take advantage of the complimentary launch, the *Wauwinet Lady* out of Straight Wharf, which frames the journey with a scenic harbor tour. Having traipsed past the croquet lawn, one enters a creamy-white dining room awash with lush linens and glorious flowers. David Daniel's cuisine delivers on the fantasy with a menu of intentional "simplicity"—if that's how you would describe a butter-basted lobster "surf & turf," for instance, in a carrot *yuzu nage* with dim sum of foie gras and Kobe beef (the latter elements entail a surcharge). The price scheme might seem a steal, were it not for portions that tend to tapas scale. But you can always fill up on the luscious brown bread (the sticky, molasses-infused kind so rarely encountered these days), and follow up with an exquisite, if minuscule dessert. ✉*120 Wauwinet Rd., Wauwinet* ☎*508/228–8768* ⊕*www.wauwinet.com* ⏴*Reservations essential* ▭*AE, D, DC, MC, V* ☾*Closed Nov.–Apr.*

$$$–$$$$ ✕**The Chanticleer.** Over the decades, Sconset's landmark res-taurant had grown a bit ossified: it needed Susan Handy and chef Jeff Worster of Black-Eyed Susan's to freshen up the menu and atmosphere alike. It's still elegant—more so, really, without the attendant fussiness. Handy knows how to extend a warm (i.e., non-Gallic) welcome, and Wor-ster has mastered the "brasserie moderne" staples, from steak frites to tarte tatin. The all-French wine cellar is as "deep" as ever, and the porch overlooking the herb garden remains the most coveted perch. ✉*9 New St., Siasconset* ☎*508/257–4499* ⊕*www.thechanticleer.net* ▭*AE, MC, V* ☾*Closed mid-Oct.–early May. No lunch Mon.*

$$$–$$$$ ✕**The Summer House Restaurant.** An integral element of the
★ rose-canopied complex of shingled shacks that epitomizes Sconset, the main dining room is also abloom, with lavish floral displays set against a background of pastel linen and white wicker. Here the cuisine is certainly polished, if on the sedate side; the Beachside Bistro, alongside the pool down below, goes in for splurgy dishes like a $22 Wagyu

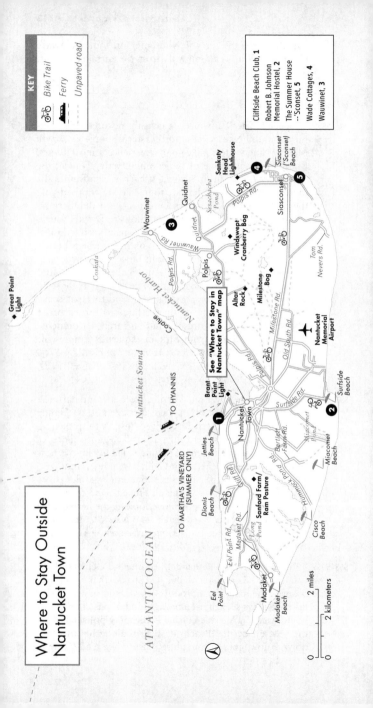

Where to Stay Outside Nantucket Town

KEY

🚲 Bike Trail
⛴ Ferry
---- Unpaved road

Cliffside Beach Club, **1**
Robert B. Johnson
Memorial Hostel, **2**
The Summer House
--'Sconset, **5**
Wade Cottages, **4**
Wauwinet, **3**

ATLANTIC OCEAN

Nantucket Sound

TO HYANNIS

TO MARTHA'S VINEYARD
(SUMMER ONLY)

Great Point
Light

Coskata

Nantucket Harbor

Coatue

Brant Point
Light

Jetties Beach

Dionis Beach

Eel Point

Eel Point Rd.

Madaket Rd.

Madaket

Madaket Beach

Cliff Rd.

Nantucket Town

Long Pond

Sanford Farm/
Ram Pasture

Hummock Pond Rd.

Cisco Beach

Miacomet Beach

Bartlett Farm Rd.

Miacomet Rd.

Surfside Rd.

Surfside Beach

Milestone Rd.

Nantucket Memorial Airport

Old South Rd.

Polpis Rd.

Altar Rock

Milestone Bog

Windswept Cranberry Bog

Polpis

Polpis Rd.

Quidnet

Quidnet

Wauwinet Rd.

Wauwinet

Sesachacha Pond

Tom Nevers Rd.

Sankaty Head Lighthouse

Siasconset
('Sconset)

Siasconset ('Sconset) Beach

See "Where to Stay in
Nantucket Town" map

0 ___ 2 miles
0 ___ 2 kilometers

Kobe beef burger and caviar on demand. It's tempting to play favorites or, while trying to decide, to bounce back and forth. ⊠*17 Ocean Ave., Siasconset* ☎*508/257–9976* ⊕*www.thesummerhouse.com* ⚄*Reservations essential* ▭*MC, V* ⊙*Closed mid-Oct.–mid-May.*

$$–$$$ ✕**Sconset Café.** It looks like a modest lunchroom, with chockablock tables virtually within arm's reach of the open kitchen. But this tiny institution, treasured by summering locals since 1983, puts out wonderful breakfasts, great lunches, and outright astounding dinners. The nightly menus shift every two weeks to take advantage of seasonal bounty. If you have trouble getting in (it's not exactly undiscovered, and reservations are accepted for the 6 PM seating only), you can always order out and feast on the beach. (Call in the shoulder season before you head out to confirm that it's open.) ⊠*Post Office Sq., Siasconset* ☎*508/257–4008* ⊕*www.sconsetcafe.com* ▭*No credit cards* ⚐*BYOB* ⊙*Mid-Oct.–mid-May.*

$$$$ ★ Fodor'sChoice ▦**Wauwinet.** This resplendently updated 1850 resort straddles a "haulover" poised between ocean and bay—which means beaches on both sides. Head out by complimentary van or launch to partake of utmost pampering (the staff-to-guest ratio exceeds one-on-one). Optional activities include sailing, water-taxiing to a private beach along Coatue, and touring the Great Point nature preserve by Land Rover. Of course, it's tempting just to stay put, what with the cushy country-chic rooms (lavished with Pratesi linens) and a splendid restaurant, Topper's. **Pros:** Solicitous staff, dual beaches, peaceful setting. **Cons:** Distance from town, overly chichi, tiny rooms on the third floor. ⊠*120 Wauwinet Rd., Wauwinet* ⚐*Box 2580, Nantucket 02584* ☎*508/228–0145 or 800/426–8718* ▭*508/228–7135* ⊕*www.wauwinet.com* ⟿*25 rooms, 5 cottages* ⚄*In-room: safe, DVD, Wi-Fi. In-hotel: restaurant, room service, bar, tennis courts, spa, beachfront, bicycles, no elevator, concierge, town shuttle, no kids under 12* ▭*AE, DC, MC, V* ⊙*Closed Nov.–Apr.* ⚑*BP.*

$$$$ ▦**Wade Cottages.** This complex of guest rooms, apartments, and cottages couldn't be better situated for beach aficionados. The buildings, in the same family since the 1920s, are arranged around a central lawn with a great ocean view, shared by most of the rooms. Furnishings tend to be of the somewhat worn beach-house school, but you'll be too busy—and happy—to waste a moment critiquing.

Pros: Old-style Nantucket, dazzling views, compatible with families. **Cons:** Shabby-chic (a plus in some eyes), not romantically inclined, very family-centric. ⊠*Shell St., Box 211, Siasconset 02564* ☎*508/257–6308* 🖷*508/257–4602* ⊕*www.wadecottages.com* ⌁*8 rooms, 4 with bath; 6 apartments; 3 cottages* ⌂*In-hotel: laundry facilities* ⊟*AE, MC, V* ⊗*Closed mid-Oct.–late May* ⍭*CP.*

$$$–$$$$ ⛫ **The Summer House–'Sconset.** Perched on a bluff overlooking Sconset Beach, this cluster of rose-covered cottages—cobbled from salvage in the 1840s—epitomizes Nantucket's enduring allure. The rooms, though small, are intensely romantic, with lace coverlets and pale pine armoires; most have marble baths with whirlpool tubs, and one has a fireplace. Contemplative sorts can claim an Adirondack chair on the lawn. Others may want to race down to the beach, perhaps enjoying lunch beside the heated pool en route. **Pros:** Romantic setting, beautiful on-site restaurants, pool right on the beach. **Cons:** 20 minutes from town, cottages snug, sounds of restaurant revelry. ⊠*17 Ocean Ave., Siasconset 02564* ☎*508/257–4577* 🖷*508/257–4590* ⊕*www. thesummerhouse.com* ⌁*10 rooms* ⌂*In-hotel: 2 restaurants, bars, pool, no elevator* ⊟*AE, MC, V* ⊗*Closed Nov.–late Apr.* ⍭*CP.*

NIGHTLIFE

BARS

The bar at the **Summer House Restaurant** (⊠*17 Ocean Ave.* ☎*508/257–9976*) is hands down the most romantic spot for a cocktail on-island. A pianist entertains devotees, who cluster around the bar or claim comfortable armchairs.

FILM

The **Siasconset Casino** (⊠*New St., Siasconset* ☎*508/257–6661*) shows first-run movies, auditorium-style, Tuesday, Thursday, and Sunday evenings at 8:30, June through Labor Day. Old hands know to bring pillows.

SPORTS & THE OUTDOORS

BEACHES

Siasconset Beach (⊠*End of Milestone Rd.*) has a lifeguard (the surf runs moderate to heavy) but no facilities; restaurants are a short walk away.

TENNIS
Siasconset Casino (✉*10 New St., Siasconset* ☎*508/257–6585*) is a private club with 11 outdoor courts. Some non-member court time is available; call ahead for information.

NANTUCKET ESSENTIALS

To research prices, get advice from other travelers, and book travel arrangements, visit www.fodors.com.

TRANSPORTATION

BY BOAT & FERRY
See ⇨Boat & Ferry Travel in Essentials in the back of this book. Nantucket has first-class marina and mooring amenities for yacht and boat owners.

Marina Contacts Madaket Marine (☎*508/228–1163* ⊕*www.madaketmarine.com*). **Nantucket Boat Basin** (☎*508/325–1333 or 800/626–2628* 🖶*508/228–8941* ⊕*www.nantucketboatbasin.com*). **Nantucket Moorings** (☎*508/228–4472* 🖶*508/228–7441* ⊕*www.nantucketmoorings.com*).

BY BUS
The Nantucket Regional Transit Authority (NRTA) runs shuttle buses in town and to Madaket, mid-island areas (including the airport and Surfside Beach), and Sconset. Service is available May to late September. Fares are $1 to $2, depending on the route. Each of the routes has its own schedule (you can pick one up at the chamber of commerce, Visitor Services, the NRTA office, or at most any bus stop); service generally begins at 7 AM and ends at 11:30 PM. All shuttle buses have bike racks and lifts. Fares are $1 in town or mid-island; $2 to Madaket, Surfside, the airport, or Sconset; seniors pay half fare and children under seven—and pets—ride free. Passes run $7 for 1 day, $12 for 3, $20 for 7, $50 for 30, and $80 for the season, with attendant discounts available. Passes for up to a week can be bought on board; longer-term passes can be purchased at the NRTA office.

Bus Information Nantucket Regional Transit Authority (NRTA) (✉*22 Federal St., Nantucket02554* ☎*508/228–7025* ⊕*www.shuttlenantucket.com*).

BY CAR

The chamber of commerce strongly discourages bringing cars to Nantucket. They're really not needed—unless you're planning to stay a week or more, and renting far out of town, off the bus routes. The town itself is entirely walkable, and keeping a car there is not practical; the longest you're allowed to park is ½ to 1½ hours at a time ("summer specials"—supplemental police personnel—are right on it, keeping tabs by PDA). The entire island is easily accessible by bike, taxi, or public transportation.

If you're still determined to rent a car while on Nantucket, book early—and expect to spend at least $109 a day during high season.

Nantucket Agencies Nantucket Island Rent A Car (⊠ *Nantucket Memorial Airport* ☎ *508/228–9989 or 800/508–9972* ⊕ *www.nantucketislandrentacar.com*).

Nantucket Windmill Auto Rental (⊠ *Nantucket Memorial Airport* ☎ *508/228–1227 or 800/228–1227* ⊕ *www.nantucketautorental.com*).

Young's Bicycle Shop (⊠ *6 Broad St.* ☎ *508/228–1151* 🖷 *508/228–3038* ⊕ *www.youngsbicycleshop.com*).

BY TAXI

Taxis usually wait outside the airport, on Steamboat Wharf, and at the foot of Main Street. Rates are flat fees, based on one person with two bags before 1 AM: $6 within town (1½-mi radius), and, from town, $11 to the airport, $17 to Sconset, and $23 to Wauwinet.

Nantucket Taxi Companies A1 Taxi (☎ *508/325–3330*). **All Point Taxi** (☎ *508/228–5779*). **Val's Cab Service** (☎ *508/228–9410*).

CONTACTS & RESOURCES

EMERGENCIES

There's no 24-hour pharmacy on the island. Call the **Nantucket Cottage Hospital** (⊠ *57 Prospect St.* ☎ *508/825–8100* ⊕ *www.nantuckethospital.org*), in case of an emergency.

For police, fire department, or emergency medical technicians dial 911.

INTERNET, MAIL & SHIPPING

The main post office is right in the center of town; if lines are daunting, try the mid-island annex on Pleasant Street. There's a UPS Store off Surfside Road. You can find a FedEx box (pickup is early: 4 PM) at the Steamship office, and another near the airport. The Atheneum offers free Internet access, including Wi-Fi, and the Even Keel doubles as an Internet café.

Internet Access **Even Keel Café** (⌧*40 Main St.* ☎*508/228–1979* ⊕*www.evenkeelcafe.com*). **Nantucket Atheneum** (⌧*1 India St.* ☎*508/228–1110* ⊕*www.nantucketatheneum.org*).

Mail & Shipping **FedEx** (☎*800/238–5355* ⊕*www.fedex.com*). **The UPS Store** (⌧*2 Windy Way* ☎*508/325–8884*). **U.S. Post Office** (⌧*5 Federal St.* ☎*508/228–4477* ⌧*Annex, 144 Pleasant St.* ☎*508/325–5682 or 800/274–8777*).

MONEY MATTERS

ATMS

ATMs are ubiquitous—you can find them at the airport, ferry terminals, and supermarkets. The following are accessible 24 hours.

24-Hour ATM Locations **Fleet Bank** (⌧*Pacific National, 15 Sparks Ave.* ⌧*Pacific Club, Main and S. Water Sts.*). **Nantucket Bank** (⌧*2 Orange St.* ⌧*104 Pleasant St.* ⌧*1 Amelia Dr.*).

TOUR OPTIONS

ADVENTURE TOURS

No matter what you want to do around Nantucket, be it kayaking, mountain biking, climbing, birding, hiking, snorkeling, or scuba diving, Eco Guides: Strong Wings can customize a small-group tour.

Tour Operator **Eco Guides: Strong Wings** (⌧*9 Nobadeer Farm Rd.* ☎*508/228–1769* ⊕*www.strongwings.org*).

NATURE TOURS

Great Point Natural History Tours, led by knowledge-able naturalists, are sponsored by the Trustees of Reservations. Group tours are about three hours long, and you see the sights via Jeep. The Maria Mitchell Association leads marine-ecology field trips and nature and bird walks weekly in the spring and early summer months and three times a week from June through Labor Day.

Tour Operators **Great Point Natural History Tours** (☎*508/228–6799* ⊕*www.thetrustees.org*). **Maria Mitchell Association** (*MMA* ⌧*4 Vestal St.* ☎*508/228–9198* ⊕*www.mmo.org*).

VAN TOURS

Sixth-generation Nantucketer Gail Johnson of Gail's Tours narrates a lively 1½-hour van tour of the island's high-lights: the moors, the cranberry bogs, and the lighthouses, in addition to Nantucket Town. The 13-passenger cran-berry-red van heads out at 10, 1, and 3 in season; pickups at in-town inns can be arranged.

Contacts **Gail's Tours** (☎508/257–6557 ⊕www.nantucket. net/tours/gails).

WALKING TOURS

Walking tours generally cover the major sights within the historic district. The Nantucket Historical Association's 90-minute Historic Nantucket Walking Tours (offered several times a day in season) provide an overview of the island's history and encompass such sites as Petticoat Row, upper Main Street, and the wharfs, churches, and library. Twelfth-generation islander Dirk Gardiner Roggeveen leads 90- to 120-minute tours in the afternoons (except Sunday); children are welcome to tag along for free.

The self-guided Black Heritage Trail tour covers nine sites in and around town, including the African Meeting House, the Whaling Museum, and the Atheneum. The trail guide is free from the Friends of the African Meeting House on Nantucket, which also leads a "Walk the Black Heritage Trail" tour by appointment in season.

Tour Operators **Friends of the African Meeting House on Nantucket** (✉York and Pleasant Sts. ☎508/228–9833 ⊕www. afroammuseum.org/afmnantucket.htm). **Historic Nantucket Walk-ing Tours** (✉Whaling Museum, 15 Broad St. ☎508/325–1894 ⊕www.nha.org).

VISITOR INFORMATION

You can stop by the Nantucket Visitor Services and Infor-mation Bureau, open weekdays 9–6 year-round, to get your bearings, as well as maps, brochures, island infor-mation, and advice. The bureau is also a great resource if you need a room at the last minute—they track cancella-tions daily and might be able to refer you to an inn with newly available rooms. It's in the center of town, within a couple of blocks of both ferry landings, each of which also has a NVS booth in season. The chamber of commerce is another great place to get maps and island information; it's open weekdays 9–5, year-round.

Tourist Information Nantucket Visitor Services and Information Bureau (✉ *25 Federal St., 02554* ☎ *508/228–0925* ⊕ *www.nantucket. net*). **Nantucket Chamber of Commerce** (✉ *48 Main St., upstairs* ☎ *508/228–1700* ⊕ *www.nantucketchamber.org*).

2

Martha's Vineyard & Nantucket Essentials

PLANNING TOOLS, EXPERT INSIGHT, GREAT CONTACTS

There are planners and there are those who, excuse the pun, fly by the seat of their pants. We happily place ourselves among the planners. Our writers and editors try to anticipate all the issues you may face before and during any journey, and then they do their research. This section is the product of their efforts. Use it to get excited about your trip to Martha's Vineyard & Nantucket, to inform your travel planning, or to guide you on the road should the seat of your pants start to feel threadbare.

GETTING STARTED

We're really proud of our Web site: Fodors.com is a great place to begin any journey. Scan Travel Wire for suggested itineraries, travel deals, restaurant and hotel openings, and other up-to-the-minute info. Check out Booking to research prices and book plane tickets, hotel rooms, rental cars, and vacation packages. Head to Talk for on-the-ground pointers from travelers who frequent our message boards. You can also link to loads of other travel-related resources.

▌ RESOURCES

ONLINE TRAVEL TOOLS
For general information, visit the Martha's Vineyard Chamber of Commerce online at ⊕*www.mvy. com* and the Nantucket Chamber of Commerce online at ⊕*www. nantucketchamber.org.* Other resources include the Cape Cod Information Center (⊕*www.all-capecod.com*) and Cape Cod Online (⊕*www.capecodonline. com*), which can provide limited information on the islands.

Transportation Smart Traveler (⊕www.smartraveler.com) provides real-time updates on traffic conditions on the approaches to Cape Cod (just click on the link for Boston, and you'll find a further link to Cape Cod), which can be handy in planning your trips out to the islands. You can look at live Web cam pictures of the Bourne and Saga-

---

WORD OF MOUTH

After your trip, be sure to rate the places you visited and share your experiences and travel tips with us and other Fodorites in Travel Ratings and Talk on www. fodors.com.

---

more bridges at the Cape Cod USA site (⊕www.capecodlivecam.com), as well as Web cam pictures of the harbor in Hyannis, from which ferries travel to the islands.

For Martha's Vineyard bus schedules, check with the Martha's Vineyard Transit Authority (⊕www.vineyard-transit.com); for the same on Nantucket, go to the Nantucket Regional Transit Authority site (⊕www.shut-tlenantucket.com).

Island ferry information and schedules are available online from the Steamship Authority (⊕www.island-ferry.com) and from Hy-Line (⊕www. hy-linecruises.com). For information on the Boston to Provincetown ferries, visit the site of Bay State Cruise Company (⊕www.baystatecruisecom-pany.com) or Boston Harbor Cruises (⊕www.bostonharborcruises.com).

Disability Access The Directory of Accessible Facilities lists accessible recreational facilities in Massachusetts (⊕www.mass.gov/dcr/univer-sal_access/index.htm).

VISITOR INFORMATION

Before you go, contact the state's office of tourism and the islands' chambers of commerce for general information, seasonal events, and brochures. For specific information on state forests and parks, the area's farmers' markets and fairs, or wildlife, contact the special-interest government offices below. You can also check Web sites on the Internet (⇨ *Web Sites*). When you arrive, stop by the local chamber of commerce for additional information—each chamber is stocked with local brochures and produces a comprehensive annual guidebook on each town.

General Islands Contacts

Martha's Vineyard Chamber of Commerce (⊠ *Beach Rd., Box 1698, Vineyard Haven 02568* ☎ *508/693–4486 or 800/505–4815* ⊕ *www.mvy. com*). **Nantucket Chamber of Commerce** (⊠ *48 Main St., 2nd fl., 02554* ☎ *508/228–1700* ⊕ *www.nantucket chamber.org*).

Massachusetts Contacts **Department of Agricultural Resources** (☎ *617/626–1700* ⊕ *www.state. ma.us/dfa*). **Department of Conservation and Recreation** (☎ *617/626–1250* ⊕ *www.mass. gov/dcr*). **Department of Fish and Game** (☎ *508/626–1500* ⊕ *www. state.ma.us/dfwele*).

Massachusetts Office of Travel & Tourism (⊠ *10 Park Plaza, Suite 4510, Boston 02116* ☎ *800/227–6277, 800/447–6277 brochures* ⊕ *www.massvacation.com*).

▌ THINGS TO CONSIDER

GEAR

Only a few restaurants on the islands require a jacket and tie; the area prides itself on informality. Do **pack a sweater or jacket, even in summer,** for nights can be cool. *For suggested clothing to minimize bites from deer ticks and to prevent Lyme disease, see* ⇨ *Health*. Perhaps most important of all, **don't forget a swimsuit** (or two).

TRIP INSURANCE

What kind of coverage do you honestly need? Do you even need trip insurance at all? Take a deep breath and read on.

We believe that comprehensive trip insurance is especially valuable if you're booking a very expensive or complicated trip or if you're booking far in advance. Who knows what could happen six months down the road? But whether you get insurance has more to do with how comfortable you are assuming all that risk yourself.

Comprehensive travel policies typically cover trip-cancellation and interruption, letting you cancel or cut your trip short because of a personal emergency, illness, or, in some cases, acts of terrorism in your destination. Such policies also cover evacuation and medical care. Some also cover you for trip delays because of bad weather or mechanical problems as well as for lost or delayed baggage. Another type of coverage to look for is financial default—that is, when your

PACKING 101

We realize that packing is a matter of style, but there's a lot to be said for traveling light. These tips help fight the battle of the bulging bag.

Make a list. In a recent Fodor's survey, 29% of respondents said they make lists (and often pack) a week before a trip. You can use your list to pack and to repack at the end of your trip. It can also serve as record of the contents of your suitcase—in case it disappears in transit.

Edit your wardrobe. Plan to wear everything twice (better yet, thrice) and to do laundry along the way. Stick to one basic look, and build around one or two neutrals and an accent (e.g., black, white, and olive green). Women can freshen looks by changing scarves or jewelry.

Be practical. Put comfortable shoes atop your list. Pack lightweight, wrinkle-resistant, compact, washable items. Stack and roll clothes, so they'll wrinkle less. Unless you're on a guided tour or a cruise, select luggage you can readily carry. Porters, like good butlers, are hard to find these days.

Check weight and size limitations. In the United States you may be charged extra for checked bags weighing more than 50 pounds. Carry-on size limitations can be stringent, too, and this is particularly true of small planes to Nantucket and Martha's Vineyard.

Check carry-on restrictions. Research restrictions with the TSA. Consider packing all but essentials (travel documents, prescription meds, wallet) in checked luggage. This leads to a "pack only what you can afford to lose" approach that might help you streamline.

Rethink valuables. Although comprehensive travel policies may cover luggage, the liability limit is often a pittance. Your homeowner's policy may cover you sufficiently when you travel—or not.

Lock it up. If you must pack valuables, use TSA-approved locks (about $10) that can be unlocked by all U.S. security personnel.

Tag it. Always tag your luggage; use your business address if you don't want people to know your home address. Put the same information (and a copy of your itinerary) inside your luggage, too.

Report problems immediately. If your bags—or things in them—are damaged or go astray, file a written claim with your airline *before leaving the airport*. If the airline is at fault, it may give you money for essentials until your luggage arrives. Most lost bags are found within 48 hours, so alert the airline to your whereabouts for two or three days. If your bag was opened for security reasons in the States and something is missing, file a claim with the TSA.

TRIP INSURANCE RESOURCES		
Insurance Comparison Sites		
Insure My Trip.com	800/487-4722	www.insuremytrip.com
Square Mouth.com	800/240-0369	www.quotetravelinsurance.com
Comprehensive Travel Insurers		
Access America	866/807-3982	www.accessamerica.com
CSA Travel Protection	800/873-9855	www.csatravelprotection.com
HTH Worldwide	610/254-8700 or 888/243-2358	www.hthworldwide.com
Travelex Insurance	888/457-4602	www.travelex-insurance.com
Travel Guard International	715/345-0505 or 800/826-4919	www.travelguard.com
Travel Insured International	800/243-3174	www.travelinsured.com
Medical-Only Insurers		
INTERNATIONAL MEDICAL GROUP	800/628-4664	WWW.IMGLOBAL.COM
International SOS	215/942-8000 or 713/521-7611	www.internationalsos.com
Wallach & Company	800/237-6615 or 504/687-3166	www.wallach.com

trip is disrupted because a tour operator, airline, or cruise line goes out of business. Generally you must buy this when you book your trip or shortly thereafter, and it's available to you only if your operator isn't on a list of excluded companies.

Expect comprehensive travel insurance policies to cost about 4% to 8% of the total price of your trip (it's more like 8%–12% if you're over age 70). A medical-only policy may be cheaper than a comprehensive policy. Always read the fine print of your policy to make sure that you are covered for the risks that are of most concern to you. Compare several policies to make sure you're getting the best price and range of coverage available.

BOOKING YOUR TRIP

Unless your cousin is a travel agent, you're probably among the millions of people who make most of their travel arrangements online.

But have you ever wondered just what the differences are between an online travel agent (a Web site through which you make reservations instead of going directly to the airline, hotel, or car-rental company), a discounter (a firm that does a high volume of business with a hotel chain or airline and accordingly gets good prices), a wholesaler (one that makes cheap reservations in bulk and then re-sells them to people like you), and an aggregator (one that compares all the offerings so you don't have to)?

Is it truly better to book directly on an airline or hotel Web site? And when does a real live travel agent come in handy?

▋ ONLINE

You really have to shop around. A travel wholesaler such as Hotels.com or HotelClub.net can be a source of good rates, as can discounters such as Hotwire or Priceline, particularly if you can bid for your hotel room or airfare. Indeed, such sites sometimes have deals that are unavailable elsewhere. They do, however, tend to work only with hotel chains (which makes them just plain useless for getting hotel reservations outside of major cities) or big airlines (so that often leaves out upstarts like jetBlue and some foreign carriers).

Also, with discounters and wholesalers you must generally prepay, and everything is non-refundable. And before you fork over the dough, be sure to check the terms and conditions, so you know what a given company will do for you if there's a problem and what you'll have to deal with on your own.

■ TIP → **To be absolutely sure everything was processed correctly, confirm reservations made through online travel agents, discounters, and wholesalers directly with your hotel before leaving home.**

Booking engines like Expedia, Travelocity, and Orbitz are actually travel agents, albeit high-volume, online ones. And airline travel packagers like American Airlines Vacations and Virgin Vacations—well, they're travel agents, too. But they may still not work with all the world's hotels.

An aggregator site will search many sites and pull the best prices for airfares, hotels, and rental cars from them. Most aggregators compare the major travel-booking sites such as Expedia, Travelocity, and Orbitz; some also look at airline Web sites, though rarely the sites of smaller budget airlines. Some aggregators also compare other travel products, including complex packages—a good thing, as you can sometimes get the best overall deal by booking an air-and-hotel package.

▌ WITH A TRAVEL AGENT

If you use an agent—brick-and-mortar or virtual—you'll pay a fee for the service. And know that the service you get from some online agents isn't comprehensive. For example Expedia and Travelocity don't search for prices on budget airlines like jetBlue, Southwest, or small foreign carriers. That said, some agents (online or not) *do* have access to fares that are difficult to find otherwise, and the savings can more than make up for any surcharge.

A knowledgeable brick-and-mortar travel agent can be a godsend if you're booking a cruise, a package trip that's not available to you directly, an air pass, or a complicated itinerary including several overseas flights. What's more, travel agents who specialize in a destination may have exclusive access to certain deals and insider information on things such as charter flights. Agents who specialize in types of travelers (senior citizens, gays and lesbians, naturists) or types of trips (cruises, luxury travel, safaris) can also be invaluable.

■TIP→ **Remember that Expedia, Travelocity, and Orbitz are travel agents, not just booking engines. To resolve any problems with a reservation made through these companies, contact them first.**

Agent Resources **American Society of Travel Agents** (☎ *703/739–2782* ⊕ *www.travelsense.org*).

▌ ACCOMMODATIONS

Accommodations on islands range from campsites to bed-and-breakfasts to luxurious self-contained resorts offering all kinds of sporting facilities, restaurants, entertainment, services (including business services and children's programs), and all the assistance you'll ever need in making vacation arrangements.

Because real-estate prices have skyrocketed here in the past few years, a few bed-and-breakfasts have been sold and converted back to private homes. The effect is that the islands have fewer lodging options than they have had in years, and lodging rates have risen a bit, too. That said, there are still plenty of overnight options.

Single-night lodgings for those just seeking a night on mainland Cape Cod before venturing out to the islands can be found at countless tacky but cheap little roadside motels, as well as at others that are spotless and cheery yet still inexpensive, or at chain hotels at all price levels; these places often have a pool, TVs, or other amenities to keep children entertained in the evening. Bear in mind that many Cape

Online Booking Resources

AGGREGATORS		
Kayak	www.kayak.com	also looks at cruises and vacation packages.
Mobissimo	www.mobissimo.com	
Qixo	www.qixo.com	also compares cruises, vacation packages, and even travel insurance.
Sidestep	www.sidestep.com	also compares vacation packages and lists travel deals.
Travelgrove	www.travelgrove.com	also compares cruises and packages.
BOOKING ENGINES		
Cheap Tickets	www.cheaptickets.com	a discounter.
Expedia	www.expedia.com	a large online agency that charges a booking fee for airline tickets.
Hotwire	www.hotwire.com	a discounter.
lastminute.com	www.lastminute.com	specializes in last-minute travel. The main site is for the U.K., but it has a link to a U.S. site.
Luxury Link	www.luxurylink.com	has auctions (surprisingly good deals) as well as offers on the high-end side of travel.
Onetravel.com	www.onetravel.com	a discounter for hotels, car rentals, airfares, and packages.
Orbitz	www.orbitz.com	charges a booking fee for airline tickets, but gives a clear breakdown of fees and taxes before you book.
Priceline.com	www.priceline.	a discounter that also allows
Travel.com	www.travel.com	allows you to compare its rates
Travelocity	www.travelocity.com	charges a booking fee for airline tickets, but promises good problem resolution.
ONLINE ACCOMMODATIONS		
Hotelbook.com	www.hotelbook.com	focuses on independent hotels worldwide.
Hotel Club	www.hotelclub.net	good for major cities worldwide.

accommodations, even simple motels, have two-, three-, and even four-night minimum stays on weekends in high season, generally from around Memorial Day through Labor Day. It's still worth checking with a property to see if you can stay for fewer days, especially if you're planning to come out for a last-minute visit, but be warned that finding a single-night accommodation on a June, July, or August weekend can prove extremely challenging.

Because of extremely high demand for accommodations on the islands, it's best to reserve especially well in advance, especially from June through early September. If you're looking to visit during the summer months or over a popular weekend, such as the Nantucket Daffodil Festival or Christmas Stroll, it's not a bad idea to book a full year in advance. Most inns on the islands require prepayment or nonrefundable deposits as well as three-night (or more) minimums in summer. And rates can be very high, averaging $250 a night or more on Nantucket and only slightly less on Martha's Vineyard.

Families may want to **consider condominiums, cottages, and efficiencies,** which offer more space; living areas; kitchens; and sometimes laundry facilities or children's play areas. Especially as single-night lodging options on the islands diminish in number, this is an increasingly popular option, although many condo and cottage rentals have one-week minimum stays, especially in summer.

The lodgings we list are the cream of the crop in each price category. We always list the facilities that are available—but we don't specify whether they cost extra: when pricing accommodations, always ask what's included and what costs extra. Properties indicated by a ×⊡ are lodging establishments whose restaurant warrants a special trip even if you're not staying there.

Most hotels and other lodgings require you to give your credit-card details before they will confirm your reservation. If you don't feel comfortable e-mailing this information, ask if you can fax it (some places even prefer faxes). However you book, get confirmation in writing and have a copy of it handy when you check in.

Be sure you understand the hotel's cancellation policy. Some places allow you to cancel without any kind of penalty—even if you prepaid to secure a discounted rate—if you cancel at least 24 hours in advance. Others require you to cancel a week in advance or penalize you the cost of one night. Small inns and B&Bs are most likely to require you to cancel far in advance. Most hotels allow children under a certain age to stay in their parents' room at no extra charge, but others charge for them as extra adults; find out the cutoff age for discounts.

Online Booking Resources

CONTACTS		
Forgetaway		www.forgetaway.weather.com
Home Away	512/493–0382	www.homeaway.com
Interhome	954/791–8282 or 800/882–6864	www.interhome.us
Vacation Home Rentals	201/767–9393 or 800/633–3284	www.vhrww.com
Worldwide		
Villas International	415/499–9490 or 800/221–2260	www.villasintl.com

■TIP→Assume that hotels operate on the European Plan (**EP**, no meals) unless we specify that they use the Breakfast Plan (**BP**, with full breakfast), Continental Plan (**CP**, Continental breakfast), Full American Plan (**FAP**, all meals), Modified American Plan (**MAP**, breakfast and dinner) or are all-inclusive (**AI**, all meals and most activities).

CATEGORY	COST
$$$$	over $260
$$$	$200–$260
$$	$140–$200
$	$90–$140
¢	under $90

All prices are for a standard double room in high season, excluding a variable state tax and gratuities. Some inns add a 15% service charge.

APARTMENT & HOUSE RENTALS

Many travelers to the islands rent a house if they're going to stay for a week or longer rather than stay at a B&B or hotel. These houses can save you money; however, some rentals are luxury properties, economical only when your party is large. Many local real-estate agencies deal with rentals, and most specialize in a specific area; see the end of each chapter for information on agents in your area.

If you do decide to rent, be sure to book a property well in advance of your trip, as many properties are rented out to the same families or groups year after year. Rental choices are often more abundant in the smaller, quieter towns, such as Up-Island on Martha's Vineyard.

BED & BREAKFASTS

Bed-and-breakfast inns have long been popular on the islands. Many of them occupy stately old sea captains' homes and other

17th-, 18th-, and 19th-century buildings; others are in newer homes.

In many cases, B&Bs are not appropriate for families—noise travels easily, rooms are often small, and the furnishings are often fragile—so be sure to ask. Many B&Bs do not provide phones or TVs in guest rooms, some are not air-conditioned, and nearly all prohibit smoking indoors (some allow smoking on the grounds).

In summer you should reserve lodgings as far in advance as possible—several months for the most popular inns. Assistance with last-minute reservations is available through the chamber of commerce's Web site (⇨ Web Sites). Off-season, rates are much reduced, and you may find that it's easier to get to know your innkeeper.

Numerous B&B reservation agencies can aid you in choosing an inn.

Reservation Services Bed & Breakfast.com (☎512/322–2710 or 800/462–2632 ⊕www.bedandbreakfast.com) also sends out an online newsletter. **Bed & Breakfast Inns Online** (☎615/868–1946 or 800/215–7365 ⊕www.bbonline.com). **BnB Finder.com** (☎212/432–7693 or 888/547–8226 ⊕www.bnbfinder.com).

Reservation Services on the Islands Martha's Vineyard and Nantucket Reservations (☎508/693–7200 ⊕www.mvreservations.com). **Nantucket Ac-**

commodations (☎508/228–9559 ⊕www.nantucketaccommodation.com). **Nantucket Concierge** (☎508/228–8400 ⊕www.nantucketconcierge.com).

CAMPING

There are a few private and state-park camping areas on Nantucket and Martha's Vineyard. For additional details on camping in specific areas, look for the ⚠ icon in that area's Where to Stay & Eat section.

HOME EXCHANGES

With a direct home exchange you stay in someone else's home while they stay in yours. Some outfits also deal with vacation homes, so you're not actually staying in someone's full-time residence, just their vacant weekend place.

Exchange Clubs Home Exchange.com (☎800/877–8723 ⊕www.homeexchange.com); $59.95 for a 1-year online listing. **HomeLink International** (☎800/638–3841 ⊕www.homelink.org); $90 yearly for Web-only membership; $140 includes Web access and two catalogs. **Intervac U.S.** (☎*800/756–4663* ⊕*www.intervacus.com*); $78.88 for Web-only membership; $126 includes Web access and a catalog.

HOSTELS

Hostels offer bare-bones lodging at low, low prices—often in shared dorm rooms with shared baths—to people of all ages, though the primary market is young travelers, especially students. Most hostels serve breakfast; dinner and/or shared cooking facilities may also be available. In some hostels you aren't allowed to be in your room during the day, and there may be a curfew at night. Nevertheless, hostels provide a sense of community, with public rooms where travelers often gather to share stories. Many hostels are affiliated with Hostelling International (HI), an umbrella group of hostel associations with some 4,000 member properties in more than 60 countries. Other hostels are completely independent and may be nothing more than a really cheap hotel.

Membership in any HI association, open to travelers of all ages, allows you to stay in HI-affiliated hostels at member rates. One-year membership is about $28 for adults. Rates in dorm-style rooms run about $15–$25 per bed per night; private rooms are more, but are still generally well under $100 a night. Members have priority if the hostel is full; they're also eligible for discounts around the world, even on rail and bus travel in some countries.

Martha's Vineyard and Nantucket each have a hostel. In season, when all other rates are jacked up beyond belief, hostels are often the only budget-accommodation option, but you must plan ahead to reserve space. You may luck out on last-minute cancellations, but it would be unwise to rely on them. *See the lodging listings in the appropriate chapters for specifics.*

Information Hostelling International—USA (☎*301/495–1240* ⊕*www.hiusa.org*).

▌ AIRLINE TICKETS

Most domestic airline tickets are electronic; international tickets may be either electronic or paper. With an e-ticket the only thing you receive is an e-mailed receipt citing your itinerary and reservation and ticket numbers.

The greatest advantage of an e-ticket is that if you lose your receipt, you can simply print out another copy or ask the airline to do it for you at check-in. You usually pay a surcharge (up to $50) to get a paper ticket, if you can get one at all.

The sole advantage of a paper ticket is that it may be easier to endorse over to another airline if your flight is canceled and the airline with which you booked can't accommodate you on another flight.

■TIP→ Discount air passes that let you travel economically in a country or region must often be purchased before you leave home. In some cases you can get them only through a travel agent.

▋ RENTAL CARS

When you reserve a car, ask about cancellation penalties, taxes, drop-off charges (if you're planning to pick up the car in one city and leave it in another), and surcharges (for being under or over a certain age, for additional drivers, or for driving across state or country borders or beyond a specific distance from your point of rental). All these things can add substantially to your costs. Request car seats and extras such as GPS when you book.

Rates are sometimes—but not always—better if you book in advance or reserve through a rental agency's Web site. There are other reasons to book ahead, though: for popular destinations, during busy times of the year, or to ensure that you get certain types of cars (vans, SUVs, exotic sports cars).

■TIP→ Make sure that a confirmed reservation guarantees you a car. Agencies sometimes overbook, particularly for busy weekends and holiday periods.

In Massachusetts you must be 21 to rent a car, and rates may be higher if you're under 25. When picking up a car, non-U.S. residents will need a reservation voucher (for prepaid reserva-

tions made in the traveler's home country), a passport, a driver's license, and a travel policy that covers each driver.

Base rates in Boston begin at $25–$40 a day and $170–$250 a week for an economy car with air-conditioning, automatic transmission, and unlimited mileage; rates tend to be slightly lower out of Providence and slightly higher out of Hyannis, but much depends on availability, which changes regularly. Keep in mind that taxes and a variety of surcharges typically add 30% to 40% to your total bill.

You can book car rentals on Martha's Vineyard through the Woods Hole ferry terminal free phone. A handful of local agencies, listed below, have rental desks at the airport. The cost is $100–$150 per day for a sedan. Renting a four-wheel-drive vehicle costs around $160 per day (seasonal prices fluctuate widely).

If you're determined to rent a car while on Nantucket, be sure to book early. Expect to spend about $100 a day during high season.

CAR RENTAL RESOURCES
Automobile Associations U.S.:
American Automobile Association (AAA ☎315/797–5000 ⊕www.aaa.com); most contact with the organization is through state and regional members. **National Automobile Club** (☎650/294–7000 ⊕www.thenac.com); membership is open to California residents only.

Cape Cod Agencies Rent-A-Wreck of Hyannis (☎508/771–9667 or 888/486–1470 ⊕www.rentawreck.com).

Martha's Vineyard Agencies AAA Island (☎508/627–6800 or 800/627–6333 ⊕www.mvautorental.com). **Adventure Rentals** (✉Beach Rd., Vineyard Haven ☎508/693–1959 ⊕www.islandadventuresmv.com).

Nantucket Agencies Affordable Rentals (✉6 S. Beach St. ☎508/228–3501 or 877/235–3500). **Nantucket Island Rent A Car** (✉Nantucket Memorial Airport ☎508/228–9989 or 800/508–9972 ⊕www.nantucketislandrentacar.com). **Nantucket Windmill** (✉Nantucket Memorial Airport ☎508/228–1227 or 800/228–1227 ⊕www.nantucketautorental.com).

Major Agencies Alamo (☎800/462–5266 ⊕www.alamo.com). **Avis** (☎800/331–1212 ⊕www.avis.com). **Budget** (☎800/527–0700 ⊕www.budget.com). **Hertz** (☎800/654–3131 ⊕www.hertz.com). **National Car Rental** (☎800/227–7368 ⊕www.nationalcar.com).

CAR-RENTAL INSURANCE

Everyone who rents a car wonders whether the insurance that the rental companies offer is worth the expense. No one—including us—has a simple answer. It all depends on how much regular insurance you have, how comfortable you are with risk, and whether or not money is an issue.

If you own a car and carry comprehensive car insurance for both collision and liability, your personal auto insurance will probably cover a rental, but read your policy's fine print to be sure. If you don't have auto insurance, then you should probably buy the collision- or loss-damage waiver (CDW or LDW) from the rental company. This eliminates your liability for damage to the car.

Some credit cards offer CDW coverage, but it's usually supplemental to your own insurance and rarely covers SUVs, mini-vans, luxury models, and the like. If your coverage is secondary, you may still be liable for loss-of-use costs from the car-rental company (again, read the fine print). But no credit-card insurance is valid unless you use that card for *all* transactions, from reserving to paying the final bill.

■TIP➔ Diners Club offers primary CDW coverage on all rentals reserved and paid for with the card. This means that Diners Club's company—not your own car insurance—pays in case of an accident. It *doesn't* mean that your car-insurance company won't raise your rates once it discovers you had an accident.

You may also be offered supplemental liability coverage; the car-rental company is required to carry a minimal level of liability coverage insuring all renters, but it's rarely enough to cover claims in a really serious accident if you're at fault. Your own auto-insurance policy will protect you if you own a car; if you don't, you have to decide whether you are willing to take the risk.

U.S. rental companies sell CDWs and LDWs for about $15 to $25 a day; supplemental liability is usually more than $10 a day. The car-rental company may offer you all sorts of other policies, but they're rarely worth the cost. Personal accident insurance, which is basic hospitalization coverage, is an especially egregious rip-off if you already have health insurance.

■TIP➔ **You can decline the insurance from the rental company and purchase it through a third-party provider such as Travel Guard (www.travelguard.com)—$9 per day for $35,000 of coverage. That's sometimes just under half the price of the CDW offered by some car-rental companies.**

▌ VACATION PACKAGES

Packages *are not* guided excursions. Packages combine airfare, accommodations, and perhaps a rental car or other extras (theater tickets, guided excursions, boat trips, reserved entry to popular museums, transit passes), but they let you do your own thing. During busy periods packages may be your only option, as flights and rooms may be sold out otherwise.

Packages will definitely save you time. They can also save you money, particularly in peak sea-

sons, but—and this is a really big "but"—you should price each part of the package separately to be sure. And be aware that prices advertised on Web sites and in newspapers rarely include service charges or taxes, which can up your costs by hundreds of dollars.

■TIP➔ **Some packages and cruises are sold only through travel agents. Don't always assume that you can get the best deal by booking everything yourself.**

Each year consumers are stranded or lose their money when packagers—even large ones with excellent reputations—go out of business. How can you protect yourself?

First, always pay with a credit card; if you have a problem, your credit-card company may help you resolve it. Second, buy trip insurance that covers default. Third, choose a company that belongs to the United States Tour Operators Association, whose members must set aside funds to cover defaults. Finally, choose a company that also participates in the Tour Operator Program of the American Society of Travel Agents (ASTA), which will act as mediator in any disputes.

You can also check on the tour operator's reputation among travelers by posting an inquiry on one of the Fodors.com forums.

Organizations American Society of Travel Agents (*ASTA* ☎ *703/739–2782 or 800/965–2782* ⊕ *www.astanet.com*). **United States**

Tour Operators Association
(*USTOA* ☎*212/599–6599* ⊕*www.
ustoa.com*).

■TIP→ Local tourism boards can
provide information about lesser-
known and small-niche operators
that sell packages to only a few
destinations.

▋ GUIDED TOURS

Guided tours are a good option
when you don't want to do it all
yourself. You travel along with a
group (sometimes large, sometimes small), stay in prebooked
hotels, eat with your fellow travelers (the cost of meals sometimes included in the price of
your tour, sometimes not), and
follow a schedule.

Whenever you book a guided
tour, find out what's included and
what isn't. A "land-only" tour
includes all your travel (by bus,
in most cases) in the destination,
but not necessarily your flights
to and from or even within it.
Also, in most cases prices in tour
brochures don't include fees and
taxes. And remember that you'll
be expected to tip your guide (in
cash) at the end of the tour.

TRANSPORTATION

▌BY AIR

Most long-distance travelers visiting islands head to a major gateway, such as Boston or Providence, RI, and then connect for a shorter flight out to the islands, or even rent a car to explore the greater Cape Cod region or drive to the various terminals with ferries out to the islands. Flying time to Boston or Providence is 1 hour from New York, 2½ hours from Chicago, 6 hours from Los Angeles, and 3½ hours from Dallas.

Boston's Logan Airport is one of the nation's most important domestic and international airports, with direct flights from all over North America and Europe (as well as other continents). Providence's efficient T. F. Green Airport receives few international flights (mostly from Canada) but offers a wide range of direct domestic flights to East Coast and Midwest destinations; it serves the western United States to a lesser extent. Discount carrier Southwest also flies out of Providence, which helps keep fares down.

There are also numerous flights to Nantucket and Martha's Vineyard from Hyannis, Boston, New Bedford, and Providence, and you can fly between Nantucket and Martha's Vineyard as well.

■TIP→If you travel frequently, look into the TSA's Registered Traveler program. The program, which is still being tested in several U.S. airports, is designed to cut down on gridlock at security checkpoints by allowing prescreened travelers to pass quickly through kiosks that scan an iris and/or a fingerprint. How sci-fi is that?

Airlines & Airports Airline and Airport Links.com (⊕ *www.airline andairportlinks.com*) has links to many of the world's airlines and airports.

Airline Security Issues Transportation Security Administration (⊕ *www.tsa.gov*) has answers for almost every question that might come up.

AIRPORTS

The island airports are Martha's Vineyard (MVY) and Nantucket (ACK). The major gateways to the islands as well as to Cape Cod are Boston's Logan International Airport (BOS) and Providence's T. F. Green Airport (PVD). Smaller airports with island service include the Barnstable (HYA) airport in Hyannis, and New Bedford (EWB) on the South Shore of Massachusetts.

Long layovers don't have to be only about sitting around or shopping. These days they can be about burning off vacation calories. Check out www.air-portgyms.com for lists of health clubs that are in or near many U.S. and Canadian airports.

Airport Information **Airline and Airport Links.com** (⊕ *www.airline andairportlinks.com*) has links to many of the world's airlines and airports. Boston: **Logan International Airport** (☎ *617/561–1806 or 800/235–6426* ⊕ *www.massport. com/logan*). Hyannis: **Barnstable Municipal Airport** (☎ *508/775–2020* ⊕ *www.town.barnstable. ma.us*). Martha's Vineyard: **Martha's Vineyard Airport** (☎ *508/693–7022* ⊕ *www.mvyairport.com*). Nantucket: **Nantucket Memorial Airport** (☎ *508/325–5300* ⊕ *www.nan-tucketairport.com*). New Bedford: **New Bedford Regional Airport** (☎ *508/991–6161* ⊕ *www.ci. new-bedford.ma.us*). Providence: **T. F. Green Airport** (☎ *401/737–8222 or 888/268–7222* ⊕ *www. pvdairport.com*).

TRANSFERS BETWEEN AIRPORTS

You can always find plenty of taxis outside the terminals of the island airports when flights arrive, and this is the easiest and fastest way to reach your accommodations.

FLIGHTS

All of the nation's major airlines—as well as many international airlines—serve Boston's Logan Airport, and all major national carriers serve Providence. Hyannis's Barnstable Municipal Airport is serviced by US Airways Express (with service to Boston and NYC's La Guardia), Nantucket Airlines (with service to Nantucket), Island Airlines (with service to Nantucket), and Cape Air (with service to Boston, Providence, Nantucket, and Martha's Vineyard).

Smaller Airlines **Cape Air** (☎ *508/771–6944 or 800/352–0714* ⊕ *www.flycapeair.com*). **Island Airlines** (☎ *508/228–7575 or 800/248–7779* ⊕ *www.islandair.net*). **Nantucket Airlines** (☎ *508/228–6234 or 800/635–8787* ⊕ *www. nantucketairlines.com*). **US Airways Express** (☎ *800/428–4322* ⊕ *www. usair.com*).

▌ BY BOAT & FERRY

Ferries to Martha's Vineyard leave Woods Hole year-round. In summer you can also catch Vineyard ferries in Falmouth and Hyannis. All provide parking lots where you can leave your car overnight ($10–$15 per night). A number of parking lots in Falmouth hold the overflow of cars when the Woods Hole lot is filled, and free shuttle buses take passengers to the ferry, about 15 minutes away. Signs along Route 28 heading south from the Bourne Bridge direct you to open parking lots, as does AM radio station 1610, which you can pick up within 5 mi of Falmouth.

Ferries to Nantucket leave Hyannis year-round. In season, a passenger ferry connects Nantucket with Martha's Vineyard, and a cruise from Hyannis makes a day trip with stops at both islands. From New Bedford you can take a ferry to Martha's Vineyard from mid-May to mid-October.

FERRIES TO MARTHA'S VINEYARD

The Steamship Authority runs the only car ferries, which make the 45-minute trip from Woods Hole to Vineyard Haven year-round and to Oak Bluffs from late May through mid-October. There are several runs per day, but fewer during the off-season. In summer and on autumn weekends, you *must* have a reservation if you want to bring your car (passenger reservations are never necessary). You should **make car reservations as far ahead as possible**; in season the reservations office is open daily 8–5, with extended phone hours in summer and during busy times from 7 AM to 9 PM. You can also make car reservations online at the Steamship Authority's Web site. In season standby car reservations are not available. One-way passenger fare year-round is $7; bicycles are $3. The cost for a car traveling one-way in season (April–October) is $65 (not including passengers); off-season cars cost $40.

The *Island Queen* makes the 35-minute trip from Falmouth Harbor to Oak Bluffs from late May through early October. Ferries run multiple times a day from mid-June through early September, with less frequent (but still daily) service in spring and fall; call for schedules. Round-trip fare is $15, bicycles $6. Only cash and traveler's checks are accepted for payment.

Begun in 2007 the Vineyard Fast Ferry offers high-speed passenger service from North Kingstown, RI (a half hour south of Providence and a half hour northwest of Newport), to Martha's Vineyard. The ride takes 90 minutes, making this a great option for those flying in to T. F. Green Airport, just south of Providence. Service is from late May through early October and costs $46 each way ($5 for bicycles).

Hy-Line offers both high-speed and conventional ferry service from Hyannis. The conventional ferries offer a 95-minute run from Hyannis to Oak Bluffs early May–late October. One-way fare is $18.50; bicycles cost $6. The high-speed runs from late May through late November, takes 55 minutes, and costs $31.50; it costs $6 for bicycles. The parking lot fills up in summer, so **call to reserve a parking space** in high season. From June to mid-September, Hy-Line's Around the Sound cruise makes a one-day round-trip from Hyannis with stops at Nantucket and Martha's Vineyard ($73.50).

The New England Fast Ferry Company makes the hour-long trip by high-speed catamaran from New Bedford to Oak Bluffs and Vineyard Haven from mid-May to mid-October, several times daily. One-way is $29, bicycles $5.

Boat & Ferry Information Hy-Line (⊠*Ocean St. dock* ☎*508/778–2600 or 800/492–8082* ⊕*www.hy-linecruises.com*). *Island Queen* (⊠*Falmouth Harbor* ☎*508/548–4800* ⊕*www.islandqueen.com*). **New**

England Fast Ferry (✉ *State Pier Ferry Terminal* ☎ *866/683–3779* ⊕ *www.nefastferry.com*). **Steamship Authority** (☎ *508/477–8600 information and car reservations, 508/693–9130 on the Vineyard* ⊕ *www.steamshipauthority.com*). **Vineyard Fast Ferry** (✉ *Quonset Point, North Kingstown, RI* ☎ *401/295–4040* ⊕ *www.vineyard fastferry.com*).

FERRIES TO NANTUCKET

The Steamship Authority runs car-and-passenger ferries from Hyannis to Nantucket year-round, a 2¼-hour trip. There's also high-speed passenger ferry service, which takes only an hour, from late March through late December. Note that there are no standby car reservations on ferries to Nantucket. One-way passenger fare is $15, bicycles $6. Cost for a car traveling one-way April through October is $180; November through April, $120. One-way high-speed passenger ferry fare is $29.50, bicycles $6.

Hy-Line's high-end, high-speed *Grey Lady* ferries run between Hyannis and Nantucket year-round in an hour. Such speed has its downside in rough seas—lots of bucking and rolling that some find literally nauseating. Seating ranges from benches on the upper deck to airline-like seats in side rows of the cabin to café-style tables and chairs in the cabin front. Make reservations in advance, particularly during the summer months or for holiday travel. One-way fare is $38, bicycles $6.

Hy-Line's slower ferry makes the roughly two-hour trip from Hyannis between early May and late October. The M/V *Great Point* offers a first-class section ($24.50 one-way) with a private lounge, restrooms, upholstered seats, carpeting, complimentary Continental breakfast or afternoon cheese and crackers, a bar, and a snack bar. Standard one-way fare is $18.50, bicycles $6.

From Harwich Port, the Freedom Cruise Line runs express high-speed 75-minute ferries to Nantucket between late May and early October, allowing you to explore the rose-covered isle without having to brave the crowds of Hyannis (another plus is that for day trips to Nantucket, parking is free; it's $15 nightly, otherwise). Round-trip fare is $57 ($38 one-way), $12 for bikes. Sightseeing and seal cruises are also offered daily.

Boat & Ferry Information **Freedom Cruise Line** (✉ *Saquatucket Harbor, Harwich Port* ☎ *508/432–8999* ⊕ *www.nantucketislandferry. com*). **Hy-Line** (✉ *Ocean St. dock* ☎ *508/778–2600 or 800/492–8082* ⊕ *www.hy-linecruises.com*). **Steamship Authority** (✉ *South St. dock* ☎ *508/477–8600, 508/495–3278 on Nantucket for reservations* ⊕ *www. steamshipauthority.com*).

▌ BY BUS

The big buses of the Martha's Vineyard Transit Authority (VTA) provide regular service to all six towns on the island, with frequent stops in peak season and quite limited service in winter. The fare is $1 per town, including the town of departure. One-day ($6), three-day ($15), and one-week ($25) passes can be purchased on the bus and at Steamship Authority terminals.

The Nantucket Regional Transit Authority (NRTA) runs shuttle buses in town and to Madaket, mid-island areas (including the airport, Sconset, Surfside Beach, and Jetties Beach). Service is available late May to early September. Fares are $1 to $2, depending on the route; passes cost $7 for one day, $12 for three days, and $20 for one week.

Bus Information Martha's Vineyard Transit Authority (*VTA* ☎ *508/693–9940* ⊕ *www.vineyard transit.com*). **Nantucket Regional Transit Authority (NRTA)** (✉ *22 Federal St., Nantucket 02554* ☎ *508/228–7025* ⊕ *www.shuttle nantucket.com*).

BUS TRAVEL TO & FROM THE CAPE COD FERRY TERMINALS
Greyhound serves Boston and Providence from all over the United States; from there you can connect to Greyhound's affiliate, Peter Pan Bus Lines, which serves several towns on Cape Cod, including the ferry terminals at Hyannis and Woods Hole.

Bus Information Greyhound (☎ *800/231–2222* ⊕ *www.grey-hound.com*). **Peter Pan Bus Lines** (☎ *508/548–7588 or 888/751–8800* ⊕ *www.peterpanbus.com*).

▌ BY CAR

To reach island ferry terminals on Cape Cod from Boston (60 mi), take Route I–93 south, then Route 3 south. For Hyannis ferries, cross the Sagamore Bridge, which puts you onto U.S. 6, the Cape's main artery, and follow it to Exit 6, which puts you onto Route 132 south to Hyannis; it's about a 25- to 40-minute drive from the bridge to the Hyannis ferry terminal, depending on traffic, and a 90-minute to two-hour drive from Boston. For Woods Hole ferries, cross the Bourne Bridge and take Route 28 south to Falmouth and Woods Hole; it's about a 20- to 25-minute drive from the bridge, and a 90-minute to two-hour drive from Boston. It's roughly a five- to six-hour drive to reach the ferry terminals by car from New York City.

On summer weekends, when more than 100,000 cars a day cross each bridge, **make every effort to avoid arriving in late afternoon,** especially on holidays. And be sure to give yourself extra time when trying to catch a ferry, especially if you're planning to park your car in one of the lots on the mainland. U.S. 6 and Route 28 are heavily congested eastbound on Friday evening, westbound on Sunday afternoon, and in both directions on Saturday (when rental homes change hands).

Traffic delays often result from congestion at the Sagamore and Bourne bridges, but in 2007 a "flyover" road was built connecting the Sagamore Bridge directly to Route 3, thus greatly reducing the traffic jams that used to result from the much-despised and now-replaced traffic rotary on the mainland side of the bridge. This development has cut travel time onto the Cape by as much as 20 minutes on busy days.

Traffic can be a challenge on the islands, especially in season. Nantucket is small enough that you can easily get around on foot or by public transportation, but on Martha's Vineyard it can be handy to have a car if you really want to see the whole island and travel freely among the different towns. Bringing a car over on the ferry in summer requires reservations far in advance, costs almost double what it does off-season, and necessitates standing in long lines—it's sometimes easier and more economical to rent a car once you're on the island, and then only for the days you plan on exploring. And consider public transportation and taxis if you're making only a few trips to different parts of the island, which has good bus service that can get you to just about every major sight, village, and beach. Where you stay and what you plan on seeing can greatly influence your transportation plans. As soon as you've booked a room, discuss the different options for getting around Martha's Vineyard with your innkeeper or hotel staff.

PARKING
Parking, in general, is a great challenge on the islands from mid-June through early September. Popular and congested downtowns, such as Oak Bluffs, Edgartown, Vineyard Haven, and Nantucket Town, prove especially tough. In general, anytime you can walk, bike, or cab it somewhere, or you're able to travel in one car instead of two or more, do so. Off-season, parking is rarely a problem anywhere on the islands.

RULES OF THE ROAD
In Massachusetts, highway speed limits are 55 mph near urban areas, 60 or 65 mph elsewhere. Speed limits on U.S. 6 on the Cape vary as it changes from four lanes to two lanes. Radar detectors are legal in Massachusetts.

Massachusetts permits a right turn on a red light (*after* a full stop) unless a sign says otherwise. Also, when you approach one of the Cape's numerous rotaries (traffic circles), note that the vehicles already in the rotary have the right of way and that those vehicles entering the rotary must yield. Be careful: some drivers forget (or ignore) this principle.

Massachusetts law requires that drivers **strap children under age five (or under 40 pounds) into approved child-safety seats.** Kids ages 5 to 12 must wear seat belts. Drivers (but not other passengers over age 12) are legally required to wear seat belts, but they can be ticketed for not wearing them only if they're pulled over for some other reason.

ON THE GROUND

∎ BEACHES

In season you must pay to park at public beaches. Parking at "restricted" beaches is available only to residents and to visitors with permits. If you're renting a house, you can usually purchase a weekly beach permit; contact the local chambers of commerce for details. Walkers and bicyclists do not need permits to use restricted beaches. The official season generally begins the last weekend in June and ends on Labor Day. Note that the lots are often open to all early in the morning (before 8) and late in the afternoon (after 4 or 5), even at resident beaches in season.

∎ BICYCLE TRAVEL

Bicycling is very popular on the islands, which have an abundance of excellent bike trails, some of them as busy as the region's roads in summer. Note that Massachusetts law requires children under 13 to wear protective helmets while riding a bicycle, even as a passenger. *For information on trails, maps, and rentals, see listings for specific towns.*

Bike Maps **Rubel Bike Maps** (✉ *Box 401035, Cambridge, MA 02140* ⊕ *www.bikemaps.com*).

∎ BUSINESS HOURS

Hours on Nantucket and Martha's Vineyard can sometimes differ from those elsewhere in New England, as many businesses and attractions are open only seasonally or have limited hours during the quieter months, from mid-fall to mid-spring.

Museum and attraction hours vary widely from place to place and from season to season. Some places are staffed by volunteers and have limited hours (open just a few hours a day several days a week) even in summer, although major museums and attractions are generally open daily in summer. Always check the hours of a place you plan to visit ahead of time.

Banks are usually open weekdays from 9 to 3 and some Saturday mornings. The post office is open from 8 to 5 weekdays and often on Saturday morning. Shops in more heavily settled areas, particularly in indoor and strip malls, typically open at 9 or 10 daily and stay open until anywhere from 6 PM to 10 PM on weekdays and Saturday, and until 5 or 6 on Sunday. Hours vary greatly, so call ahead when in doubt.

On major roads and in some densely populated areas, you'll usually find at least one or two pharmacies and gas stations open

24 hours. Throughout the region, most bars and discos stay open until 1 or 2 AM.

▌DAY TOURS & GUIDES

BOAT TOURS

A couple of boat tours offered on the Cape are worth checking out even if you're out on the islands, as they're offered by companies that have island ferry service and are thus easily reached from the islands. Patriot Boats has two-hour day and sunset cruises from Falmouth Harbor on the 74-foot schooner *Liberté II* in July and August. Another sunset cruise, which operates on Friday and Saturday evenings, passes six lighthouses in the Falmouth area. Fishing charters are also available. Hy-Line runs one-hour narrated boat tours of Hyannis Harbor, including a view of the Kennedy compound. On Sunday, you can embark on a Ben & Jerry's make-your-own-sundae "ice cream float" through Lewis Bay; ticket prices for all tours range between $14 and $15.

Fees & Schedules **Hy-Line** (⊠ *Ocean St. dock, Pier 1, Hyannis* ☎ *508/778–2600 or 800/492–8082* ⊕ *www.hy-linecruises.com*). **Patriot Boats** (⊠ *227 Clinton Ave., Falmouth* ☎ *508/548–2626 or 800/734–0088* ⊕ *www.theliberte.com*).

WALKING TOURS

Liz Villard's Vineyard History Tours leads walking tours of Edgartown's "history, architecture, ghosts, and gossip," including a stop at the Vincent House.

Tours are run from April through December; call for times. Liz and her guides also lead similar tours of Oak Bluffs and Vineyard Haven. Walks last a little over an hour. Sixth-generation Nantucketer Gail Johnson of Gail's Tours narrates a lively 1½-hour van tour of the island's highlights.

Fees & Schedules **Gail's Tours** (☎ *508/257–6557* ⊕ *www.nantucket. net/tours/gails*). **Vineyard History Tours** (☎ *508/627–8619* ⊕ *www. mvpreservation.org/tours.html*).

▌EATING OUT

The restaurants we list are the cream of the crop in each price category. Note that ordering a lobster dinner, which can be far more expensive than other menu items, may push your meal into a higher price category than the restaurant's price range shows. Properties indicated by a ✕▨ are lodging establishments whose restaurant warrants a special trip.

For information on food-related health issues, see Health below.

CATEGORY	COST
¢	under $10
$	$10–$16
$$	$17–$22
$$$	$23–$30
$$$$	over $30

Per person for a main course at dinner.

CUTTING COSTS

Even the best of the region's restaurants offer slightly scaled-down portions of pricier dinner menus during lunchtime. Any time of day you can indulge in fresh local seafood and clambakes at **seat-yourself shanties** for a much lower price than their fine-dining counterparts. Often the tackier the decor (plastic fish on the walls), the better the seafood. These laid-back local haunts usually operate a fish market on the premises and are in every sizable town on the islands.

RESERVATIONS & DRESS

Regardless of where you are, it's a good idea to make a reservation if you can. In some places (Hong Kong, for example), it's expected. We mention them specifically only when reservations are essential (there's no other way you'll ever get a table) or when they are not accepted. For popular restaurants, book as far ahead as you can (often 30 days), and reconfirm as soon as you arrive. (Large parties should always call ahead to check the reservations policy.) We mention dress only when men are required to wear a jacket or a jacket and tie.

Contacts OpenTable (⊕*www. opentable.com*). **DinnerBroker** (⊕*www.dinnerbroker.com*).

WINES, BEER & SPIRITS

In Massachusetts you can generally buy alcoholic beverages (wine, beer, and spirits) in liquor stores, known locally as package stores. A few exceptions allow some grocery stores to sell wine and beer. All of the towns on Martha's Vineyard except Oak Bluffs, Edgartown, Vineyard Haven, and Aquinnah are "dry" and don't sell alcohol.

▌ EMERGENCIES

Both Nantucket and Martha's Vineyard have hospitals. For rescues at sea, call the Coast Guard. Boaters should use Channel 16 on their radios.

Emergency Services Ambulance, fire, police (☎*911 or dial township station*). **Coast Guard** (☎*508/888–0335* ⊕*www.uscg.mil*).

Hospitals Martha's Vineyard Hospital (✉*Linton La., Oak Bluffs* ☎*508/693–0410* ⊕*www.marthas-vineyardhospital.com*). **Nantucket Cottage Hospital** (✉*57 Prospect St., Nantucket* ☎*508/825–8100* ⊕*www.nantuckethospital.org*).

Late-Night Pharmacy Leslie's Drug Store (✉*65 Main St., Vineyard Haven* ☎*508/693–1010*).

▌ GAY & LESBIAN TRAVEL

Although most gay visitors to the region think immediately of Provincetown, at the tip of Cape Cod, with its wealth of gay inns and nightlife, Martha's Vineyard has a few gay-owned inns and B&Bs, and both islands are generally quite gay-friendly. Martha's Vineyard, although lacking any gay-specific nightlife, has a number of gay-friendly businesses and has become increasingly popular as a gay vacation spot in recent years. Nantucket is also quite tolerant but has less of a gay following than the Vineyard. In 2004 Massachusetts became the first state in the nation to legalize same-sex marriage.

Gay- & Lesbian-Friendly Travel Agencies Different Roads Travel (☎760/325–6964, 800/429–8747 Ext. 14 ✉lgernert@tzell.com). **Kennedy Travel** (✉130 W. 42nd St., Suite 401, New York, NY 10036 ☎800/237–7433 or 212/840–8659 📠212/730–2269 ⊕www.kennedy travel.com). **Now, Voyager** (✉4406 18th St., San Francisco, CA 94114 ☎415/626–1169 or 800/255–6951 📠415/626–8626 ⊕www.now voyager.com). **Skylink Travel and Tour/Flying Dutchmen Travel** (☎707/546–9888 or 800/225–5759), serving lesbian travelers.

▌ HEALTH

LYME DISEASE
Lyme disease, so named for its having been first reported in the town of Lyme, Connecticut, is a potentially debilitating disease carried by deer ticks, which thrive in dry, brush-covered areas, especially on Cape Cod. Always **use insect repellent;** outbreaks of Lyme disease all over the region make it imperative that you protect yourself from ticks from early spring through summer. To prevent bites, **wear light-color clothing and tuck pant legs into socks.** Look for black ticks about the size of a pinhead around hairlines and the warmest parts of the body. If you have been bitten, **consult**

a physician, especially if you see the telltale bull's-eye bite pattern. Influenza-like symptoms often accompany a Lyme infection. Early treatment is imperative.

PESTS & OTHER HAZARDS
Cape Cod's greatest insect pest is mosquitoes, which are at their worst after snowy winters and wet springs. The best protection is **repellent containing DEET.** A particular pest of coastal areas, especially salt marshes, is the greenhead fly. Their bite is nasty, and they are best repelled by a liberal application of Avon Skin So Soft.

Poison ivy is a pervasive vine-like plant, recognizable by its leaf pattern: three shiny green leaves together. In spring new poison-ivy leaves are red; likewise, they can take on a reddish tint as fall approaches. The oil from these leaves produces an itchy skin rash that spreads with scratching. If you think you may have touched some leaves, **wash**

as soon as you can with soap and cool water.

SHELLFISHING

Martha's Vineyard and Nantucket attract seafood lovers who enjoy harvesting their own clams, mussels, and even lobsters; permits are required, and casual harvesting of lobsters is strictly forbidden. Amateur clammers should be aware that New England shellfish beds are periodically visited by red tides, during which microorganisms can render shellfish (excluding lobsters, scallops, and all fin fish) poisonous. To keep abreast of the situation, inquire when you apply for a license (usually at town halls or police stations) and pay attention to red tide postings as you travel. The region had a particularly devastating red tide breakout in 2005, but there have been relatively few problems since.

Lyme Disease Info **Massachusetts Department of Public Health** (☎508/947–1231, 866/627–7968 public health hotline ⊕www.state. ma.us/dph). **National Centers for Disease Control and Prevention** (☎888/232–3228 general information, 877/394–8747 travelers' health line, 800/311–3435 public inquiries ⊟888/232–3299 ⊕www.cdc.gov).

▌MEDIA

NEWSPAPERS & MAGAZINES

Glossy regional magazines include *Cape Cod Life* (⊕www.capecod life.com) and *Cape Cod Magazine* (⊕www.capecodmagazine. com), which both have articles about people and places on the Cape and the islands. The *Cape Cod Times* (⊕www.capecodonline.com) is a daily newspaper with news from around the Cape and islands.

The *Martha's Vineyard Times* (⊕www.mvtimes.com) and *Vineyard Gazette* (⊕www.mvgazette. com) are the main news sources on Martha's Vineyard. On Nantucket, look for the free tabloidformat weekly *Yesterday's Island* (⊕www.yesterdaysisland.com) and the regular island newspaper, the *Inquirer and Mirror* (⊕www.ack.net).

▌MONEY

Prices throughout this guide are given for adults. Substantially reduced fees are almost always available for children, students, and senior citizens. *For information on taxes, see ⇨Taxes.*

CREDIT CARDS

Throughout this guide, the following abbreviations are used: **AE**, American Express; **D**, Discover; **DC**, Diners Club; **MC**, MasterCard; and **V**, Visa.

It's a good idea to inform your credit-card company before you travel. Otherwise, the credit-card company might put a hold on your card owing to unusual activity—not a good thing halfway through your trip. Record all your credit-card numbers—as well as the phone numbers to call if your cards are lost or stolen—in a safe place, so you're prepared should something go wrong. Both MasterCard and Visa have general numbers you can call (collect if you're abroad) if your card is lost, but you're better off calling the number of your issuing bank, since MasterCard and Visa usually just transfer you to your bank; your bank's number is usually printed on your card.

Reporting Lost Cards **American Express** (☎800/528–4800 in U.S., 336/393–1111 collect from abroad ⊕www.americanexpress.com). **Diners Club** (☎800/234–6377 in U.S., 303/799–1504 collect from abroad ⊕www.dinersclub.com). **Discover** (☎800/347–2683 in U.S., 801/902–3100 collect from abroad ⊕www.discovercard.com). **MasterCard** (☎800/627–8372 in U.S., 636/722–7111 collect from abroad ⊕www.mastercard.com). **Visa** (☎800/847–2911 in U.S., 410/581–9994 collect from abroad ⊕www.visa.com).

▌ RESTROOMS

In each town on the islands, the tourist information office or chamber of commerce office *(see ⇨Visitor Information)* has a restroom or can refer you to the nearest facilities. Gas stations usually have restrooms as well. If you're driving between Boston and the Cape on Route 3, there are restrooms in the Tourist Information Center at Exit 5.

Find a Loo **The Bathroom Diaries** (⊕www.thebathroomdiaries.com) is flush with unsanitized info on restrooms the world over—each one located, reviewed, and rated.

▌ SPORTS & THE OUTDOORS

For further details on enjoying the outdoors, including water sports, see ⇨the appropriate regional chapter.

BICYCLING

Martha's Vineyard has superb terrain for biking—you can pick up a map that shows the island's many dedicated bike paths from the chamber of commerce. Several shops throughout the island rent bicycles, many of them close to the ferry terminals.

FISHING

Charter boats and party boats (per-head fees, rather than the charters' group rates) fish in season for bluefish, tuna, marlin, and mako and blue sharks. Throughout the year there's bottom fishing for flounder, tautog, scup, fluke, cod, and pollack.

▌ TAXES

The state hotel tax varies from town to town but never exceeds 9.7%.

SALES TAX

Massachusetts state sales tax is 5%.

▌ TIME

Martha's Vineyard and Nantucket are in the Eastern Standard Time zone. When it's noon here it's 9 AM in Los Angeles, 11 AM in Chicago, 5 PM in London, and 3 AM the following day in Sydney.

TIPPING

The customary tipping rate for taxi drivers is 15%–20%, with a minimum of $2; bellhops are usually given $2 per bag in luxury hotels, $1 per bag elsewhere. Hotel maids should be tipped $2 per day of your stay. A doorman who hails or helps you into a cab can be tipped $1–$2. You should also tip your hotel concierge for services rendered; the size of the tip depends on the difficulty of your request, as well as the quality of the concierge's work. For an ordinary dinner reservation or tour arrangements, $3–$5 should do; if the concierge scores seats at a popular restaurant or show or performs unusual services (getting your laptop repaired, finding a good pet-sitter, etc.), $10 or more is appropriate.

Waiters should be tipped 15%–20%, though at higher-end restaurants, a solid 20% is more the norm. Many restaurants add a gratuity to the bill for parties of six or more. Ask what the percentage is if the menu or bill doesn't state it. Tip $1 per drink you order at the bar, though if at an upscale establishment, those $15 martinis might warrant a $2 tip.

INDEX

NOTES

KELLY house
2 double beds

harbor View Inn				Edgar-
SEP 3 - 6	4	3		oak Bloff
2 dll 249	385	385		
$ 1,117.83	1-800-225-6005			

KELLEY house double - sep 3-209
$964.27   sep 4 335
        sep 5 335
Sep - 209   4 335   5 335

Cancellation Aug 23

harbu side

steamship: authority.com
508-495-3278

PVD   -PF Green airport

how far from woodhole Ma.
to Providence Rhode island

massachusetts

-> 7042-78293
Acct #   BlJo203hotmail.comm
1-800 724-9988

Armed Force Vacation Club

NOTES

Cancelation # for Hyanniss

Budget rent a Car
praidence Rhode island
Cnf· 1921 4725 4629
AmX trip ZD

NOTES

NOTES

Wood hole

OB - Oak Bluff

NOTES

NOTES

Portsmouth   Portsmouth

65	37	15
65	33	15
130	66	

Hyannis mU $69.00
        75.00

NOTES

ABOUT OUR WRITERS

Former Fodor's staff editor and longtime Cape Cod contributor Andrew Collins updated the Martha's Vineyard chapter for this edition, as well as the information in the front of the book. Andrew grew up in New England and has visited Cape Cod for many years, writing about it for *Fodor's Gay Guide to the USA,* several other Fodor's titles related to New England, and a number of newspapers and magazines. He has contributed to *Fodor's New Mexico, Travel & Leisure, Out Traveler, Sunset,* and *New Mexico Magazine,* and teaches a course on travel writing for New York City's Gotham Writers' Workshop.

Nantucket resident Sandy MacDonald is a seasoned travel writer who has written several New England guidebooks and contributed to others. She has also written about the island for publications such as *Boston Magazine* and *New England Travel & Life.* For this book, she covered Nantucket's good life—including dining, lodging, nightlife, the arts, and shopping.